150° 158°

U A   N E W   G U I N E A   0°

ANUS

NEW IRELAND

BOUGAINVILLE

RCK

ARCHIPELAGO

ADANG

SOLOMON

MOROBE

WEST
NEW BRITAIN

EAST
NEW BRITAIN

ISLANDS

SOLOMON SEA

8°

NORTHERN

MILNE BAY

CORAL SEA

CENTRAL

16°

KEY

------- DISTRICT BOUNDARY

---·--- INTERNATIONAL BOUNDARY

Scale

0   100   200   300   400 Miles

0   200   400   600 Km.

150° 158°

ANTHROPOLOGY IN PAPUA NEW GUINEA

Anthropology in Papua New Guinea

READINGS FROM
THE ENCYCLOPAEDIA OF PAPUA AND NEW GUINEA

EDITED BY

Ian Hogbin

Professorial Fellow in Anthropology
Macquarie University

MELBOURNE UNIVERSITY PRESS
1973

First published 1973

Printed in Australia by
Wilke and Company Limited, Clayton, Victoria 3168 for
Melbourne University Press, Carlton, Victoria 3053
USA and Canada: ISBS Inc., Portland, Oregon 97208
Great Britain and Europe: Angus & Robertson (UK) Ltd, London

Registered in Australia for transmission by post as a book

ISBN 0 522 84051 5
Dewey Decimal Classification Number 301.2995

To the Memory of
Barbara M. Ramsden

Preface

The idea of an *Encyclopaedia* for Papua and New Guinea came as an inspiration to Peter Ryan, Director of Melbourne University Press. Early in 1966, when thinking over possible members of an editorial committee, he asked me whether I would be willing to take charge of the entries coming under the heading of Anthropology, an invitation I accepted.

I am the sort of person who, if he were a minister of religion, would be in a state of constant anxiety if his Sunday sermon was not written by the preceding Monday, and as a result I so intimidated my chosen contributors with direst threats and cajoled them with promises of early publication that the majority had sent in their assignments by the end of 1967. But not every section editor was burdened with such an inconvenient horror of procrastination, and we had to wait for more than four years for the appearance of the work in print. During this long interval it occurred to me that many students and those members of the public specially concerned with Papua New Guinea affairs—I refer as much to New Guineans themselves as to Europeans—might welcome the issue in a separate volume of a few of the articles having a wide general appeal. Peter Ryan agreed, and this is what I am now offering.

The obvious choice for the core of the book was the couple of papers a knowledge of whose subject matter was indispensable for an understanding of the people and the way their lives are organized. I refer to Marie de Lepervanche's 'Social Structure' and Lewis Langness's 'Political Organization'. As to the rest, I had to bear in mind the limit of about 80 000 words—which I have in fact exceeded. Some of the articles, although definitive, could be excluded on the grounds of their being intended primarily for reference—hence Douglas Newton's exhaustive survey under the title 'Art' was ruled out—and certain others had too narrow an interest—Edward Wolfers's fascinating account of 'Counting and

Numbers', for example, and Donald Laycock's of 'Gambling'. But I still had too much and was obliged to reject and reject again. Ronald Berndt's 'Social Control' was the last casualty. This article is of some length, and had it been admitted two others would have had to go. My consolation is that he has stated his intention of expanding the material into a book, also designed for students. I hope that he will not delay too long.

The lapse of time between 1967 and 1972 meant that some of the papers were no longer up to date. Most of them have now been extensively revised. I note that Marie de Lepervanche has consulted more than thirty extra books and journals and Lewis Langness almost twenty. (*Man in New Guinea*, issued quarterly by the Department of Anthropology and Sociology, University of Papua New Guinea, lists all new anthropological publications.)

A point not mentioned anywhere in the text may be referred to here. It occurred to me only after the book was in the printer's hands, too late to pass on for comment to the relevant authors. Recent fighting in Chimbu and the Western Highlands may well have been precipitated in part by acute land shortages. Both districts have always been heavily populated, and in pre-contact days expanding groups as a regular procedure took up arms and destroyed their less numerous neighbours in order to gain control of extra areas to meet increasing needs. With the establishment of administrative control, however, the boundaries as they were at that moment were frozen, and orders went out for raiding to cease. In the intervening decades two things have happened: numbers have gone up still further, in some places actually doubling, and the introduction of commercial crops has made land even more valuable. Redistribution or resettlement are possible solutions to the problem.

As Peter Ryan pointed out in his Introduction to the *Encyclopaedia*, occasionally slight differences of view upon the same topic may be found between one article and another. I made no attempt to bring the authors into line. They are all authorities, and where they disagree the reader can assume that so far consensus has not been achieved.

There are difficulties in the use of the names Papua, New Guinea, and the recently adopted official title Papua New Guinea. These are partly the result of the several changes that have occurred. British New Guinea became Papua; German New Guinea, first the Mandated Territory and then the Trust Territory of New Guinea; and Dutch New Guinea, West Irian and, in 1973, Irian Jaya. Further, the main island itself is called New Guinea. 'Papua New Guineans' is such a mouthful that the writers have preferred to speak simply of New Guineans. (I refrained from exercising my editorial rights and substituting the current local spelling Niuginians, which I personally prefer.)

The book is dedicated, with the deepest respect and considerable affection, to the memory of Barbara M. Ramsden, former chief editor for Melbourne University Press, who died in the middle of the production of the *Encyclopaedia*, though mercifully not until she had been through the anthropological entries. We worked together in complete harmony and without a single disagreement, and she earned my regard not only for her absolute devotion to scholarship but also for her sympathetic personality—though she had a wonderfully sharp and acidulous tongue when confronted with verbal pomposity whether written or spoken. The explicit aim of the *Encyclopaedia*, as set out in the Introduction, was to be within the comprehension of the intelligent general reader. Miss Ramsden refused to pass professional jargon or anything that was in the least abstruse, unclear, or capable of misunderstanding. If some of my authors write like angels, as I have been assured that they do, then it is she who deserves much of the credit.

When Miss Ramsden confessed to me that the surgeon had told her that only a few more months remained I begged that she would let me dedicate to her the proposed *Readings*. Reluctantly, and then only at the penultimate moment, she agreed. I think she would have approved the finished volume, and I hope that it will do honour to her name.

Macquarie University   *Ian Hogbin*
February 1973

Contributors

Ann Chowning
Professor of Anthropology, University of Papua New Guinea

Marie de Lepervanche
Department of Anthropology, University of Sydney

A. L. Epstein
Professor of Anthropology, Sussex University

T. Scarlett Epstein
Professor, Institute of Development Studies, Sussex University

Leonard B. Glick
Professor of Anthropology, Hampshire College, Amherst, Mass.

Murray Groves
Professor of Sociology, University of Hong Kong

Thomas G. Harding
Professor of Anthropology, University of California, Santa Barbara

L. L. Langness
Professor of Anthropology, University of California, Los Angeles

Peter Lawrence
Professor of Anthropology, University of Sydney

D'Arcy Ryan
Department of Anthropology, University of Western Australia

Charles A. Valentine
Professor of Anthropology, Washington University, Saint Louis

Contents

xi

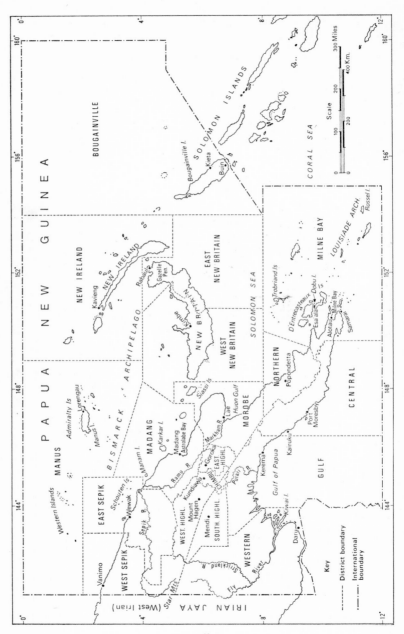

xii

Social Structure

Marie de Lepervanche

INTRODUCTION

The people of Papua New Guinea speak hundreds of different languages. Their traditional societies are small-scale and lack any kind of centralized political or administrative organization that could be called a government. In anthropological terms, they are stateless social systems. The expressions 'society' and 'social system' refer to a group of persons speaking the same language and having a similar culture. The members do not normally think of themselves as a unit, rarely have a name for themselves, form no socially coherent or autonomous body, and are not united politically. In these respects they differ from many African societies that lack chiefs or central administrative apparatus. The Sudanese Nuer, for example, are divided into a series of segmentary patrilineal descent groups which are associated with territorial segments, including tribes and their sections. Evans-Pritchard's analysis distinguishes Nuer clan organization from their tribal or territorial arrangements but shows the relationship between the two. The members of each Nuer tribe 'besides recognizing themselves as a distinct local community affirm their obligation to combine in warfare against outsiders, and acknowledge the rights of their members to compensation for injury' (p. 5). Because there are no tribes in this sense in Papua New Guinea, Hogbin and Wedgwood suggested the term 'phyle' for the cultural-linguistic units. In lowland areas the population of the phylae usually ranges from a few hundred to four or five thousand. In the Highlands there may be sixty thousand members in a phyle, although some are smaller.

This does not mean that ethnographers have refrained from using the term 'tribe' in accounts of these societies. They have done so, but inconsistently. Read referred to the Gahuku-Gama political unit as a district (1951–2) but later called the same group a tribe (1952–3). According to Brookfield and Brown the Chimbu are

1

divided into tribes of different kinds, namely phratry-tribes comprising 'members of a single phratry' and alliance-tribes 'composed of two or more sub-tribes with a tradition of independent origin and more recent alliance' (Brookfield and Brown, p. 79). Although they say Chimbu tribes 'are among the largest political units in New Guinea', fighting within tribes occurred frequently (pp. 79–80). A. Strathern refers to Melpa tribes being divided into clans and says that clan level is of 'central importance in political action' (1971, p. 23). These examples illustrate a tendency to blur the analytic distinction Evans-Pritchard and Hogbin and Wedgwood drew between descent organization on the one hand and territorial organization on the other.

Most phylae are divided into a number of homologous territorial and social segments. These are the autonomous local groups usually called parishes (Hogbin and Wedgwood). The population rarely exceeds five hundred: some in the Highlands are larger, and others in the lowlands number less than one hundred. The relatively small size of these units seems to be related to ecology and to the need for efficient division of labour in agricultural and other co-ordinated tasks. The type of country and the requirements of shifting cultivation limit the size of the group. Even a small population needs a relatively large amount of garden land for the type of horticulture practised. Too many people, and thus too great a dispersal of gardens, would prevent convenient assembly for communal tasks and defence. But where people are widely dispersed over a considerable area of country during the gardening cycle, as are the Sio, associations of gardeners often had to defend their territory and 'considerations of military defence became an integral part of the food quest' (Harding 1963–8, p. 403).

Parish residents live together in one or more villages, in scattered homesteads, or in houses clustered together in hamlets. Villages are more common on the coast and in the Eastern Highlands, whereas the hamlet or homestead pattern is typical of the Western Highlands. The parish is usually named, its members are associated with a particular territory, they frequently act together in ritual affairs and unite in attacking similar groups and for defence. Within the parish there is usually some means of settling disputes by compensation payments. Thus it is the largest local group that can be regarded as having any permanent political unity. The Gahuku-Gama distinguish explicitly between *hina*, fighting within the political unit controlled by rules, and *rova*, open warfare between political units (Read 1951, p. 157). Other peoples make similar distinctions (Berndt and Lawrence; Barth).

With few exceptions, there are no political offices. Leaders are emergent. A big-man reaches his position through his own initiative and in competition with his peers, and during his lifetime he may achieve prominence as a warrior or garden magician or ritual leader, or he may become successful in economic exchanges with others. Whatever the basis of a big-man's prestige, he must also develop a reputation for generosity by helping others and sponsoring feasts. By so doing he accumulates debtors and dependants and a certain amount of political power. But however respected a leader is in his own community, his influence rarely extends far beyond it, although his name may be well known.

Almost everywhere the people are subsistence horticulturalists and pig-keepers. Men, and boys particularly, also hunt small game, although most ethnographers have not described this pastime in great detail despite the fact that some peoples use hunting strategies for warfare (Bulmer 1967–8). In certain coastal areas, such as Mailu (Central District) and Siassi Islands, the basic diet is fish, and horticulture is limited (Malinowski 1915; Harding 1965). The lagoon-dwelling Manus daily trade their fish for vegetable food from the mainland Usiai (Mead 1942), and in the Sepik area the Tchambuli also rely on frequent exchanges of fish for other kinds of food (Mead 1938). Elsewhere on the coast, fish usually supplements the staples of taro, yams or sago. In the Highlands the main staple is sweet potato. Throughout the country pigs are eaten on ceremonial rather than everyday occasions.

Almost the only divisions of labour are those based on age and sex, and economic life is fairly uniform. But particular regions tend towards economic specialization. The Arapesh and Mundugumor exchange food for manufactured objects (Mead 1938). The Mailu and Siassi Islanders make big sailing canoes and undertake long journeys to trade them. Their objective is to acquire pigs, which neither group breeds. And in the Huon Gulf, near Lae, the Busama produce a surplus of food, the Lutu provide stone for making tools, and the Labu make grass bags. These coastal villages trade with each other on the basis of gift exchanges; transactions are between kinsmen or through established partnerships. The coastal dwellers also exchange goods with the hill peoples for tobacco, but in this case dealings are with casual strangers and bartering is the rule (Hogbin 1951). In the Gazelle Peninsula ecological diversity permits localized production which provides the basis for a complex system of internal trade among the Tolai people (Epstein 1962–3, 1964–5). And trading in various utilitarian objects accompanies the ceremonial *kula* exchanges between the Trobriand, Dobu and other islanders in the Milne Bay District (Seligman; Malinowski 1922; Fortune 1932).

Common ethnographical themes emerge, but the area presents variety as well as uniformities. Exchanges of food are important, particularly on ceremonial occasions or at stages of the life cycle such as initiation or marriage. This is not surprising where people produce a small surplus but do not store food. Exchanges at a marriage may also help forge political links between the bride and groom's kin, or establish long-term partnerships between a man and his brother-in-law. Giving away valuables, whether shells, pigs or women, can also set sign to a truce after warfare or earn prestige for a man and his group. But, depending on the society and what people value, the nature and consequences of such exchanges differ.

Accompanying any exchange there is co-operation to produce goods and usually competition in giving them. Those who co-operate or compete with one another differ from society to society, as do the goals to which the people aspire. The big gift exchanges, such as the *moka*, are systems of total prestations with economic, religious, aesthetic and political components: 'The prestations are made between groups which are in an unstable state of alliance with each other: the only way they can maintain their alliance is by continuing positive, ceremonial exchanges of valuables. This is literally the way in which they "come to terms" with each other' (A. Strathern 1971, p. 214).

Gifts are often exchanged for reasons that Westerners may describe as superstitious: for example, to ward off illness, to appease a ghost, or to restore a man's bodily integrity from female pollution after sexual intercourse. The last is particularly important in Highland societies where the male-female distinction is marked. Ethnographers have argued about this sexual antagonism and have related its incidence and nature to certain kinds of rituals, cults and to warfare (Read 1954; Meggitt 1964; Allen; Langness 1966–7; A. Strathern 1968).

New Guineans often use pedigrees, kin terms, horticultural, local, or bodily idioms such as blood, substance or semen, to express their relations of co-operation, competition and exchange. Translating these indigenous concepts into anthropological terms has been part of the task of writers on social structure. Another part of the same task has been to distinguish between a people's ideology, their rules for behaviour or group formation, what they actually do, and where apparent discrepancies between their ideas and actions lie. Then it is important to show how all these aspects of social life are interrelated, but not necessarily in any kind of neat functional fit. The task is not easy, and many puzzles remain. But the indigenous idioms may shed light on some of the problems in the ethnographies.

SOCIAL RELATIONS

Anthropologists do not readily accept any one definition of social structure, but common to many accounts of Papua New Guinea societies is the notion that social structure refers, inter alia, to the pattern of relations between people acting in social roles and to the pattern of relations between social groups. Sex and age are important principles for distinguishing social roles, as writers on male-female antagonism have demonstrated. The relation of local groups vis-a-vis each other is also significant. And writers have emphasized the influence of kinship, and have depicted social structure, particularly of Highland societies, as a hierarchical arrangement of segmentary descent groups such as clans, sub-clans and lineages. But expedient and inconsistent use of these terms has created problems in the literature. For instance, Langness admits when writing on Bena Bena marriage that he uses 'the idiom of lineage and clan advisedly and for want of a better language', but the units of social structure he outlines 'bear only superficial resemblance to lineages and clans as they are usually described' (1969, p. 38).

What does Langness mean by 'usually described'? The usual descriptions are themselves problematic. Brookfield and Brown use the term 'clan' for a type of Chimbu group that Nilles calls a 'sub-clan'. Barnes suggests that 'Enga use genealogies at [sub-clan] level merely to state the facts of contemporary organization, not as evidence to be cited in support of contemporary struggles, as with the Tiv [peoples of northern Nigeria, West Africa]' (1967–8, p. 38). Barth, referring to peoples living in the Fly headwaters whose social life includes much secret ritual in male cult houses, argues that 'the presence of a clan organization in some parts of Faiwolmin primarily reflects a particular organization of the ancestor cult and is thus intimately associated with highly secret and mystical notions of garden fertility rather than distinctive ideas about descent and kinship' (p. 177).

One aspect of social life that is evident in the ethnographies is that New Guineans are flexible in conceptualizing their social relations; but the anthropological analytical vocabulary is perhaps too rigid and inflexible. Barnes has called for more care in concept formation and use, and for greater analytical rigour in constructing models of Papua New Guinea social structure, and A. Strathern has tried to apply some of Barnes's suggestions in dealing with the

Melpa material. The Melpa people in certain circumstances use the notion 'one father' to describe what Strathern calls a patrilineal descent group, such as a clan, and its solidarity. They also refer in other contexts to the idea of 'one blood', that is, maternal substance, when speaking of clansmen. This ambiguity, Strathern says, accommodates the fact that matrifilial as well as patrifilial recruitment to these social groups occurs (1972, p. 221). But the one-father notion can also apply, depending on context, to a whole tribe or a small lineage as well as to a clan (1971, p. 34). Yet the lineage may also be described as a 'one-semen group' or 'one-blood group' (p. 34). Strathern demonstrates that context is crucial in discussing Melpa structure, but even he uses terms like 'clan' and 'group' without always making it clear what the exact referents are.

Another area of ambiguity arises from the fact that New Guineans sometimes refer to the same group, depending on context again, either in descent or local terms. A Melpa clan 'is spoken of emphatically as *tepam tenda* = "(founded by a) single father", and this dogma is referred to as the basis for rules of exogamy, and co-operation in warfare and ceremonial exchange'. But the people also use the reference *pana ru*, meaning 'garden ditch', and this 'compares the clan either to a ditch between gardens or to shallower divisions between different plots in a garden, thus aptly symbolising the fact that the tribe is segmented into a number of clans' (A. Strathern 1971, p. 33). In an attempt to link Melpa idioms with anthropological terms appropriate to these groups, Strathern also says (p. 34) that

> at the highest and the lowest levels a kinship model is used to conceptualise groups and their inter-relations, while in between, at the level of the clan and sub-clan, there is additional stress on territorial and residential idioms: the clan is a 'field ditch', sub-clans and sub-sub-clans are 'men's house groups'. The terminology here reflects the importance of territoriality and residence in political relations between, and in affiliation to, groups at this level; and it is the clan and the sub-clan which are also the major co-operating groups in *moka* exchanges.

Elsewhere he posits that the notion of 'men's house group' (*rapa*) bridges the dysjunction between the Melpa agnatic model of their important social groups and the 'mundane genealogical facts about lineage composition' (1972, p. 92). Alternatively, it describes the Melpa view of 'the functions of their group segments' (1972, p. 53).

The last example introduces another problem, namely that some writers have tried to reconcile morphological and functional definitions of categories and groups but have not always made the distinction clear and consistent (Barnes 1967–8, p. 34). The Enga, according to Meggitt, have a lineage system but, as well, 'group status is at least partly determined by the size and the function of the group' (1965, p. 55). Strathern shows that Melpa sub-clan segmentation and naming do not follow any prescribed pattern—as a hierarchical descent-group model of social structure may suggest —but that big-men change sub-clan names in their own interests during exchange transactions. If leaders can get away with inventing new groups to receive pork distribution they do so (1971, pp. 28, 51; 1972, pp. 42, 51). Although Strathern is aware that the use of descent-group terms and a morphological definition of groups can mask the process of group formation, not all writers are. The importance of grasping the meaning of indigenous concepts is relevant here. As Barnes has argued, the Enga vernacular names 'suggest that the Enga perceive their categories in relative rather than absolute terms' (1967–8, p. 34). Glasse and Lindenbaum also stress the elasticity of 'we' and 'they' categories, and that such categories are not absolute among the South Fore (p. 365).

In writing about South Fore marriage, Glasse appears to have faced the same impasse as did Langness when writing on Bena Bena marriage (see p. 5). Glasse says that the fit between the South Fore data and the unilineal models of Africanists is a bad one; but 'for want of a better set of terms', he refers to Fore corporate groups as clans, sub-clans and lineages, even though clans have local and not ancestral names. Glasse adds that 'the Fore conceive of their corporate groupings as descent hierarchies, but to use unilineal terminology suggests a greater concern with formal principles than the people manifest in their speech and behaviour' (1969, p. 20). Glasse and Lindenbaum, in a later article, emphasize that the South Fore terminology for the groups indicates an association between groups and topographical features or botanical species connected with group territory. The Fore do have notions of descent from ancestors, and use the idea of one blood to express this, but 'in a sense they use "descent" as a means of conceptualizing residence' (p. 366).

This brief excursion into some of the difficulties ethnographers have encountered in dealing with Papua New Guinea social structure points to a real need for an extensive re-examination of the whole ethnographic corpus before a sophisticated and useful definition of social structure can emerge. Or, possibly, the search for any universally useful concept is pointless. Perhaps Barth (p. 191) is more perceptive in writing of the variations in the cult systems of the Fly headwaters when he says:

> In the analysis of traditional social systems of New Guinea, it is important to be mesmerized neither by the unity nor the diversity of the area. To put in perspective the striking idiomatic and sectorial similarities in the cultures and societies of different parts of New Guinea, we need to define and contrast total syndromes constituted by ritual, kinship, economic, and ecological elements, and to explore the basic differences and similarities in the systems so constituted.

Although the ethnographic data is rich, and calls for a major reassessment, the task is beyond the scope of this article. But from the empirical data available it is possible to construct patterns of social relations and see regularities in social behaviour. At a low level of analysis this article will attempt to emphasize some of these patterns and focus occasionally on the kinds of difficulties already mentioned.

In the small-scale societies of Papua New Guinea, social relations are primarily kinship relations. This means first of all that closely related people tend to live together and associate with each other in various enterprises and, second, that the people see and express their relationships in kinship terms regardless of actual genealogical connection. Within the parish, people are related to each other by ties of kinship or marriage, or they believe themselves to be. Other kinsmen and affines live in neighbouring settlements, but beyond a certain geographical range all men are strangers and therefore potentially hostile—unless trading relations exist between widely separated partners. Then, kinship ties are recognized or extended to facilitate communication, as among the Lakalai, or a relation of institutionalized friendship of the quasi-kin type is established between partners, as in Manam (Wedgwood 1958–9). Thus a man travelling away from home can always stay with someone he trusts.

The Lakalai of New Britain are divided into more than sixty matrilineal clans. The members of any one clan acknowledge a bond of common descent in the female line, presumably from a common ancestress although she is not remembered. They call each other by kin terms despite the fact that exact genealogical links are not always known. Not all the members of a clan live together: they are scattered throughout a number of parishes. But each clan is associated with a food taboo, and when a Lakalai needs a trading partner in a remote settlement he seeks a clan mate who shares his food taboo. This man he calls brother. People can thus extend their kinship relations indefinitely and overcome the limitations of distance which frequently determine where the line between kin and non-kin is drawn (Chowning).

Kinship is much more extensive in these societies than among Western peoples. Persons who do not know their precise genealogical connection may call each other by kin terms. In fact, relations we describe as economic, political, or even friendly, are usually phrased in a kinship idiom. So too are enmities: the Enga say 'we marry the people we fight' (Meggitt 1965, p. 101). Where Westerners differentiate individuals or classes of individuals by their social role (for example, according to their economic status as employers or employees, or by the kind of authority they exercise over us as teachers, policemen, judges and so on), the people of Papua New Guinea usually express social differentiation in kinship terms. Among the Kuma a man's followers are known as his children (Reay 1959a). In the Trobriand Islands it is customary for a leader to receive a certain kind of tribute (*pokala*) from his junior clansmen in recognition of his seniority. But clan kinship and *pokala* are not felt to ensure political allegiance. On the other hand, the harvest gift (*urigubu*) a leader receives from his wife's brother is bound up with political allegiance, and in certain circumstances clan kinship may be replaced by fictitious affinal relationship for tributary purposes. Those with power to do so may manipulate kinship relations in this way so that the actual social relations between two persons, in this case between a leader and his follower, are expressed in appropriate kinship terms which indicate differential status and political obligation (Powell).

The people of Tangu believe that married siblings of the same sex should co-operate, and those of opposite sex should make exchanges. Thus the husbands of households that exchange with each other are 'brothers-in-law' and the men of households that co-operate are 'brothers'. Moreover, a leader can make 'brothers' for himself by recruiting men to assist him. The co-operative relationship itself establishes the bond of 'brotherhood' (Burridge). In other words, individuals may come and go, but the pattern of social relations, which are here kinship relations, tends to persist.

PATTERNS OF KINSHIP ORGANIZATION
Western people sometimes extend kinship terms like 'aunt' and 'uncle' to a few selected family friends with whom there is no known genealogical connection. In primitive societies, kin terms are usually extended to whole classes of persons; further, relatives that

Westerners would differentiate are often classified together. Among Westerners a distinction is made between father, mother, son and daughter (lineal relatives) and aunts, uncles, cousins, nephews and nieces (lateral relatives). The people in many primitive societies do not make this distinction, and have what is called a classificatory kinship system. The distinguishing feature of such systems is that certain lineal and collateral relatives are merged terminologically. In one type of classificatory system a man addresses his father's brother by the term he uses for his father. The father's brother's children are then called by the terms for brothers and sisters. The father's sister has another term applied to her, and her children are addressed by a different term from that for brothers and sisters. Another classificatory type of nomenclature emphasizes differences in generation so that a man calls all relatives of his parents' generation by the terms he uses for his mother and father, and all relatives of his own generation are classed as siblings. There are other types of classificatory system, and a close correlation between terminology and social behaviour tends to exist in the way the examples below illustrate.

Although all Papua New Guinea societies are organized on a kinship basis and bilateral ties are everywhere recognized, the way kinship is reckoned varies. Different patterns of relationships depend on which ties are emphasized and for what purpose. In general the people believe that all kinsmen, and often affines, should be loyal and helpful. In addition to this underlying kinship morality, each society uses some specific kinship or descent criteria to delineate important social categories and groups. In most cases binding obligations exist between close kinsmen who share membership in one of these units. There is no legal system comparable to our own through which the rights of individuals and groups are defined and contracts made, but each kin term generally has appropriate conduct associated with it so that the use of these terms expresses the rights and obligations between men.

In some societies people stress the importance of patrilineality. Groups of men and their sisters who claim to be patrilineally related then form socially significant units. For instance, members of each patrilineal descent group, or patri-clan, abide by a rule of exogamy whereby spouses are chosen from outside. After marriage a wife usually goes to live with her husband and his agnates (patrilineal kinsmen), a type of residence known as patri-virilocal. The male members of the patri-clan hold land in common and often live together in one settlement. They help each other in work, ritual enterprises and exchange dealings. Here the tie between brothers is strong and expresses mutual assistance. Those who co-operate may be called brothers, and even local groups may be conceived as groups of brothers, although some men who claim agnatic relationship with each other may not be able to trace the precise genealogical links. With few exceptions, the Huli being one, all Highland social systems have this ideology in varying degrees of brotherhood or patrilineal stress, and further examples are found in the lowlands. But as Barnes has pointed out, a distinction between patrilineal or agnatic descent on the one hand, and patrifiliation on the other, should be made more often, as this distinction approximates more closely to certain differences Highland peoples themselves make (1967–8).

Some societies from the coast emphasize matrilineality, that is, tracing descent in the female line from a common ancestress. Here a man belongs to his mother's group not his father's, and he inherits land from his mother's brothers. He may live as a child in his father's settlement, but to activate land rights he must join his matri-kinsmen. He may be given permission to garden on his father's land, but he will not be allowed to transmit these rights to his heirs unless the society recognizes a formal purchase that enables him to do so. Among the Siuai of Bougainville a man can acquire his father's land provided he gives the mortuary feast for his father and relieves his father's matrilineage of the responsibility (Oliver 1949).

Where matrilineality is stressed it is common for the people to conceive of their whole society as divided into several matrilineal clans whose members are dispersed throughout a number of parishes. The Trobriand Islanders (Malinowski 1929) say they are divided into four clans, the Lakalai (Chowning) into more than sixty, and the Siuai (Oliver 1949) into six. In none of these societies do all the members of any clan live together or co-operate in any joint undertaking, but they may share a common name (Lakalai, Trobriand Islanders), a totem (Trobriand Islanders), or own certain sacred places (Lakalai, Siuai), and in this sense share common property. Usually the matri-clans are exogamous, but in Lakalai they are not. The land-holding groups are often segments of the wider clans, and the members of these smaller units tend to form the nuclei of local groups or parishes. But depending on the rules of residence, which vary more in matrilineal than patrilineal systems, the composition of the parishes also varies. Where a man goes to claim land in his mother's brothers' settlement and there brings his wife at marriage, as in the Trobriands, the form of residence is avunculo-virilocal. In Lesu (Powdermaker) a man goes to live at marriage with his wife and her matrilineal kin. Residence in Dobu (Fortune 1932) is bilocal. The combination of kinship and residence rules is thus an important factor affecting the composition of local groups.

Although many societies stress either matrilineality or patrilineality, some use both kinds of unilineal criteria, though for different purposes. The people of Wogeo are divided into two phyle-wide exogamous matrilineal moieties. The members of both are dispersed throughout all the parishes, and moiety affiliation does not impinge to any great extent on everyday life. Wogeo local groups, on the other hand, exhibit a patrilineal emphasis. Rights in agricultural land usually pass from father to son and, with few exceptions, residence is patri-virilocal (Hogbin 1970). The Ngaing also use both kinds of unilineal reckoning. Their parishes consist of several named groups each of which inhabits a defined territory, has exclusive rights to certain tracts of land, is exogamous, and possesses certain ritual property. Membership of these groups, which may be called patri-clans, is determined primarily by patrilineal descent, although the component patrilineages of each clan do not claim a further putative common ancestor. Residence after marriage is patri-virilocal. With two exceptions, each parish is associated with a war god who is also inherited patrilineally. But the Ngaing recognize in addition a number of categories, the members of which say they are related to each other by virtue of descent in the female line from a common ancestress. Clansmen so related never combine for group action but are scattered throughout a number of local groups. They jointly possess a totem and are forbidden to marry each other. If a man is killed his matrilineal clansmen living in other local groups, as well as the members of his patri-clan and parish group, must be compensated. Ngaing links with matri-clansmen are also invoked when anyone is travelling away from home and needs protection, and in some enterprises a man may call on his matri-clansmen for help (Lawrence 1965).

Even though a people may stress the patriline or matriline for descent or inheritance, this does not rule out ambiguity. The Tolai, for instance, belong to matrilineal descent groups, but not all members of a matrilineage reside together. Virilocal residence is a principle of Tolai social structure, and over time and depending on who lives where, matrilineages can become locally linked to each other by patrilateral ties. When this happens, Epstein (1969, p. 109) notes:

we observe the attempts of one group to assert its dominance over another by claiming to have 'fathered' it, and of the rival party to declare its independence and full rights to ownership of its hamlet sites by denying the claim. Behind these efforts to secure the hamlet base lies the further struggle to establish rights to the allocation, control, and disposal of gardening and other lands. In these circumstances conflict smoulders not very far beneath the surface, and frequently erupts in bitter quarrels and disputes over land.

A third variety of reckoning relationships stresses neither male nor female line but gives equal weight to cognatic links traced through males or females indifferently. In some cases reckoning is ancestor-focused, and a man traces relationship to others by virtue of their common descent through males or females, or males and females, from a common ancestor. Or the focus for reckoning cognatic links may be the individual himself and not an ancestor. In either case, cognatic criteria alone cannot define discrete categories or groups as unilineal criteria can, because each individual or set of siblings belongs to a different category. But peoples who reckon relationships cognatically sometimes conceive their landholding or local units as groups of cognates all descended from a common ancestor. The Möwehafen people of New Britain think of their parishes as cognatic or non-unilineal descent groups in this way (Todd). In this type of system a man may inherit land in several lines and choose, within these limits, where he wants to live. If he takes up rights by virtue of descent from one of his father's ancestors, he may still have potential rights to land through descent from one of his mother's ancestors. It is often to his advantage to exercise his rights in his father's group if he has lived there since birth. He then remains with people he has known all his life and consolidates his interests. Should he wish to move elsewhere, his choice in fact is often restricted, ideology not withstanding, by such factors as a group's willingness to accept him.

Kunimaipa emphasis on cognatic kinship is particularly strong, but unlike the Möwehafen these people do not assert that all parish members are descended from a common ancestor. A Kunimaipa has a wide range of specific obligations to all his close cognates and their spouses; after he marries, the close cognates of his wife and their spouses are brought within the same category as his own cognates. To more distant kin he has fewer obligations, and to anyone outside that circle none at all. The make-up of these categories, for which the Kunimaipa have distinctive terms, varies for each individual, as they consist of people related to him through both parents and wife. Those included in a category never form a group in any sense: they live scattered in many hamlets in a number of parish territories.

In the course of his life a man lives in a series of hamlets, in each of which he is likely to reside with a different collection of his cognates and affinal kin. A man gains status and prestige by founding a hamlet and sponsoring, together with his fellow residents, feasts and ceremonies in it. Those who join a hamlet should remain there until, many years after the hamlet was founded, the group organizes a special big ceremony there. Usually after that the site is abandoned and families move to other hamlets or join in founding a new one.

Most men who have brothers, patrilateral parallel cousins, or more distant agnates, generally live with them for a long period in a succession of hamlets. That is, most men establish patri-virilocal domicile. A few who quarrel with their agnates, or who have none, establish their domicile with other cognates or with affines. A man's effective obligations are to the hamlet group with which he lives and to the brothers of close kinsmen of his spouse. For most men that means their own agnates and their wife's agnates. A man also has obligations to other residents within the parish territory. In disputes between parishes a man avoids his close kin when fighting.

The Kunimaipa also recognize named categories of kin which they designate by the word *kapot*. Some of the people consider a *kapot* to be a non-unilineal descent category with an apical ancestor, others say they do not know the origin of their *kapot*. The Kunimaipa are not interested in ancestors or genealogies, and some of the links said to exist between members of any one *kapot* cannot be traced. A person claims to belong to the *kapot* of his father, to that of his mother, and often to others as well, but in each generation there is a tendency for the offspring of a couple to emphasize the *kapot* of the parent with whose kin the family establishes domicile. That is usually the father's, but the process is one of relative emphasis only, and it can be reversed at any time, even in successive generations. The general result is that the alignment of kin in local groups tends to show an agnatic bias, but this is not inevitable, nor do the people emphasize the patriline in their ideology (McArthur 1961).

A combination of cognatic reckoning for one purpose and a unilineal emphasis for another is common. In Busama, land is inherited in the matriline, but close cognatic kinsfolk with a grandparent in common are distinguished as one blood (*da-tigeng*), whereas those linked by more remote ancestors are one stem

(*hu-tigeng*) (Hogbin 1963). In the Highlands the Huli conceive their
local units as non-unilineal descent groups but distinguish as a category those persons descended in the male line from the patrilineal
ancestors of the parish, although some of them may not be parish
members. This distinction is socially relevant only with respect to
exogamy and in certain ritual contexts. Thus the agnatic category
of kin to whom the rules of exogamy apply is differentiated from
the non-unilineal residential and political group (Glasse 1954–62,
1965).

The western Motu (Groves) are another example of people who
use different criteria for different purposes, in this case for allocat-
ing rights to land on the one hand and to valuable assets such as
fishing nets on the other. These people recognize a number of
dispersed named categories of kin, called *iduhu*, whose members
are said to be the descendants of ancestors who left an original
village in Port Moresby to found the western Motu settlements. The
members of any one of these categories never act together as a
group, although they possess a name and certain ritual insignia in
common. Localized fragments of these dispersed categories form
the component sections of nucleated villages, but sometimes an
immigrant group not claiming affiliation with one of the *iduhu* also
forms a village section.

The Motu use '*iduhu*' in a generic sense and also as a term for
village sections. At this level the *iduhu* is a named group. Its
members are associated with a residential locality, garden land,
certain trading vessels, fishing nets, and ritual paraphernalia. They
engage in overseas trading expeditions and feast giving. As a
residential unit, the primary members of the *iduhu* are agnates, and
the group leader succeeds by agnatic primogeniture.

Rights in a man's estate pass from father to son, and residence
after marriage is patri-virilocal. But there are other relatives, such
as male affines, usually attached to each *iduhu*. Their status is less
than that of primary members. They do not share the rights and
duties connected with the different assets that constitute the *iduhu*
estate unless they have been incorporated as full members of the
group. This may occur if a man renounces his affiliation with his
natal *iduhu* and then works for and supports the host group. To
manage its estate effectively, an *iduhu* must be of a certain numerical
strength. When membership decreases, outsiders may be recruited,
although Motu ideology suggests that primary members should
constitute an agnatic lineage. Thus the actual composition of the
group may deviate from the norm, but the agnatic idiom is used to
delineate primary members who alone share such scarce assets as

houses and heavy fishing nets; and only sons of primary members are admitted to the group's ritual estate.

Different criteria operate with respect to Motu land rights. All the cognatic descendants of the original cultivator of any tract may claim rights to it. Land is plentiful and is not important in the ancestor cult. But houses, nets, and the ritual associated with net manufacture, are of great importance; their ownership is confined to agnates. Thus with respect to different kinds of rights in *iduhu* estates, different kinds of criteria are invoked.

These examples illustrate how Papua New Guinea peoples use different, but in each case specific, kin ties to link individuals together in a number of ways: as members of exogamous units, as a privileged section of a community, as landowners or custodians of ritual property, as members of residential groups, and so on. In this way kinship and descent criteria serve to delineate significant social categories and groups. Kinship relations are social relations, and the acknowledgment of a specific kin tie between individuals entails their recognition of the appropriate set of rights and obligations attached to that tie.

When anthropologists analyse kinship systems, they usually include marriage relations, rules and regularities as part of such systems. In Papua New Guinea both monogamous and polygynous marriages are found, but the rates vary from one society to another. In Nupasafa, amongst the Bena Bena, 'between 25 and 30 per cent of married men have more than one wife at a time' (Langness 1969, p. 48). The South Fore, on the other hand, lack women, and polygyny is now rare (Glasse and Lindenbaum, p. 363).

Unlike some Australian Aboriginal or South East Asian peoples, New Guineans do not have prescriptive marriage rules of the kind discussed by Lévi-Strauss (1969), but prohibitions on marriage between certain kinds of kin, such as those who share one blood, are common. Among the Daribi those who share wealth cannot marry, and sister exchange is disapproved (Wagner 1969, pp. 60–1). In addition to prohibitions on certain kinsfolk marrying, the Fore and Bena Bena also prohibit marriage between those who live together (Glasse 1969, p. 28; Langness 1969, p. 44). The Maring also have marriage prohibitions but, according to Rappaport, have one prescription—'that one of a woman's granddaughters (a son's daughter) should marry into her natal subclan. This is called "returning the planting material"' (1969, p. 126). Some people have preferences: in South Fore 'ego has a "preference" to wed not only the daughters of his MB's [mother's brothers] but also of his MB's age-mates' (Glasse 1969, p. 32). Among the Trobriand Islanders a father's sister's daughter is the preferred spouse for a chief (Malinowski 1929).

Marriages are often linked with exchange relationships, alliances between groups, and warfare; and the circulation of pigs, cooked pork and other valuables usually marks the occasion of a union (Glasse and Meggitt). The Chimbu regard marriage as a way of cementing relations between groups (Brown 1969, p. 90). Tsembaga men recruit allies through affinal ties (Rappaport 1969, p. 121). Melpa affines ideally are exchange partners and should visit each other, and 'the tendency to establish intense *moka* exchange relations with allies and former minor enemies fits with the clustering of marriages between them' (A. and M. Strathern, p. 154). Unlike Enga and Siane, Melpa have 'a preference for marrying into allied rather than traditional-enemy groups' (A. Strathern 1971, pp. 156–7), but these groups appear to be men's house groups rather than clans, despite an earlier statement to the effect that 'clans tend to avoid marrying their traditional enemies' (A. and M. Strathern, p. 154). Ambiguity in the Melpa material is further illustrated by the following statements (A. Strathern 1972, pp. 131-2):

> Once a marriage has taken place between two 'men's house groups' (*manga rapa*, sub-divisions of a clan) and children have been born of the marriage, there can be no further intermarriage between the two *rapa* for from three to five generations . . . The implications of this rule have to be established separately for every clan, since there is some ambiguity about which levels of segmentation are to be taken as relevant for the calculation of prohibitions. This in turn is connected with the ambiguous status of the men's house subdivisions in certain clans . . .

There is also some confusion about which groups are concerned and the extent to which they are allied through marriage and exchange relations in any case. When referring to wife-taking between the *rapa* of certain Melpa clans, A. Strathern says: 'At this micro-level it is unlikely that wife-taking will rigidly follow inter-group alliances, since marriage arrangements are partly an individual affair, and men can have exchange partnerships outside the main sequences of exchange in which their clans are involved' (1972, p. 137). Perhaps a key to unravelling the Melpa material lies in making clear and consistent distinctions between morphological and functional definitions. As M. Strathern has stated: 'The analytical ascription of any one named group to a structural category (such as a clan) depends on the kinds of functions which cluster around it and its interaction with other groups' (p. 7).

The same author has described the crucial position of women in Melpa society. They are in between their group of origin and the group into which they have married. The women facilitate exchanges between men of both groups, but they can also obstruct men's business: women, then, are peripheral to the power structure of the society but are participant intermediaries as well. But not all New Guineans see marriages as fostering group relations, cementing political alliances, or enhancing exchange partnerships. Bena Bena marriages are ties between individuals not groups (Langness 1969, pp. 50–1), as are those of the Telefolmin people (Craig, p. 196).

ASSOCIATIONS ON THE BASIS OF AGE AND SEX

Although kinship is the major organizing principle, other types of associations exist in which members are recruited primarily on the basis of age and, to a greater extent, sex. Among the Gahuku-Gama, according to Read, the ties uniting age-mates are frequently stronger than those between kin, and age is a significant organizing principle (1951–2). Brookfield and Brown also mention age-mates among the Chimbu but do not elaborate on the extent to which age differences permeate that society (p. 73). Fore boys who are born at the same time or who are initiated together become age-mates, and strong ties of loyalty exist between them. Although the age-mate relation resembles a close kinship tie, the Fore think of the age bond as one with its own validity: 'they thereby acknowledge the importance of a tie based not on true kinship but with obligations and rights resembling those of kinsmen' (Lindenbaum and Glasse, p. 172). Fore women also become age-mates, but these bonds do not have the importance of those between men. The Baktamin people organize initiation in seven grades through which the males pass as age-sets, and similar ritual organizations are shared by neighbouring peoples (Barth, p. 180).

Some societies recognize a division into two sections for ceremonial or cult purposes. Abelam males belong to one or other of two non-localized sections (*ara*), which are connected with cult initiation and competitive exchange of yams. These sections are not kin groups in the sense that specific kinship criteria determine membership, although men often belong to the same section as their fathers. Ideally, the clans of one hamlet should belong to one section and exchange yams with men of the other section in a neighbouring hamlet (Kaberry). Among the Kwoma all males belong to one of two yam cult sections. Boys are initiated into the cult and may choose their section. Men of the same clan need not all belong to the same section (Whiting and Reed). In both Abelam and Kwoma, then, the cult sections link together men of different descent groups; at the same time, cult ties can divide men with the same descent affiliations.

A characteristic institution of many societies is the men's club house. It provides a focal point for male pursuits, and usually women and children are not allowed entry. In most phylae each parish has one or more of these ceremonial houses, and as a rule men belong to the club house nearest their dwelling. Where patri-lineality and patri-virilocality are stressed, boys ordinarily join their father's club house because they are living with their father on patrilineal land. And in such a society an incorporated outsider belongs to his host's club house. Where descent is reckoned matri-lineally the residence rules vary, as do club house affiliations. A Lakalai male belongs to his father's club house while the latter is still alive. Upon the father's death he may move with his brothers or brothers-in-law to found a new hamlet and establish a new men's house. Hamlet membership depends on club house affiliation.

In Busama, where land is inherited matrilineally and kinship reckoned bilaterally, residence is by choice, and a man belongs to the club house nearest to where he is living. He may therefore join his father's club, his mother's brother's club, or the club of an affine or distant cognate (Hogbin 1951). In Siuai also, land is inherited in the matriline; but in addition a man may purchase some from his father's matrilineage and become a member of his father's parish. Here there is no fixed rule of residence: hamlet composition is mixed, and club members are related to each other in a variety of ways. An ambitious man gains prestige by sponsoring the construction of his own club house. During the work he recruits as many helpers as he can reward (Oliver 1949).

Ritual affairs are the prerogative of males, and often entail an attempt at communication between men and non-empirical beings (Lawrence and Meggitt). The Tsembaga say 'they perform their rituals to rearrange their relations with spirits' (Rappaport 1967a, p. 237). Although a detailed mention of the relation between humans and what Westerners call supernatural entities is beyond the scope of this article, it is relevant to note that in a number of societies the people do not make the distinction Western people do between the natural and supernatural: humans, ghosts, spirits and so on live together on one plane (Lawrence and Meggitt).

Observable social behaviour anywhere is related to what the

people believe, and Wagner's ethnography of the Daribi is one example of an attempt to link the people's belief in supernatural entities to their system of social action (1967). This material will be referred to later, but, for the moment, the illustrations will be of sex distinctions and of relations between the sexes which often entail ritual.

Boys are often initiated into the men's cult at puberty (Read 1952–3; Allen). Adolescent Elema boys are secluded for six to twelve months to hasten maturity (Williams 1940). Among the Mae Enga the bachelors take part in purificatory rituals (Meggitt 1964). Iatmül boys are scarified at initiation, and all males are organized into a system of age grades (Bateson).

In a number of societies, particularly in the Highlands, relations between the sexes are strained, and the sexual dichotomy is underlined by the men's sleeping in the club house or separate houses, and the women, children, and sometimes pigs, in the domestic dwellings. Men usually regard women as polluting influences and take precautions, including ritual ones, when contact with females is necessary. Frequent sexual congress is considered bad for a man's ritual and physical wellbeing, and men regard menstruating women as dangerous (Read 1953–4; Meggitt 1964; Allen; Langness 1966–7). Taboos on sexual intercourse for a woman after childbirth are also common. For a Bena Bena woman, coitus is forbidden from the time she is pregnant until her offspring cuts its second tooth (Langness 1969, p. 48). But the existence of such prohibitions is open to different interpretations by different writers. Those authors mentioned above associate the taboos with hostility between the sexes, pollution fears on the part of men, the need for male solidarity or wellbeing: that is, an intense preoccupation with sexual relations and their dangers. But Heider, writing on the Dani people, says they 'lack the male-female antagonism which is so common to the east, and indeed have a minimal interest in sex, as evidenced by a generally-observed five-year post-partum sexual abstinence' (p. 170).

Read commented in 1954 on the pervasiveness of male-female hostility in the Highlands, and writers since have attempted to link this phenomenon with other aspects of social life. Meggitt, emphasizing Enga attitudes and practices, correlates a strong stress on female pollution with male purificatory cults and marriages between people whose groups are potential enemies. He also argues that in societies where people marry into friendly groups, such as the Kuma and Chimbu, there is much less fear of female pollution. He adds: 'it is significant that women's status is highest in those societies which do not sharply conceptualize long-term hostility between affinally related groups and do not stress the initiation of youths into male associations' (1964, p. 222). The ultimate opposition in male-female relations that Meggitt extracts from the Highland ethnography is that 'one reflects the anxiety of prudes to protect themselves from contamination by women, the other the aggressive determination of lechers to assert their control over recalcitrant women' (p. 221). It is tempting to speculate here on the fact that both Reay and Brown, who have written extensively on the Kuma and Chimbu respectively, are women. And Marilyn Strathern's account of Melpa females' roles underlines the fact that men and women probably see their own social situations and those of the opposite sex differently.

In Allen's analysis of male cults he concentrates on ritual in which those initiated constitute a clearly defined social group. He argues that a pronounced sex division is most likely in areas where parishes are associated with the members of one exogamous patrilineal descent group. The effective male members of the descent group are then solidary vis-a-vis their incoming wives and outmarrying sisters and daughters. Langness, on the other hand, puts forward the view that a functional nexus exists between warfare, male solidarity, sex and dependency needs, and hostility between the sexes, including 'the broadest expression of such hostility in daily life as well as in belief and ritual' (1966–7, p. 163). There is no radical disagreement between these writers, and it would appear on the evidence available that residential separation, and the emphasis on male ritual unity, are possibly associated with the custom of fostering male solidarity in a region where warfare is endemic. Training in the arts of war is usually an essential preoccupation of the young Highland initiate (Langness 1966–7).

LEADERS AND FOLLOWERS

Another form of association is that between a leader and his followers. Leaders or big-men achieve their position largely through their own efforts, though birth may be an advantage. Men who are senior members of the kin and landholding groups are in a good position to enter the leadership contest. In some societies the ideology states that birth status and membership of a local landholding group are prerequisites. But there are always exceptions, and a number of big-men succeed without formal qualifications.

To make a name and retain prestige a leader must continue to be successful. Aspirants must have initiative and be industrious. They need to have access to valuable resources and be in a position to distribute them judiciously. In this way a man puts others in his debt and builds up a body of dependants. A big-man's followers usually include his close kin, other kinsmen, and affinal members of his local group who are willing to assist him or who depend on him in some way. In many cases a man and his supporters belong to the same club house.

Although leadership is everywhere achieved in competition with rivals, the nature of the competition varies. And depending on the enterprises to which male prestige attaches, the role of big-man also varies. There are significant differences between the Highlands and the coast with respect to leadership qualities, and there are variations within each area too.

In the Highlands the phylae are larger and the population density higher than on the coast. Land is often in short supply and competition for it keen. The main staple, sweet potato, grows in a variety of regions and supports more people than either yams or taro. Its intensive cultivation has possibly contributed to the development of larger local groups than in the lowlands and, as a result, the greater proximity of settlements and the pressure on land has probably increased the frequency and intensity of warfare (Watson 1965). But the archaeological evidence does not indicate a sudden population explosion in the Highlands with the introduction of sweet potatoes, as Watson originally suggested (Brookfield and White).

Even where taro cultivation is important and the population density not so great, warfare occurs. Amongst the peoples of the Fly River headwaters, sorcery, for instance, requires revenge, and 'though war was not continuous, the fear and threat of attack was, and no mechanisms for institutionalizing periods of truce or peace are known. Detailed census material indicates warfare as the cause of death of 35% of the population' (Barth, p. 175). In the Highlands, warfare is endemic and the successful warrior or man of violence often has high status, especially in the eastern region. But men who are able to settle disputes, arrange truces, and make compensation payments to everyone's satisfaction, also attract attention and are important as leaders (Read 1959; Salisbury 1964; A. Strathern 1971).

The accent on warfare is not merely for defensive purposes; ambitious men attempt to gain status through staging successful offensive operations. In these conditions local-group strength is important. To fight battles or defend home territory, leaders need active male supporters and are keen to recruit them, especially if the group has suffered previous losses. Followers on their part look

to a noted big-man for protection and security. But to retain
allegiance a leader must offer more than reflected glory in warfare.
He therefore attempts to put as many young men as possible in his
debt by helping them with their bride price or exchange dealings,
or by lending or giving them land. To do this he must have access
to land and have accumulated wealth in pigs through successful
exchanges.

In the Western Highlands, where the big ceremonial pig
exchanges take place, profitable manipulation of the inter-parish
exchanges also confers prestige. In the Eastern Highlands the
ceremonial exchanges are on a smaller scale, and among the Kainantu people fighting prowess is emphasized as the important
attribute for leadership (Berndt 1962). But a Fore big-man concentrates on developing a network of ties beyond his parish which
'ensure multiple exchange partners and places of refuge, rather than
a force of fighting men which can be quickly drafted into service'
(Glasse and Lindenbaum, p. 376).

Where exchanges are important, big-men not only build up their
local-group strength, but also attempt to establish partners in other
parishes. Among the Enga (Meggitt 1965), Mendi (Ryan 1961) and
Kyaka (Bulmer 1960–1), marriages are contracted between as many
different groups as possible so that affinal ties are spread wide and
new exchange partners created. A Kyaka man can sometimes rely
on his partners as allies in warfare. But such alliances are for the
most part unstable. And because both warfare and exchanges are
competitive, a leader at any particular time may have before him
the choice of trying to increase his prestige by attacking another
parish or by scoring points in his exchange dealings with its leaders.
Alternatively, he may need the help of ordinary men outside his
parish. The *moka* of the Western Highlands provides a fertile field
for status competition, and formerly the payment of war compensa-
tions could initiate exchanges (A. Strathern 1971, pp. 94–5).
Today, *moka* is an alternative to physical violence in which the war
of status continues (p. 129), and for a leader, ties with partners
outside his own local group are often more important than a strong
local base (Strathern 1971; 1972, p. 86). Moreover, *moka*, and
probably *te*, leaders concentrate on controlling transactions and
credit rather than production itself. Melpa leaders arrange the
distribution of pigs without having the bother of feeding and keeping the animals (Strathern 1969–70; 1971, pp. 131–2). This latter
strategy resembles in some respects the calculations of Siuai leaders.

With few exceptions inter-parish relations in the Highlands

fluctuate between states of enmity, amity or neutrality, and seem to depend to a large extent on the relationships between neighbouring big-men (de Lepervanche). This view is supported by Strathern's statement (1971, p. 220):

> The *moka* system reveals a situation which is common in New Guinea Highlands societies. There are well-defined social groups, in relations of opposition to, and alliance with, each other, and it is possible to analyse the political system of the society at least partly in terms of these groups and their interrelations. But crossing over all the boundaries of opposition there are networks of exchange ties between individuals, developed to a high degree of organisation.

Not only do leaders try to maximize clan prestige in exchanges; they also use their networks to score off other important individuals. Thus these networks increase the possibilities for rivalry between leaders. That is, networks free the big-man to some extent from his 'segmentary enclavement' because he does not have to depend entirely on either a limited amount of physical resources or a limited number of helpers for making his prestations. But, Strathern argues, these networks 'also tend to make political relations unstable' (1971, p. 221). The relative instability of political and group relations is also underlined by Strathern's statement that the Melpa clan, Eltimbo, is in danger of losing its separate identity because the members live with closely related men of the more powerful Kitepi and Oklembo clans, even though 'Eltimbo leaders struggle to maintain themselves as in some ways separate from Kitepi leaders' (1972, p. 242).

These examples highlight again some of the problems of analysing Papua New Guinea social systems: the necessity of keeping in mind the distinction between morphological and functional definitions of groups and their relations; the interaction between ideology, rules for group recruitment, and actual group formation and dissolution. The relation between groups and between individuals, set against the ideal arrangements the people often allegedly have, suggests also that the vocabulary of traditional structural analysis is inadequate to portray the richness of social life.

One other interesting emphasis in recent analyses of Papua New Guinea social behaviour has been the relation between traditional life styles and what some Westerners are inclined to categorize as modern developments. Brunton has argued that cargo movements are generated by native attempts to deal with problems, including imbalances, in traditional exchange systems: 'These problems arose mainly, though not necessarily solely, as a result of European contact, bringing, as it did, new and larger supplies of wealth articles' (p. 115). These cults 'occur in societies where exchange relations form the most important basis of the political system and where, for one reason or another, these relations can no longer be maintained as previously' (p. 127). Brunton's thesis, originally presented in 1969, is supported by Strathern's empirical data from the Mount Hagen area. Here reference is made to big-men seizing upon the Administration's arrival, and the entry of shell valuables, to enlarge their exchange dealings. But the influx of shells also made these valuables available 'to men other than those who in the past had dominated the *moka* by their exchange partnerships' (Strathern 1971, p. 76, 108; 1970–1).

The skills of a Highland leader are essentially secular, and he usually gains prestige through constant competition with his peers in fighting and exchange. Today, warfare is officially suppressed, and there are indications that energy and initiative formerly devoted to warfare is channelled into the exchange systems and into entre-preneurial business dealings (Finney). But the Maring people distinguish 'ancestor spirit men' 'who are able to "hear the talk" of clan ancestor spirits' from important men who were marked for killing by an enemy but managed to survive, and from 'fight medicine men' who look after sacred fight objects and care for young warriors during warfare (Lowman-Vayda).

The coast has had a long history of contact with Europeans, and warfare has been prohibited for many years. Chronic hostility between parishes seems to have been common in the past (Wedgwood 1930–1) but, even so, the recurrent warfare typical of the Highlands does not seem to have been characteristic. Population densities are comparatively low, and there is little or no history of land shortage. Although some sweet potatoes are grown, the staples are basically taro, yams and sago, none of which has sustained large or expanding populations. With few exceptions (Tolai 37000, Orokaiva 9000, and Motu 9000), lowland phylae do not exceed a few thousand souls at most.

Lowland fighting seems often to have been associated with ritual requirements. A Kiwai men's house was not complete until an enemy had been killed for it and his head brought back (Landtmann). In order to reach man's highest estate, a Kwoma had to acquire an enemy's head. Raiding parties stealthily attacked a distant group to lessen the likelihood of retaliation. But Kwoma leaders also were and are active in the peaceful pursuits of the yam cult. Only the men of highest status plant yams, which have ceremonial significance, and their cultivation is associated with taboos and ritual (Whiting and Reed).

The emphasis on ritual expertise in general is marked on the coast, and prestige often attaches to the man who is skilled in ritual knowledge. Usually a considerable amount of magic is associated with economic pursuits. In gardening, fishing and trading, magical performances are felt to ensure success, and the man who knows how to invoke the responsible deities or who possesses potent magic is influential and attracts adherents. The highest Trobriand rank is confined to those sub-clans whose members are said to possess special magical powers. In Kiriwina the Tabalu sub-clan, which controls the weather magic, has particularly high status as the people believe subsistence ultimately depends on the effective magical control of the elements. The prerogatives of high rank also include the right of males to marry polygamously. This entails additional economic and political privileges. In the Trobriands a brother is obliged to support his sister, and a man with many wives has a number of brothers-in-law supplying him with tribute. He is then in a position to use this wealth to provide resources against natural disasters. In this way a potential leader puts others in his debt and secures more political dependants. But despite any initial advantages conferred by birth, a man does not inherit his predecessor's dependants. He has to build up his own following and contract marriages that will benefit him (Malinowski 1935; Powell). A Trobriand leader's success in *kula* trading is also crucial if he wants to maintain his status (Uberoi). Fortune says of Dobu leaders who excel in *kula* that they are clever competitors anyway and that 'The belief in the potency and necessity of magical knowledge appears in the *kula* to create its own reality, at least in some measure' (1932, p. 232).

Among the Garia the mastery of ritual knowledge is a prerequisite of leadership. Garden leaders attract dependants because people are keen to join work teams supervised by an influential man whose ritual is effective and who knows how to make gardens productive (Lawrence 1967). The Ngaing also recognize the importance of ritual skills, and a monopoly of sacred knowledge is essential for a leader. An important man attracts followers even from outside his own patri-clan (Lawrence 1965).

In Abelam the cultivation and distribution of long yams are intimately connected with the male cult, and skilled yam growers enjoy the highest prestige. They are renowned for their magical powers, which the people believe induce the biggest yams to grow, and gardens are made under their direction. A clan that does not do well in the yam exchanges loses members to other leaders. Thus any big-man has amongst his supporters kinsmen other than his own clansmen who depend on him for magic. A leader also enlists the support of kinsmen outside his group so that he will have sufficient labour to retain the initiative in producing a surplus of bigger and better yams for the competitive exchanges.

Formerly the Abelam encouraged warlike qualities in their leaders and welcomed newcomers to the local group to swell the fighting strength, but today they say they fight with yams and not with spears. The traditional hostility between parishes, which in the past was expressed in warfare, is now channelled into the competitive exchanges, and for a man to be known as a peacemaker today enhances his prestige (Kaberry). A similar situation obtains on Goodenough Island (Young).

The emphasis on the leader as peacemaker is common in the lowlands and may have increased since pacification. But there are indications that this stress already existed in some areas, and to a much greater extent than in the Highlands. Lakalai leaders had to prove their capacity as warriors before being elected to village leadership, but once this status was achieved they were expected to negotiate disputes and keep the peace. There were taboos against quarrelling in the leader's presence; he was not allowed to carry weapons himself, and his role as elected leader was to mediate and prevent hostilities within his village and between his village and others. Today, Lakalai leaders achieve their position through competing successfully with rivals in financing ventures and giving feasts.

The ability to accumulate and dispose of wealth has always been essential for leadership, and one way for a Lakalai to gain power is to become the head of a trust group. He then manages its wealth tokens and ceremonial paraphernalia, and must give his consent to any transactions requiring the expenditure of this wealth. And because membership of any trust group is not confined to a single sub-clan or hamlet, a trustee can extend his influence beyond his own close kinsmen and throughout his parish (Chowning and Goodenough).

Everywhere emergent leadership means constant competition between men to recruit supporters and keep them. But the nature of the competition varies and, accordingly, so does the kind of following a big-man seeks to build up. It is expedient in most Highland societies for big-men to have allies or exchange partners in other parishes, but another important concern appears to be local-group strength. It is to a big-man's advantage in the latter case to have his followers concentrated in one parish. If land is scarce, and a man is in a position to lend or give it away, he is likely to make use of this asset to recruit followers. Outsiders are admitted into local groups and often incorporated into the parish clan itself, provided they transfer their allegiance to the host group.

In lowland societies like the Abelam, where a man's prestige also depends on the labour he can secure to assist him in his pursuits, outsiders are also assimilated into local and descent groups. In this area, land itself is not in short supply, but an ambitious man depends initially on his patrilineal descent group for inheritance and secure tenure. The attraction for newcomers is a leader's ritual and gardening skill.

Scarce and valuable resources in many other lowland societies are pigs, wealth tokens, and shell money—that is movable property. The ability to accumulate such assets and dispose of them prudently, particularly in sponsoring feasts, confers status and secures dependants. Among the Lakalai (Chowning and Goodenough), Siuai (Oliver 1949, 1955) and Tolai (Epstein 1964–5, 1966) land is not short; in many cases a man can acquire land or cultivation rights by agreement with its owners or by some form of purchase, although ideally it is inherited in the matriline. Pigs, wealth tokens, or shell money, on the other hand, are not inherited matrilineally: a man can give or leave them to his sons, who in turn strive to accumulate more through successful trading ventures. Thus an aspiring leader does not rely solely on his descent-group mates for help nor on his matrilineage land as the major source of riches. The transfer of wealth tokens acquired through trade validates Lakalai marriages and helps settle feuds. By extravagant gifts a wealthy man can put others in his debt, humiliate his rivals, and enhance his own prestige. The Siuai also regard feast giving as an important avenue to prestige, and a Siuai leader eclipses his rival by honouring him with a lavish feast. Unless the rival can reciprocate with a bigger and better performance, his influence wanes. Siuai and Tolai big-men continually attempt to expand their trading contacts and accumulate shell money which they use as currency to finance their enterprises and, in the case of the Siuai, to buy allies.

In these circumstances a man can be successful and influential even though his supporters and those indebted to him are not concentrated in one local group. Indeed, it is to his advantage to have supporters and established trade contacts in groups other than his own. A Siuai leader farms out pigs so that his followers will feed them. And a Tolai big-man travels about a great deal and does not always live in the hamlet where his matrilineage owns land.

LOCAL ORGANIZATION AND PARISH STRUCTURE

Because achieved leadership necessarily entails the creation of a following, local groups may be viewed in one sense as composed of leaders and their supporters (Chowning and Goodenough; Powell). In some cases the local groups are named after the leader, and the inhabitants referred to as his people (Oliver 1949; Hogbin 1967). And because followers are attracted to successful leaders, men sometimes change their local, political or cult affiliations. This frequently entails a change in kinship or descent group affiliation.

Put another way, the actual genealogical relationships between parish members do not always conform to the stated norms of parish composition. But kinship in primitive societies is a social phenomenon and not simply biological; it is not even based solely on the peoples' ideas of procreation. As social relations between individuals change, so kinship affiliations may also change.

This flexibility does not mean that the peoples' conception of their social groups is necessarily uncertain. In most parishes a number of different kinds of kinsmen may be found; yet in no phyle are the parishes conceived as heterogeneous collections of kin. Parish membership rests on land rights, and in most phylae there is a patterned distribution of landholding units. Each parish is associated with a particular territory that the people say is owned by a certain group or groups of kinsmen. The members claim hereditary rights to this land and regard themselves as belonging to the parish. (The Garia are an exception: they do not recognize local groups of the parish type, and individual strips of territory are said to be owned by patrilineages (Lawrence 1967).)

Land is the basis of subsistence, and rights to settle and cultivate land depend on a man's kinship status. Land rights are usually transmitted according to the rule which governs descent. In most cases the landowners are men, and frequently groups of close kinsmen hold land in common. They allow women to make gardens, though occasionally, as in Lesu (Powdermaker) and Manam (Wedgwood 1958–9), a woman inherits land herself. In some cases mechanics exist for the permanent transfer of land, but this usually entails the acceptance of the kinship obligations attached to ownership of that land. Thus each society has its ideology and exhibits a definite pattern of social relations. Resources are allocated in a particular way, landholding units tend to persist as corporate entities, and definite rules guide social behaviour. Because of this, it is possible to discern within each society a type of parish that is relatively constant for each phyle and depends to a large extent on how kinship organization and local organization interlock.

In comparison with the Highlands, the lowlands exhibit greater variety in the interrelationship between kinship and local organization, and so greater variety in parish type, although everywhere parishes are small and the patterns of social relations relatively simple. In the Highlands there is less variation in the interlocking of kinship and local organization at parish level, but some anthropologists have maintained that the patterns of relations between parishes are more complex, although these complexities have not always been clearly delineated. Some writers have also tended to make comparisons with societies in Africa rather than with coastal Papua New Guinea social systems. Certainly the use of African models has obscured many characteristics that are common to Papua New Guinea in general (Barnes 1962).

Throughout the country the notion of 'place' is often used to identify a group, but the idea of 'place' also tends to restrict social horizons. In few societies, the Huli being one (Glasse 1954–62), is there any inclusive idea of social or territorial unity. It is rare for any people to be able to delineate their phyle boundaries. The notion of defined territory usually applies only to parishes. Even where the people say they belong to a series of phyle-wide descent categories with members in many parishes, clan ties may be invoked for trading or ceremonial purposes or for soliciting aid. But the existence of such ties does not mean that all the members of the descent categories unite for any concerted action, nor do the ties preclude the members of one parish fighting clan-mates in another. In Highland systems where the inhabitants of two or more parishes are said to be linked by bonds of brotherhood into a wider political community, parish autonomy regularly asserts itself, and hostilities break out between such groups. In general, units wider than the parish have no permanent social or political unity.

Effective kinship and marriage relations, and relations of alliance and enmity, tend to exist between territorially close or contiguous parishes. There are differences in the manner and degree to which social horizons extend beyond the parish. These depend to a large extent on such factors as whether or not the parish consists of one or more exogamous unilineal descent groups, marriage patterns, the existence or otherwise of phyle-wide descent categories, and the presence or absence of specific residence rules. It is not possible to give here an exhaustive summary of parish types, but some are listed below (Hogbin and Wedgwood).

PARISH TYPES

Type 1

In most Highland societies each parish consists ideally of an exogamous patri-clan whose members claim exclusive rights to parish territory. Residence is patri-virilocal and ideally parish members consist of males of the one clan, plus their unmarried sisters, wives and children. At marriage a sister goes to live with her husband on his parish land. In practice each Highland parish includes, in addition to incoming wives, outsiders who are birth members of other parishes. Survivors from devastated settlements seek refuge with matrilateral kin or affines and are often welcome to augment parish strength. As well, big-men actively recruit followers, such as their wives' brothers or their sisters' children, from outside their own clan (Meggitt 1965; A. Strathern 1972, p. 111).

The status of outsiders varies. Among the Siane (Salisbury 1962), Korofeigu (Langness 1964), Kyaka (Bulmer 1960–1) and Ipili (Meggitt 1954–62) they appear to suffer no disadvantage provided they co-operate with their hosts. But among the Enga (Meggitt 1965) and Chimbu (Brown 1962), if the sponsor of an immigrant is an important man and the newcomer transfers his allegiance to his host's group (behaves, that is, as a brother to the other members), he or his agnatic descendants are accepted as clan members with rights to parish land. But a man who joins his wife's clansmen among the Enga and Chimbu is never recognized as a full member of that group. In other words, the status of outsiders appears to depend on sponsorship, and the agnatic idiom expresses differential status within the parish. Yet in relations between parishes the political community is conceived as one clan vis-a-vis other like units, although not all members can trace their genealogical relationships to each other.

Because of the rules of exogamy, which incorporated outsiders must often obey, each parish is dependent on others for brides. Spouses are chosen from neighbouring groups, and among the Mendi (Ryan 1961), Kyaka (Bulmer 1960–1), Enga (Meggitt 1965), and peoples of the Wage and Lai Valleys (Meggitt 1956–7) marriages are contracted with as many different neighbouring communities as possible. Affines exchange pigs, and in order to widen the exchange network more than one marriage between two groups is prohibited. Thus from each parish, affinal and cognatic ties spread out in different directions to neighbouring parishes. But these rather tenuous links do not form the basis of enduring alliances.

Affinally linked groups, like brother groups, may fight each other. The Enga and Siane say explicitly 'we marry the people we fight', although marriages are contracted while the groups concerned are at peace. The Mendi, on the other hand, assert that affines are friends; yet fights occur between them. In general, where marriage prohibitions have the effect of establishing new bonds with each union, relations between intermarrying groups are potentially hostile or friendly.

Unlike the Highland societies already mentioned, the Chimbu (Brookfield and Brown) and Kuma (Reay 1959a) permit more than one marriage between the same two groups. Among the Kuma, sister exchange is practised. In both societies land loans are often made to affines, and brothers-in-law who live together are mutually loyal and helpful.

In general, each Highland parish, particularly through the efforts of its big-men, tries to maintain its strength and reputation, retain its autonomy, and simultaneously ensure its own security by keeping some channels of exchange open and by entering into alliances with neighbours. Having friendly matrilateral kin and affines in other parishes also provides refuge in the event of defeat in warfare. But alliances are not permanent, and hostilities can easily break out between contiguous communities. Thus each parish, necessarily linked to others because of the rules of exogamy, is related in varying degrees of intensity by kinship, marriage, exchange, alliance and hostility to similar neighbouring or not-too-distant units.

Parishes composed of a single landowning exogamous unilineal descent group are typical of the Highlands but rare in the lowlands. There it is more common to find societies in which marriage can and regularly does take place within the parish. But the interrelationship between kinship and local organization that produces this situation varies, as the examples below indicate.

Type 2 (i)

In phylae where each parish consists of more than one landowning exogamous unilineal descent group no parish is dependent on others for marriage partners, and unions between parish members are common. A few spouses may be chosen from neighbouring groups, thereby establishing some affinal and cognatic links between parishes, but in comparison with those communities of the first type, these parishes are potentially more self-contained and include fewer affinal members.

Among people who stress patrilineality and patri-locality, parishes of this second type are found in the Eastern Highlands among the Gahuku-Gama (Read 1951–2, 1952–3) and in the Kainantu area (Berndt 1962). Among the Kamano, for instance, intra-parish marriage creates a network of affinal and cognatic ties that link the members of the different descent groups. Inter-parish unions also occur, but these do not create permanent links between groups. Instead, such marriages are usually fraught with tension, and fighting between parishes is common (Berndt 1962).

In the lowlands the Abelam and Ngarawapum provide further examples of this type of parish. In Abelam, parish residents live in a number of hamlets, each of which consists of two or three named sections. Associated with each section is a small exogamous land-owning descent group whose members say they are related patri-lineally even though not all links can be traced. Only about 60 per cent of the married males are in fact fully incorporated members of their father's clans and live on clan lands. The rest are living else-where with affines or maternal uncles. Each parish therefore contains men who are not natal members of the clans on whose land they live. This state of affairs is not necessarily to a man's dis-advantage. The Abelam welcome newcomers, and an immigrant may reverse his original clan membership and become incorporated into a host clan and acquire rights to its land. In this respect the situation resembles that in the Highland societies, all of which provide for the assimilation of outsiders. But the Abelam ideal, like that in the Highland systems mentioned, is patrilineal affiliation and patri-virilocal residence. Their social organization is based on this pattern, and the actual movements of individuals are fitted into this scheme. Occasionally stranger clans are also incorporated into the village organization.

Because each Abelam parish consists of a number of exogamous descent groups, there is frequent intra-parish and even intra-hamlet marriage. Thus the majority of parish members, including women, live their whole lives in the same territory, and the members of different descent groups are linked to each other by the bonds of common residence and by a multiplicity of affinal and cognatic ties.

Competition within the parish is formalized in the exchange of yams. The *tambaran* cult and yam exchanges provide focal points of interest for Abelam males, and for cult purposes all males of the parish are divided into two non-localized sections (*ara*). The dual organization creates bonds between men of different descent groups and hamlets.

This constellation of ties and associations within the parish produces a potentially self-sufficient community, and social horizons tend to be more restricted than in parishes of the first type. But even so, Abelam parishes are not isolated entities. Each forms the nexus of a system of political relations with neighbouring parishes that are either friendly or hostile. During periods of truce between enemies, yams are exchanged, but those concerned in these affairs are not ceremonial partners as is so with exchanges within the parish. The association between two friendly parishes tends to persist, and the alliance is reinforced by intermarriage between the two groups. The linkage facilitates inter-parish co-operation, important in a society where parish unity and self-containedness tends to be strong (Kaberry).

In the Ngarawapum district of the Markham Valley the people favour intra-parish marriage between members of the component patrilineal descent groups. Social horizons tends to be restricted and, like the Abelam, the Ngarawapum have a yam complex. The ceremonial procedures connected with this are parish-centred and enhance local group co-operation and unity (Read 1949–50). But in some cases a village contracts an alliance with another outside its parish territory. The tie across the border then rests on the exchange of women between the two groups, and the affinal links between brothers-in-law, who are usually friendly, provide avenues for trade and exchange (Read 1946–7).

Type 2 (ii)

Some parishes resemble those in Abelam in certain respects, but the self-sufficiency and discreteness of each parish is tempered by the existence of ties of common descent linking members of different local groups throughout the whole phyle. Depending on the nature of the phyle-wide descent categories, the degree to which social horizons extend varies.

In Wogeo each parish is divided into a pair of residential clusters. The people say all cognates are important, but inheritance of land passes in most instances from father to son, and in each separate cluster the majority of members are agnates or believe themselves to be. Marriage can take place within the parish, and residence is patri-virilocal. Effective male membership of the parish does not fluctuate much, and the bonds of common residence are reinforced by joint participation in the affairs of the men's club house.

Yet the existence in Wogeo of phyle-wide matrilineal moieties means that all the members of any parish recognize matrilineal ties with persons in other territories; hence their social universe necessarily extends beyond their own village. But these matrilineal links are only relevant for exogamy and certain kinds of ritual collaboration (Hogbin 1944–5, 1967).

Ngaing parishes resemble those in Wogeo and Abelam in that each consists of a number of separate landowning exogamous patrilineal groups. Residence is also patri-virilocal, and the men's club house provides a focal point for male enterprises. In these respects the Ngaing parish is potentially self-contained and discrete, but the people are also divided into a number of exogamous matrilineal clans. The dispersed clan members never unite for concerted action, but in comparison with Wogeo the matrilineal links are more often invoked and thus provide regular channels for extending social ties beyond the parish territory. Some links between parishes are established by marriage, and formal trade relationships, inherited patrilineally, create permanent alliances between adjacent parishes (Lawrence 1965).

In all the parishes mentioned in this section so far, the people stress patrilineality in defining their landowning units, and the residence pattern is uniformly patri-virilocal. Thus, ideally, male membership of the autonomous political communities is coincident with membership of one or more patrilineal descent groups such as clan, sub-clan or lineage. But in reality each parish includes male outsiders as well as incoming wives, and clan membership is in fact reversible. There appear to be some discrepancies here between the patrilineal ideology of these societies and actual practice. But there is no problem for the New Guinean. He performs in his lifetime a number of different social roles—as son, brother, husband, father, exchange partner, follower, perhaps leader, and so on. He may leave the natal group of his own accord and join a neighbouring settlement where he has matrilateral kin or affines prepared to accept him. If he transfers his allegiance to his host group he may be permitted to remain there permanently, particularly if extra labour is needed. In time he may even renounce his natal affiliation and be accepted by his hosts as a clansman. Or if the immigrant himself does not achieve this status his descendants almost certainly will. When an ambitious man becomes a leader he attempts to build up a following first of all amongst the close kin with whom he lives. He may then try to recruit others from outside his group. If he is influential, his efforts to establish outsiders as parish members and even members of his clan will go unopposed. In this way, men with power manipulate the society's norms, which are primarily those of kinship, and are instrumental in assigning to newcomers the requisite kinship status appropriate to the community, even in those societies like the Enga, where the people draw a sharp distinction between agnates and others.

Because the people express their relationships to each other in kinship terms, even though exact genealogical connections cannot always be traced, kinship relations cannot be considered as something existing apart from other kinds of relations. People often say they live together and co-operate because they are kin, but a man can achieve kinship with others by living and co-operating with them (Hogbin 1963; Langness 1964). In these small-scale societies with little economic or political differentiation, kinship is not a thing in itself divorced from the economic and political context: the people use kinship to define property rights, allocate scarce resources, exclude others from enjoying certain privileges, regularize marriages, delineate status relations, and express their solidarities, allegiances and obligations.

This does not mean that kinship or bodily substances associated with kinship are the only expressions of relationship. Place, parts of plants, or the planting procedure itself, are among the alternatives and will be mentioned later.

Although each society adopts certain kinship criteria to order its social relations, not all peoples use the same criteria for the same purposes; nor are residence rules uniform. There are various combinations, some of which produce a parish structure basically of the second type listed and others which are different.

Type 2 (iii)

The Trobriand Island parishes are variants of the second type. Here descent is reckoned in the matriline, and the people say they are divided into four phyle-wide exogamous matri-clans. But the effective local units are sub-clans. These are the landholding units, and as far as rank is concerned, sub-clan, not clan, affiliation is important. Indeed, Malinowski (1932) said that although men of the same sub-clan regard each other as real kinsmen, men of the same clan but of different sub-clans consider themselves pseudo-kinsmen. (See also the controversy on Trobriand kinship between Leach and Lounsbury.)

The majority of Trobriand villages, which are the autonomous local units, are associated with two or more sub-clans, each of which occupies a section of the village (Leach). One is always recognized as senior in status, and its head is also the parish leader (Powell). Typically, an aggregate of villages forms a cluster whose component members tend to co-operate in various enterprises and regard themselves as a unit vis-a-vis other clusters. One of the landowning sub-clans of the cluster is regarded as senior to the rest, and its leader may become cluster head. But after a cluster leader's death the wider unit may lose its organized unity as a political group. Yet the social identity of the group remains and is reflected in the distribution of marriage gifts (*urigubu*) between cluster members.

Because descent and inheritance of land are matrilineal, a man claims rights to land from his mother's brothers and at puberty moves to their settlement from his father's settlement where he spent his childhood. At marriage a man's wife comes there to live, a form of residence known as avunculo-virilocal. Exogamy rules demand that a man marry a woman from outside his own group, but usually she comes from within the cluster. Figures available indicate a high frequency of intra-cluster *urigubu* prestations. This reflects the close interrelation by intermarriage of the populations of the cluster villages. Yet the number of gifts between residents of the same village exceeds 50 per cent of the total of all prestations given and received, a fact which points to 'the fundamental autonomy and independence of the component villages within the framework of cluster unity' (Powell, p. 125).

The necessary shifts in residence required of individuals throughout their life cycle affects the composition of Trobriand local groups. Each parish includes male landowners who have spent part of their lives in other communities. Moreover, the males of any sub-clan are required by the institution of *urigubu* to provide gifts and services to the husbands of the women of their sub-clan, so that an adult male retains links with his father's settlement until his parents die, and also with the various settlements in which his married sisters live. He is also linked to his wife's brother's settlement as this relative provides him with *urigubu*. The bonds arising from common residence and joint participation in various enterprises unite members of different sub-clans within the parish; but through kinship, marriage and *urigubu* obligations each male is linked to other settlements outside his village, usually communities within the cluster.

Effective social relations in the Trobriands, particularly between important men, are not confined within the cluster. A man with the appropriate sub-clan rank who aspires to cluster leadership attempts to establish a nuclear following within the cluster and also acquires wives from outside. The brothers of these women then become tributary affines to their sisters' husband. In this way a leader secures dependants beyond his cluster and extends his political influence. A prominent leader's participation in successful *kula* ventures is also important. Provided he can maintain a balance between satisfying his followers at home and abroad, and regularly exhibits his wealth by feast giving, a leader's influence is strong. He may also recruit outsiders who depend entirely on him and whom he employs to keep order and manage his affairs. The leader's own sons are sometimes among his adherents and live in their father's local group rather than on their own sub-clan land. But should a cluster leader lose his power or die, his successor does not inherit an office but must build up his own following.

All parishes of this second type are associated with two or more exogamous descent groups, each of which has its social centre within the parish territory. These units may be either patrilineal or matrilineal, and they persist as landowning corporations. Common residence and co-operation in various tasks unite men of different descent-group affiliations within the community, and regular marriages between members of the same parish give rise to a multiplicity of cross-cutting affinal and cognatic links. Unlike those of the first type, these parishes are not necessarily dependent on others for marriage partners. Admittedly some links between parishes always exist, but these can rest on ties between members of phyle-wide descent categories, or between trading or exchange partners instead of, or in addition to, ties established by marriage.

Type 3

This type of parish is found in societies where the unilineal descent groups are not related to the parishes. The Lakalai (Chowning and Goodenough; Chowning), Siuai (Oliver 1949, 1955) and Tolai (Epstein 1964–5, 1966) parishes are examples. All three peoples recognize phyle-wide matrilineal descent categories, and land is in theory inherited in the matriline, but there is no fixed rule of residence. In many cases men live patri-virilocally, and cognates and affines outside the landowning units are frequently granted cultivation rights. The result is that although land within any parish territory is said to be owned by a number of small matrilineal descent groups, which are sectors of phyle-wide matrilineal categories, neither the male nor female members of these units necessarily reside together. Thus the social centre of any descent group is not permanently fixed as it is in societies with parishes of the first and second type, and membership of a political unit is not conterminous with membership of one or more specific descent groups.

There tends to be some association between membership of small hamlet groups within a parish territory and membership of a particular clan or lineage, but the majority of Lakalai men ignore the convention that they should live on clan land. Hamlet membership is based on men's-house affiliation, and village (parish) membership is based on residence in one of its hamlets. In Siuai, two out of five households garden on land in which they do not possess full or residual title, and leaders are place leaders not clan leaders. Among the Tolai people of Matupit not all descent group members live where the group has land, nor in many cases does the unit leader.

The occurrence of intra-parish marriages, which are relatively stable in these societies, means that a man's matrilineal and patri-lateral relatives often live within the same parish. In Matupit, members of a number of descent groups live in any one parish, and even though some men live in their father's settlement they are still close to their mother's brothers' land and have access to it. Others who live too far away from their sub-clan land are given permission to garden in their hamlet of residence, although theoretically this land cannot be inherited by their heirs. But if a Tolai man is wealthy and wishes to establish himself securely he may in fact purchase land from a matrilineage not his own, particularly his father's, and thereafter these plots pass to his heirs. The Siuai make similar arrangements.

It is the duty of a Lakalai male to stay with his father or father surrogate while the older man lives. Thereafter he is entitled to live where his lineage controls land, where his senior clan-mates are, or where he was raised. By agreement he may even live where the lineages of his father's grandfather or brothers-in-law control land. Regardless of descent-group ties, members of a hamlet consider themselves to be closely related. Whatever the actual relationship between hamlet members, a man includes in his close-kin category his consanguinal kin, fellow villagers who are also his descent-group mates, and the other residents of his hamlet, even if these are adopted outsiders. The hamlet thus becomes a kin group as well as a local group, and by living in one of its hamlets a man is entitled to village membership. Within the village, residents also recognize each other as kinsmen.

Several neighbouring Lakalai villages whose members maintain peaceful relations constitute a wider community or territory. Primary citizens of the territory are residents who have rights to its land by descent, but the percentage of landowning members living in a territory is relatively low. The other inhabitants are residents who live there by arrangement but have land rights by birth in other territories.

The distinction between citizen and resident appears to have been primarily significant in the past for eligibility to leadership. A formal prerequisite for war leader (*suara*) or village chief (*volipoi*) was membership of a land-controlling lineage of the village; but there were exceptions, and a non-citizen could gain political power.

Moreover, a man could be sponsored for induction as a war leader by members of his father's rather than his own clan.

Choice of residence and ease of access to other's land in these three societies result in considerable individual mobility and mixed parish composition. But although land is plentiful and available, it is not lightly regarded. In Matupit, disputes arise in the context of political struggles between rival matrilineage claimants who try to secure a hamlet as base with exclusive rights to its garden land. The parties 'in pressing their arguments appeal to the same body of customary law, but like litigants in our own system, each relies on different, though equally valid, principles or rules' (Epstein 1970–1, p. 169). The point at which a lineage is patrilaterally attached to another is the common focus for disagreement over land rights. If, for example, a son purchased in the past some of his father's land, the father's and the son's matrilineal descendants may dispute ownership. Depending on the strength of the contesting groups and their ability to support their claims with genealogical knowledge, the father's descendants successfully establish their rights, or the son's patrilateral rights are converted into matrilineal ones and his matrilineal descendants establish themselves as rightful owners. In Matupit, according to Epstein, 'there is an ambiguity in the social structure, based on the combination of the principles of matriliny and patrivirilocal residence' and this provides fruitful ground for disputes over land (1969, p. 5).

In Siuai the comparative ease with which land transfers are made also gives rise to frequent disputes. The relative rank of the contestants is often a deciding factor in the quarrel, and a long genealogy validating a claim carries considerable weight. But continuous utilization may also enhance a claim. Where a matrilineage has been associated for a long period with a tract of land it initially acquired by purchase, a myth may develop asserting that the plots are derived from an ancestress. In these societies, kinship norms are not merely static ideological entities, 'they are also strategic rhetorical resources in the process of social organization' (Scheffler, p. 294).

It is significant that in Matupit and Siuai, land is plentiful but is not the major source of wealth. A man may receive pigs from his father, and there are thus advantages in living patrilocally. Or he may accumulate shell money or other prized valuables from trading ventures, so he is not completely dependent on his matrilineage or its land in his pursuit of status. In this context, disputes over land may be seen partly as attempts by leaders of established, competing groups to consolidate their interests further.

In all these three societies, members of the descent groups are dispersed throughout a number of parishes, and membership of the political community cross-cuts descent-group affiliations. As everywhere in Papua New Guinea, a man's effective loyalty is to his place of residence and to the people with whom he co-operates from day to day in the hamlet or parish; but for the Lakalai, Tolai and Siuai, local or political allegiances are not conceived entirely in the descent idiom. An incorporated outsider in a Lakalai local group does not change his descent-group affiliation but is included in the close kin categories of those with whom he lives. A Siuai divides his relatives into those who help him to acquire renown, whatever their kinship links to each other and to him, and all others.

Matrilineality in these societies defines the landowning and exogamous units, and membership of a descent group carries with it certain social and ritual obligations; but despite ideological statements to the effect that descent-group members must help each other and be loyal, hostility between parishes is common. Members of the same matrilineal descent group who reside in different parishes may in fact fight each other. Yet parishes are not continually at war, and the matrilineal ties and trading partnerships linking members of different local groups extend social horizons and provide channels for inter-parish co-operation.

Type 4

This type of parish exists in societies that lack any kind of defined unilineal groups. Kunimaipa parishes provide an example. Kinship is reckoned cognatically, and there is no fixed residence rule. A man never has to decide irrevocably to live with specific people or in a particular place.

A person inherits potential membership of the parishes of which his parents were members. About half of all marriages are between men and women domiciled in different parish territories, so about half of the population are potentially members of two parishes. Each becomes a member of that parish in which he establishes domicile; he retains potential rights in the other. Thus parish membership (being 'a person of the place') is established by birth and domicile.

The residential groups or hamlets within parish territory are essentially ceremonial groups. The goal towards which the hamlet group's co-operative efforts are geared is the big ceremony which they will sponsor in their hamlet. The more people they can attract to come and live with them, the bigger their ceremony is likely to be. For that reason they welcome anybody who wishes to join them.

Thus in a typical hamlet group the men are related by a variety of cognatic and affinal ties. Frequently but not invariably a hamlet contains a nucleus of agnatically related men.

Most men live at least once in their lives in a parish other than their own. If it is a parish in which a man does not have rights to land and potential membership, he is provided with areas for gardening by the men of the hamlet in which he lives. He takes part in the affairs of the parish and stays until the big ceremony is held in his hamlet. After that most men return to their own parish to live, but a few do not. Should a man continue to live in a foreign parish for about fifteen years or more he gradually becomes a 'naturalized' member of that parish. His children who grow up there have potential rights to membership of that parish. They also retain potential rights in the parish from which their father came.

The wide choice of residence is associated with an adequate supply of land, its flexible inheritance, and a lack of population growth. This does not imply any necessary connection between population density and specific patterns of social relations. The uniformities as well as the cultural and social variations in Papua New Guinea make arguments that rest on ecological determinism difficult to support (Meggitt 1965; Barnes 1967–8; Rappaport 1967; Kelly; A. Strathern 1968; Barth).

Amongst the Kunimaipa a man's eldest son inherits his land. Younger sons inherit from both patrilateral and matrilateral kinsmen who have no heirs. Pigs are highly valued but are owned jointly by man and wife. All these factors, together with the importance the Kunimaipa attach to establishing new hamlets and recruiting residents to participate in ceremonial feasts, encourage individual mobility. The fluidity in social organization is reflected in the cognatic ideology that does not provide criteria for delineating distinct or bounded groups but enables the indefinite bilateral extension of kinship relations.

In addition, inter-parish marriage extends the network of ties, and social horizons are broad. Parish cohesion is loosened by fluctuations in the composition of its residents, but the accent on sponsoring or participating in ceremonies militates against a state of permanent hostility between parishes and contributes to inter-parish cohesion (McArthur 1961).

CONCLUSION

Culture and custom differ from place to place in Papua New Guinea, as do the attitudes between the sexes, the kinds of age distinctions made, the details of local grouping and kinship systems; but throughout the area there are broad similarities in the patterns of social relations. In general the uniformities rather than the total range of variations have been stressed here: the four parish types have been set out to provide a guide to some of the structural forms of the societies.

The concept structure in this article has been one of low-level abstraction, almost synonymous with the pattern of social relations. But this is not really satisfactory, as the examples of anomalies and contradictions illustrate. The form or structure alleged to exist in many societies is a segmentary lineage one; yet this is problematic, as various writers have indicated. Indeed, the imposition of such rigidity upon the empirical data, so that the alleged form of group relations does not consistently explain the data themselves, raises the question of the value of many usages of the concept 'social structure'.

Some recent writers have been acutely aware of the problem and have tried to work their way through the apparent contradictions inherent in the material they are analysing and, in addition, to grapple with the limitations of traditional anthropological terms. A. Strathern is an example. Others have tried different approaches.

In *Pigs for the Ancestors* Rappaport has depicted a functional relation between ritual and ecology among the Maring. But there are significant blanks in this work, just as there are in the Enga material, and considerable confusion as well. What emerges is a Panglossian analysis of Maring ritual and social life, set in an arbitrarily defined ecosystem. At one stage he delineates the Tsembaga by ritual criteria: 'It is on the basis of their coordination of some of these [*rumbin* and subsequent] rituals and their joint and exclusive participation in others that we may distinguish the Tsembaga as a single congregation distinct from all others' (p. 19). That may cope with the men, but the Tsembaga group is not endogamous: 'there is an explicit and statistical preference for marriage to women of proximate origin. Of the fifty wives and widows residing on Tsembaga territory in 1963, 44% were Tsembaga in origin, and an additional 22% came from the Tuguma immediately to the east. The remaining 34% came from nine other local groups, in most cases occupying territories across the river or over the mountain' (pp. 18–19). Later in the book Rappaport uses yet another criterion: he distinguishes them from other like units by their joint participation in warfare, which 'seems to have defined the borders of Tsembaga territory' (p. 28). But in the same book, 'the Tsembaga have been taken to be an ecological population in an ecosystem bounded by the limits of what is recognized as their territory' (p. 96).

Another approach that incorporates the traditional and the experimental is Wagner's study of the Daribi. Although he refers to clans without always making it clear what unit he means, he is more interested in explaining unit definition and interrelationship than in imposing clan or lineage structures on his material. He tries to elicit from the Daribi symbol system the underlying principles that order and generate the elements of their society. This entails an excursion into their belief system. The Daribi believe that a child inherits paternal substance (semen) from his father and maternal substance (blood) from his mother; and their religion includes a number of procedures for counteracting external 'influences' that 'take hold' of a person's soul. On a kinship level, a man can curse his sisters' sons, indicating that he retains, or tries to, some kind of influence over his nephews. But to recruit his own children to his clan a man must make payments to his wife's brother—the child's mother's brother (*pagebidi*). They see these payments as countering the maternal substance and possible malevolent influences such as sorcery. With these notions in mind, Wagner argues that 'sharing wealth' rather than descent or filiation is the Daribi criterion for clan membership. This is opposed to exchanging wealth with matrilateral kin in other clans. Consanguinity—Wagner's translation of substance—relates a child equally to both parents and hence links clans in alliance, whereas exchange defines the clan. He writes (1967, p. 223) that the Daribi themselves

> do not recognize general principles such as consanguinity or exchange, for the exigencies of their social existence do not require them to draw distinctions on that level, yet they do recognize and differentiate such principles as connection through paternal substance, connection through maternal substance, sharing of meat, etc. Further, they apply these principles to kinship relationships in certain culturally prescribed ways; thus, one exchanges wealth with relatives through maternal substance (the pagebidi relationship) and shares wealth with relatives through paternal substance (normative patriliny).

According to Wagner, the *pagebidi* relationship is the focal point of recruitment to clans and alliance between them and 'embodies the fundamental opposition between consanguinity and exchange, the two basic principles of Daribi social structure' (p. 93). Put another way, 'Just as exchange provides the criterion by which clans exist as discrete units, so consanguinity provides the idiom by which clan boundaries are transcended, and the two, working in opposition, generate the social system' (1969, p. 64).

The influence of Lévi-Strauss's notions of social structure, as well as those from British social anthropology, are evident in Wagner's ethnography. The approach is interesting, although he does not provide enough empirical material for an independent check on some of his assertions. His emphasis on certain ideas is provocative: those of maternal and paternal substance, the implications of reciprocity, and—contrary to the usual interpretations—that of consanguinity 'linking' and exchange 'defining' groups. A comparison illustrates why.

A. Strathern says of the *moka* exchanges, which are based on balanced reciprocity, that they can be made between clansmen as well as between men of different clans (1971, p. 113). Also, there is 'a flow of prestations between a number of partners: A gives to B, C to D, D to E, and so on. Whenever a segment of this series is planned out by participants in the exchange system we can speak of an explicit chain of exchanges . . . [such] chains are thus parts of the general "ropes of moka" which Hageners see as linking their groups together' (p. 121). The Melpa people, whose clans are recruited predominantly by the patrifiliation, also have strong links with matrilateral relatives. A man 'should make a number of payments on behalf of his children to their maternal kinsfolk . . . [he] thus safeguards his children's health by making the payments' (Strathern 1972, pp. 20–1).

There are similarities then between the Daribi and the Melpa, but where Wagner sees exchange as defining units, Strathern refers to the *moka* ropes as linking groups. Where Wagner interprets a Daribi's payments to his child's matri-kin as an attempt to ward off malevolent influences, Strathern sees similar payments among the Melpa as safeguarding the child's health, although he recognizes similarities between Melpa and Daribi (1972, p. 23).

The interpretations of similar phenomena by the peoples themselves and by their ethnographers appear contradictory; but perhaps all are meaningful, and the apparent contradictions can be resolved. This assertion rests upon the possibilities presented by Papua New Guinea social life itself, especially those of the relation between ideas and social action. And one of the most important social actions is exchange.

Exchange means giving and receiving, and hence separateness of givers and receivers; exchanges take place over time, thus entailing continuity. But when exchanges are between groups, as is common in Papua New Guinea, the givers and receivers often think of themselves as a unit vis-a-vis each other. Exchange thus includes relations of solidarity and co-operation as well as of separateness and differentiation. The people also think of their social groups as persisting over generations. Put simply, exchanges flow on, but link and separate at two levels. First, individuals within a giving or receiving group are linked by their joint enterprise but separated in many cases by the extent of their giving or receiving, particularly when big-men give and receive more than their followers. Second, exchange links and separates simultaneously the giving and receiving groups. At both levels, men remember gifts of the past and think of exchange as a continuing process. Even if exchanges are made between individuals, a man usually thinks of his kinsmen—often his sons—as carrying on similar partnerships.

New Guineans use a number of different idioms and the identical idioms in different contexts, to talk about sameness, difference and continuity. Busama close-cognates with whom a man can expect co-operation are his 'one-blood' relatives, as distinct from a wider category of cognates, his 'one-stem', members of which he would not call upon so easily. The Kunimaipa word '*kapot*' can mean the base of a tree trunk, a kinship category, or the source or origin of something, in the sense of its background. The people also think the members of a group are like the roots that come out of the base of a tree. The Melpa use a number of idioms to refer to immigrants, one of which, a 'taken and (re-) planted man', means a person with no direct filial ties with his new clan group (A. Strathern 1972, p. 19). If the immigrant is a sister's son to a man in the host group, the newcomer 'is thought of as having roots (*pukl*) in his mother's land, just as he has a kin-tie . . . with his mother's people' (p. 20). Melpa tribal segments (of the Kawelka tribe), which Strathern calls 'clans', 'sub-clans' etc., have names ending in the suffix '-*mbo*', which means 'stock', 'shoot' or 'something planted'. The allusion is that such segments 'are "planted by" women of different tribes who married into the Kawelka tribe' (p. 42). He also says that the -*mbo* idiom 'provides a useful model of differentiation, and it is often linked to the notion that the clan had a single father who was a polygynist and whose wives founded separate sub-clans' (p. 43).

Images like stem, root, tree-trunk, and planting are hardly surprising amongst horticulturalists; they can represent common ancestry, as Strathern indicates (1972, p. 19). But stems, roots and plants all grow, die, put out new shoots, or can be cut down and taken elsewhere. These images are apt for relations of inclusion, separation, continuity or exchange, although not all are used by the same people. But the Maring say of their rule that one of a woman's son's daughters should marry into the grandmother's natal sub-clan, that this is 'returning the planting material' (Rappaport 1969, p. 126).

More common than horticultural images are those referring to bodily fluids. Here there is wonderful scope for ambiguity and symbolic manoeuvres, in fact more than Douglas suggests. Had ethnographers recorded more vernacular terms, some apparent paradoxes might be easier to resolve, although many others would probably have emerged. Given the kind of social systems New Guineans have, a flexibility in conceptualizing their social relations would seem to be inevitable. The following examples indicate the kind of ambiguities the ethnographies present, particularly with respect to the blood or one-blood image.

New Guineans exchange women in marriage, pigs and other foodstuffs, promises of alliance, ceremonial articles, compensation payments—to name only a few. But sexual intercourse itself is also an exchange, or at least appears to be so conceived by some peoples. The Enga believe that the foetus in the womb results from a mixing of semen and menstrual blood. The woman has thus received the semen; but the Enga man must ritually decontaminate himself from intercourse, i.e. from the polluting fluids of the female (Meggitt 1965, pp. 163, 122). Wogeo females, after copulation, are relieved from male contamination by menstruation, but the males must engage in artificial menstruation by 'gashing the penis to induce profuse bleeding', and so cleansing themselves of female pollution (Hogbin 1970, p. 88). Mount Hagen people say that a child results from semen surrounding woman's menstrual blood, though men still live in fear of this blood. A man should not copulate with his wife while she is menstruating because her fluids can make his blood rise to his neck and kill him (A. Strathern 1969–70, p. 152; 1971, p. 82; 1972, pp. 9–10).

Blood that comes away from the female body in menstruation and childbirth is dangerous, and the notion that women can pollute men with it is common, especially in the Highlands. The blood that comes away from the 'menstruating men' of Wogeo is also polluting, although the act of blood-letting is cleansing, as is the blood-letting during a Bena Bena initiation of youths (Hogbin 1970, p. 88; Langness 1969, p. 39). There is not much reference in the literature to men polluting women with their bodily fluids, but Hogbin says it is true of Wogeo, and cites the Arapesh as another example (p. 96).

The semen and blood exchanged during copulation, and which stay in the womb, are productive of a new child and not thought of as dangerous. And semen and blood are used in other contexts to represent non-dangerous as well as feared possibilities. A Bena Bena father does not take charge of negotiations for his daughter's marriage because 'it is wrong for a man to take pay for his own semen' (Langness 1969, p. 42). The members of an Enga clan are 'begotten by "the one penis" of the clan founder' (Meggitt 1965, p. 8). A Melpa man's semen and strength make his sons (A. Strathern 1972, p. 13); and 'clansmen share the "grease", or semen, of an original male ancestor' (p. 221).

But the blood image is more commonly used to signify unity, solidarity and endurable relationship, as well as the polluting, dangerous and frightening—although not all peoples think of women as polluting. This contrasts with the use by some African peoples with matrilineal descent of the images of breast or womb when talking about their social relations. Richards says of the Central Bantu that they believe blood is passed through women rather than men, but 'The metaphors of kinship stress the ties between people "born from the same womb" or "suckled at the same breast"' (p. 207). The Ashanti say 'one lineage is one blood', but lineage segments may be described as 'the children of one womb' (Fortes, pp. 257–8). The Dobu do use the breast or milk term '*susu*', and contrast the matrilineal grouping they call '*susu*' with the marital group. They also insist upon 'the comparison between human child-bearing and yam seed fertility . . . Each *susu* . . . has its own line of seed', and 'Seed yams are not inherited outside the *susu* or given away outside the *susu*—this fact assumes in native expression an aspect of a human line of descent that is served and can be served only by one certain yam line of descent —the faithful retainers of the human line, faithless to other human family lines' (Fortune 1932, p. 108). Here the horticultural and bodily images are intimately linked, and the Dobu attribute personality to their yams.

Perhaps it is not unusual that New Guineans should refer to blood more often than to breast when characterizing female attributes. At least the ethnographies indicate that there is more scope for symbolic play with blood than with breast. Many New Guineans think of women as polluting; but they are also necessary for child-bearing. Their menstrual blood, which does not produce life when shed, is feared. And, to speculate momentarily, if this spilt blood is ever associated with wounding and death, the women who regularly shed it could be seen as threatening, especially where warfare is an important preoccupation. At the same time, they also think that with the birth of children, blood provides continuity.

They sometimes conceive their local units as groups of persons linked by blood.

Where manpower is important and when men engage in fighting, blood rather than the breast provides a range of associations from birth to death, and its several possible connotations allow for flexible use when contradictions are inherent in social life itself. The Highland fighting men probably enjoy both warfare and sexual intercourse; but as Langness suggests, 'the exigencies of warfare have made it necessary to sacrifice the satisfaction of certain individual needs. This affects males differently from females but results in mutual hostility and antagonism' (Langness 1966–7, p. 176). Everywhere, child-bearing is important and men are born of women: blood unites. But the circumstances surrounding preparedness for fighting and warfare itself require separation of the males from the females, and perhaps the attributes of danger and fear accompany the women. But when fighting stops, the people continue to marry and exchange, and with each union children may be born. Blood again flows in the continuity of generations, but with new life there also comes the possibility of new wounds.

Frequently ethnographers are not clear and consistent in using the English word 'blood' as a translation of indigenous concepts; nor do they all give the vernacular terms or innuendoes that may differentiate ideas symbolized by the same term. In English, for instance, the term 'consanguinity' means blood relationship, and the expression 'blood is thicker than water' refers to the closeness of the kin tie. English speakers may also speak of enmity between people by saying, 'bad blood exists between them', or the expression 'blood will out' can refer to a skeleton in the family cupboard. It would appear that in Papua New Guinea as many, if not more, ambiguities or seeming contradictions surround the term or terms translated as 'blood'.

The idea that blood signifies close kinship is common, but the kind of kinship may vary even within the one society, depending on the context. Among the Melpa 'one-blood' ('*mema tenda*') can refer 'to a range of cognatic relationships traced back to a single female ancestor' (Strathern 1972, pp. 14–15), and 'In most contexts "one blood people" are actually extra-clan non-agnatic kin' (p. 221). But in addition to the notion that clansmen are 'of one father'—solidary and united, co-operative in warfare and exchanges—'is the idea that they are "of one blood", that is, that they share a maternally-given substance . . . Calling clansmen by this term thus confuses the initial distinction between agnatic and cognatic kinship and accommodates the facts of recruitment to the native model which is the symbol for clan unity and one of the means of articulating clans within the tribe' (p. 221). The blood image copes with events such as matrifilial and patrifilial recruitment to a group, which in turn is conceived as ideally a body of agnates, or at least a solidary unit. Strathern also mentions that although the Melpa often regard distant cognates as being beyond the range of kinship, in some cases it may be expedient to remember a remote connection as 'the presumed fact of sharing blood converts a person from a stranger into an exchange partner' (p. 16).

The blood of an Enga woman makes a child's skin and flesh, and the woman 'continues to share "one blood" with her brothers who retain a residual interest in her to the extent of discouraging her husband from wantonly spilling this blood' (Meggitt 1965, p. 163). The blood image here refers to matrifiliation, and the woman's brothers also have a continued interest in her child's welfare. 'This in Mae terms is phrased as their right to demand compensation whenever ghosts of dead agnates of their sister's offspring injure the flesh and blood that the children got from their mother' (p. 164). Yet the Enga also use the blood image to express agnatic relation and patrifiliation: thus 'All the members of a man's patrilineage are thought to share one blood with him and are in this respect his siblings' (p. 94). The genitor of a child is held to be the best choice as husband for a pregnant girl because 'Then the child truly shares one blood with the members of the patrilineage of its pater' (p. 104). Moreover, an elderly man may ask a younger male to impregnate his wife, but the chosen man 'must be of the husband's patrilineage so that the resulting child shares the same blood as the pater and is thus a proper heir to his estate' (p. 144). The Enga also fear the blood of women. Menstrual blood and the blood of parturition is dangerous and polluting, and contact with women is hedged with many taboos (Meggitt 1964).

Before the depredations of *kuru* on the Fore female population, men and women were residentially separated, and boys lived with their mothers until initiation. Today women are more highly valued, because they are in short supply, and the sex antagonism typical of the Highlands may be lessened (Glasse and Lindenbaum). But the Fore do not permit marriage between persons they regard as sharing one blood, although they 'have no precise theory about how blood is shared and with whom' (Glasse 1969, p. 28). Marriage restrictions between such persons exist among other New Guineans including the Busama, Melpa, Chimbu and Wogeo. Thus the Fore use the one-blood idiom to delineate marriage categories, and also the idea of blood ties to express parish unity—that is, relations of co-residence and group solidarity vis-a-vis other like groups (Glasse and Lindenbaum).

These examples suggest that the ambiguities inherent in such use of blood are appropriate in societies where individuals and groups exchange with each other, and where groups commonly form around emergent leaders and dissolve under the exigencies of warfare or because defeat or natural disasters make regrouping expedient. Blood is thought to flow on, to link and to separate. It links a woman to her child *in utero* and thereafter, but once the child is born there are two separate people. Blood can express continuity, similarity but separateness, and difference. Hence in many parts of Papua New Guinea it signifies that which provides continuity in group membership over generations, that which links members of a group to each other at any one time, and that which links members of different groups. The last is especially apt when the semen, penis or father image is used to express group unity, and when it is important to stress that matri-kin are dispersed in different groups.

When the one-blood idiom means a link joining members of a group, it can be, and frequently is, opposed to marriage—one-blood people should not marry. But alliances between groups are important and so are the exchanges that accompany the unions. As a symbol for the links between members of different groups the blood link can become, and often does, a channel for exchanges between matrilateral kin.

Just as blood can be seen as incorporating or delineating boundaries, so too can it be viewed as crossing boundaries and linking people in different groups. Similarly, exchanges can be seen as entailing co-operation between members of a group who come together to give or receive; and this action may define the group. Alternatively, exchange forms a link between groups of men who co-operate. Put simply, relating, whether by blood or exchange, also entails continuity, separation and differentiation. In some cases these apparent contradictions may be so expressed; but possibly a single image such as blood may represent for the same people a bundle of ideas that are contradictory and foster ambiguity. Why not? Wagner sees exchanges as defining clans and A. Strathern says that the same action links groups. Both are probably true assessments, but given the way Daribi and Melpa people talk about blood, the exchanges could also link Daribi clans and define Melpa groups.

Not all New Guineans are preoccupied with bodily fluids. Nor do they all conceive their local groups as having 'one blood' or belonging to 'one penis', etc. For some, sex is not polluting either, and no formalized antagonism between the sexes exists. But there are other types of ambiguities. The Kunimaipa provide an example. These people greatly value pigs and ceremonies. They also believe in spirit beings, *rizohol*, which include human spirits, pig spirits, *bolrizohol*, and spirits of the forest. When questioned about their spirits they often appear evasive. McArthur says they are vague about where the *rizohol* dwell and answered her questions concerning their whereabouts with 'I don't know, I've never been there— have you?' (1971 p. 179). She also says that 'the possibility of using a single word for *bolrizohol* and for *rizohol* of the forest, of living people and of the dead, obviates any need for a native speaker to indicate precisely which he is talking about, and leaves the way open for him and his listeners to interpret as they please' (p. 185). Moreover, the people are inconsistent about what they say of the dead and are not worried by this. Instead they reply to questions about the dead with, 'We don't know what *rizohol* do; we don't see them. These are only things we say.' (p. 186).

McArthur concedes that her account of the Kunimaipa and their spirits may be untidy, but then any people's social life, including our own, could be so described. The imposition of continual congruences between action and ideas does not reveal order, although such methodological practices can impose an illusory order upon any data. Fortunately she resists the temptation to tidy up and argues that presumably Kunimaipa 'statements about *rizohol* do what people require. They recognize that each makes good sense in context. Nobody knows for sure what happens to *rizohol*, so if you can score a point in a quarrel by asserting that they hang around waiting for a pig-killing, you say so. The fate of *rizohol* is really irrelevant; what matters is failure to kill pigs' (p. 186). In short, their talk about spirits is a useful way of talking about what people do, which may or may not be consistent.

This article began by emphasizing uniformities and ended with ambiguities of one kind or another. But throughout, examples of variations in social life appeared. Focus on one kind of society typical of, but not exclusive to, the Highlands showed certain similarities such as antagonism between the sexes, ambivalent attitudes to blood, an accent on warfare and exchanges, and an emphasis on patrilineality for indicating group solidarity. Elsewhere other constellations of customs appear, similar but different to those mentioned. Everywhere kinship and exchange are important; but among the Lakalai, Siuai, Tolai, Dobu and Trobriand Islanders, matrilineality is pervasive. Major social groups linked by matrilineal

ties are dispersed, sometimes over wide areas; local-group strength
and access to land do not appear to be the main basis of a leader's
strength. On the contrary, trading or exchange of movable valuables
seems the most important source of wealth and prestige. The *kula*
is the most striking institution in this respect.

Everywhere in Papua New Guinea politics, ritual and exchange
are predominantly men's business, but these lowland areas offer a
rich field for exploring the relation between the affairs of men and
the emphasis on kin ties through females. 'Relation' here does not
mean that social action and ideas must be squeezed into a neat Pro-
crustean bed of functional fit. If people say they are descended from
one father or one ancestress, that they share blood, have spirits, or
that their yams have personality, their statements do not have to
be true or consistent, only useful. The job is to find out how and in
what context. In any society there is interplay between ideas and
action, and looking for the extent of manoeuvrability, the range of
ambiguity, indeed the dialectics of social life itself, is an essential
part of the anthropologist's task. But an understanding of the
differences as well as the similarities in cultural traits, together with
an appreciation of the force in ambiguity, is surely essential for an
understanding of the transformation that Papua New Guinea social
life is currently undergoing.

Bibliography

Allen, M. R. 1967. *Male Cults and Secret Initiations in Melanesia*.
   Melbourne.
Barnes, J. A. 1962. 'African models in the New Guinea Highlands',
   Man, vol. 62. Reprinted in Hogbin and Hiatt (eds), *Australian
   and Pacific Anthropology*, 1966.
—— 1967-8. 'Agnation among the Enga', *Oceania*, vol. 38.
Barth, F. 1970-1. 'Tribes and intertribal relations in the Fly head-
   waters', *Oceania*, vol. 41.
Bateson, G. 1931-2. 'Social structure of the Iatmul people of the
   Sepik River', *Oceania*, vol. 2.
Belshaw, C. S. 1957. *The Great Village*. London.
Berndt, R. M. 1962. *Excess and Restraint*. Chicago.
—— 1964. 'Warfare in the New Guinea Highlands', *American
   Anthropologist*, vol. 66, special publication.
Berndt, R. M. and Lawrence, P. (eds) 1971. *Politics in New Guinea*.
   Perth.

Brookfield, H. C. and Brown, P. 1963. *Struggle for Land*. Melbourne.
Brookfield, H. C. and White, J. P. 1968. 'Revolution or evolution in the prehistory of the New Guinea Highlands: a seminar report', *Ethnology*, vol. 7.
Brown, P. 1962. 'Non-agnates among the patrilineal Chimbu', *Journal of the Polynesian Society*, vol. 71.
―――― 1967-70. 'The Chimbu political system', *Anthropological Forum*, vol. 2.
―――― 1969. 'Marriage in Chimbu', in Glasse and Meggitt (eds), *Pigs, Pearlshells, and Women*.
Brown, P. and Brookfield, H. C. 1959-60. 'Chimbu land and society', *Oceania*, vol. 30.
―――― 1967. 'Chimbu residence and settlement', *Pacific Viewpoint*, vol. 8.
Brunton, R. 1971-2. 'Cargo cults and systems of exchange in Melanesia', *Mankind*, vol. 8.
Bulmer, R. N. H. 1960-1. 'Political aspects of the moka ceremonial exchange system among the Kyaka people of the Western Highlands of New Guinea', *Oceania*, vol. 31.
―――― 1965. 'The Kyaka of the Western Highlands', in Lawrence and Meggitt (eds), *Gods, Ghosts and Men in Melanesia*.
―――― 1967-8. 'The strategies of hunting in New Guinea', *Oceania*, vol. 38.
Burridge, K. O. L. 1963-6. 'Tangu political relations', *Anthropological Forum*, vol. 1.
Chowning, A. 1963-6. 'Lakalai kinship', *Anthropological Forum*, vol. 1.
Chowning, A. and Goodenough, W. H. 1963-6. 'Lakalai political organization', *Anthropological Forum*, vol. 1. Reprinted in Berndt and Lawrence (eds), *Politics in New Guinea*.
Craig, R. 1969. 'Marriage among the Telefolmin', in Glasse and Meggitt (eds), *Pigs, Pearlshells, and Women*.
de Lepervanche, M. 1967-8. 'Descent, residence and leadership in the New Guinea Highlands', *Oceania*, vol. 38.
Douglas, M. 1970. *Natural Symbols*. London.
du Toit, B. M. 1964-5. 'Filiation and affiliation among the Gadsup', *Oceania*, vol. 35.
Elkin, A. P. 1952-3. 'Delayed exchange in Wabag Sub-district, Central Highlands of New Guinea', *Oceania*, vol. 23.
Epstein, A. L. 1962-3. 'The economy of modern Matupit', *Oceania*, vol. 33.
―――― 1964-5. 'Variation and social structure', *Oceania*, vol. 35.

———— 1966. Power, Politics and Leadership. Paper given to a seminar on local-level politics, Burg Wartenstein, July 1966.

———— 1969. *Matupit: land, politics and change among the Tolai of New Britain*. Canberra.

———— 1970-1. 'Dispute settlement among the Tolai', *Oceania*, vol. 41.

Evans-Pritchard, E. E. 1940. *The Nuer*. Oxford.

Finney, B. R. 1968. 'Bigfellow man belong business in New Guinea', *Ethnology*, vol. 7.

Fortes, M. 1950. 'Kinship and marriage among the Ashanti', in Radcliffe-Brown and Forde (eds), *African Systems of Kinship and Marriage*.

Fortune, R. F. 1932. *Sorcerers of Dobu: social anthropology of the Dobu Islanders*. London.

———— 1947. 'The rules of relationship behaviour in one variety of primitive warfare', *Man*, vol. 47.

Glasse, R. M. 1958-9. 'The Huli descent system', *Oceania*, vol. 29.

———— 1954-62. 'Revenge and redress among the Huli', *Mankind*, vol. 5.

———— 1965. 'The Huli of the Southern Highlands', in Lawrence and Meggitt (eds), *Gods, Ghosts and Men in Melanesia*.

———— 1968. *The Huli of Papua*. Paris.

———— 1969. 'Marriage in South Fore', in Glasse and Meggitt (eds), *Pigs, Pearlshells, and Women*.

Glasse, R. M. and Lindenbaum, S. 1971. 'South Fore politics', in Berndt and Lawrence (eds), *Politics in New Guinea*.

Glasse, R. M. and Meggitt, M. J. (eds) 1969. *Pigs, Pearlshells, and Women: marriage in the New Guinea Highlands*. Englewood Cliffs.

Goodenough, W. H. 1953. 'Ethnographic notes on the Mae people of New Guinea's Western Highlands', *Southwestern Journal of Anthropology*, vol. 9.

Groves, M. 1963. 'Western Motu descent groups', *Ethnology*, vol. 2.

Harding, T. G. 1965. 'Trade and politics: a comparison of Papua and New Guinea traders', in J. Helm (ed.), *Essays in Economic Anthropology*, Seattle (Proceedings of the 1965 annual spring meeting of the American Ethnological Society).

———— 1963-8. 'Ecological and technical factors in a Melanesian gardening cycle', *Mankind*, vol. 6.

Heider, K. G. 1971-2. 'The grand valley Dani pig feast: a ritual of passage and intensification', *Oceania*, vol. 42.

Hiatt, L. R. and Jayawardena, C. (eds) 1971. *Anthropology in Oceania: essays presented to Ian Hogbin.* Sydney.

Hogbin, H. I. 1944-5. 'Marriage in Wogeo, New Guinea', *Oceania*, vol. 15.

—— 1951. *Transformation Scene.* London.

—— 1963. *Kinship and Marriage in a New Guinea Village.* London.

—— 1967. 'Land tenure in Wogeo', in Hogbin and Lawrence, *Studies in New Guinea Land Tenure.*

—— 1969-70. 'Food festivals and politics in Wogeo', *Oceania*, vol. 40.

—— 1970. *The Island of Menstruating Men: religion in Wogeo.* Scranton.

Hogbin, H. I. and Hiatt, L. R. (eds) 1966. *Readings in Australian and Pacific Anthropology.* Melbourne.

Hogbin, H. I. and Lawrence, P. 1967. *Studies in New Guinea Land Tenure.* Sydney.

Hogbin, H. I. and Wedgwood, C. 1952-4. 'Local grouping in Melanesia', *Oceania*, vols 23-4.

Kaberry, P. M. 1963-6. 'Political organization among the northern Abelam', *Anthropological Forum*, vol. 1. Reprinted in Berndt and Lawrence (eds), *Politics in New Guinea.*

Kelly, R. C. 1968-9. 'Demographic pressure and descent group structure in the New Guinea Highlands', *Oceania*, vol. 39.

Landtmann, G. 1927. *The Kiwai Papuans of British New Guinea.* London.

Langness, L. L. 1964. 'Some problems in the conceptualization of Highlands social structure', *American Anthropologist*, vol. 66, special publication. Reprinted in Hogbin and Hiatt (eds), *Readings in Australian and Pacific Anthropology.*

—— 1966-7. 'Sexual antagonism in the New Guinea Highlands', *Oceania*, vol. 37.

—— 1969. 'Marriage in Bena Bena', in Glasse and Meggitt (eds), *Pigs, Pearlshells, and Women.*

Lawrence, P. 1965. 'The Ngaing of the Rai coast', in Lawrence and Meggitt (eds), *Gods, Ghosts and Men in Melanesia*, Melbourne.

—— 1963-6. 'The Garia of the Madang District', *Anthropological Forum*, vol. 1.

—— 1967. *Land Tenure among the Garia.* Canberra, 1955. Republished in Hogbin and Lawrence, *Studies in New Guinea Land Tenure.*

Lawrence, P. and Meggitt, M. J. (eds). 1965. *Gods, Ghosts and Men in Melanesia.* Melbourne.

Leach, E. R. 1958. 'Concerning Trobriand clans and the kinship category tabu', in J. R. Goody (ed.), *The Developmental Cycle in Domestic Groups*. Cambridge.

Lévi-Strauss, C. 1963. *Structural Anthropology*. Translated by C. Jacobson and B. Schoepf. New York.

—— 1969. *The Elementary Structures of Kinship. (Les Structures élémentaires de la Parenté*, Paris, 1949.) Translated by J. H. Bell et al. Revised ed., London.

Lindenbaum, S. 1970-1. 'Sorcery and structure in Fore society', *Oceania*, vol. 41.

Lindenbaum, S. and Glasse, R. M. 1968-9. 'Fore age mates', *Oceania*, vol. 39.

Lounsbury, F. G. 1964. 'Another view of the Trobriand kinship categories', *American Anthropologist*, vol. 67, special publication.

Lowman-Vayda, C. 1963-6. 'Maring big men', *Anthropological Forum*, vol. 1. Reprinted in Berndt and Lawrence (eds), *Politics in New Guinea*.

McArthur, M. A. 1961. The Kunimaipa. Ph.D. thesis, Australian National University.

—— 1966-7. 'Analysis of the genealogy of a Mae-Enga clan', *Oceania*, vol. 37.

—— 1971. 'Men and spirits in the Kunimaipa Valley', in Hiatt and Jayawardena (eds), *Anthropology in Oceania*.

Malinowski, B. 1915. 'The natives of Mailu', *Royal Society of South Australia Transactions and Proceedings*, vol. 39.

—— 1922. *Argonauts of the Western Pacific*. London.

—— 1929. *The Sexual Life of Savages in North-Western Melanesia*. London.

—— 1935. *Coral Gardens and their Magic*. 2 vols. London.

Mead, M. 1938. *The Mountain Arapesh I : an importing culture*. Anthropological Papers of the American Museum of Natural History, vol. 36.

—— 1942. *Growing up in New Guinea*. London.

Meggitt, M. J. 1956-7. 'The valleys of the Upper Wage and Lai Rivers', *Oceania*, vol. 27.

—— 1957-8a. 'The Ipili of the Porgera Valley', *Oceania*, vol. 28.

—— 1957-8b. 'The Enga of the New Guinea Highlands', *Oceania*, vol. 28.

—— 1954-62. 'Enga political organization', *Mankind*, vol. 5.

—— 1964. 'Male-female relationships in the Highlands of Australian New Guinea', *American Anthropologist*, vol. 66, special publication.

—— 1965. *The Lineage System of the Mae-Enga of New Guinea*. Edinburgh.

—— 1967-70. 'The pattern of leadership among the Mae Enga of New Guinea', *Anthropological Forum*, vol. 2.

Murphy, R. 1972. *The Dialectics of Social Life*. London.

Newman, P. L. 1965. *Knowing the Gururumba*. New York.

Nilles, J. 1950-1. 'The Kuman of the Chimbu Region, Central Highlands, New Guinea', *Oceania*, vol. 21.

Oliver, D. L. 1949. *Studies in the Anthropology of Bougainville, Solomon Islands*. Papers of the Peabody Museum, Harvard University, vol. 29.

—— 1955. *A Solomon Island Society*. Cambridge, Mass.

Pouwer, J. 1964. 'A social system in the Star Mountains', *American Anthropologist*, vol. 66, special publication.

—— 1966. 'Towards a configurational approach to society and culture in New Guinea', *Journal of the Polynesian Society*, vol. 75.

Powdermaker, H. 1933. *Life in Lesu*. London.

Powell, H. A. 1960. 'Competitive leadership in Trobriand political organization', *Journal of the Royal Anthropological Institute*, vol. 90.

Radcliffe-Brown, A. R. 1952. *Structure and Function in Primitive Society*. London.

Radcliffe-Brown, A. R. and Forde, D. (eds) 1950. *African Systems of Kinship and Marriage*. Oxford.

Rappaport, R. A. 1967a. *Pigs for the Ancestors*. New Haven.

—— 1967b. 'Ritual regulation of environmental relations among a New Guinea people', *Ethnology*, vol. 6.

—— 1969. 'Marriage among the Maring', in Glasse and Meggitt (eds), *Pigs, Pearlshells, and Women*.

Read, K. E. 1946-7. 'Social organization in the Markham Valley, New Guinea', *Oceania*, vol. 17.

—— 1949-50. 'The political system of the Ngarawapum', *Oceania*, vol. 20.

—— 1951-2. 'The Gahuku-Gama of the Central Highlands', *South Pacific*, vol. 5.

—— 1952-3. 'Nama cult of the Central Highlands, New Guinea', *Oceania*, vol. 23.

—— 1953-4. 'Marriage among the Gahuku-Gama of Eastern Central Highlands, New Guinea', *South Pacific*, vol. 7.

—— 1954. 'Cultures of the Central Highlands, New Guinea', *Southwestern Journal of Anthropology*, vol. 10.

———— 1959. 'Leadership and consensus in a New Guinea society', *American Anthropologist*, vol. 61.

Reay, M. 1959a. *The Kuma*. Melbourne.

———— 1959b. 'Individual ownership and transfer of land among the Kuma', *Man*, vol. 59.

Richards, A. 1950. 'Some types of family structure amongst the central Bantu', in Radcliffe-Brown and Forde (eds), *African Systems of Kinship and Marriage*.

Ryan, D. J. 1955-6. 'Clan organization in the Mendi Valley', *Oceania*, vol. 26.

———— 1958-9. 'Clan formation in the Mendi Valley', *Oceania*, vol. 29.

———— 1961. Gift Exchange in the Mendi Valley. Ph.D. thesis, University of Sydney.

Sahlins, M. D. 1963. 'Poor man, rich man, big-man, chief', *Comparative Studies in Society and History*, vol. 5. Reprinted in Hogbin and Hiatt (eds), *Readings in Australian and Pacific Anthropology*.

Salisbury, R. F. 1956. 'Unilineal descent groups in the New Guinea Highlands', *Man*, vol. 56.

———— 1962. *From Stone to Steel*. Melbourne.

———— 1964. 'Despotism and Australian administration in the New Guinea Highlands', *American Anthropologist*, vol. 66, special publication.

———— 1965. 'The Siane of the Eastern Highlands', in Lawrence and Meggitt (eds), *Gods, Ghosts and Men in Melanesia*.

Scheffler, H. W. 1965. *Choiseul Island Social Structure*. Berkeley.

Seligman, C. G. 1910. *The Melanesians of British New Guinea*. Cambridge.

Strathern, A. J. 1966. 'Despots and directors in the New Guinea Highlands', *Man*, vol. 1 (new series).

———— 1968. 'Descent and alliance in the New Guinea Highlands: some problems of comparison', *Proceedings of the Royal Anthropological Institute*.

———— 1969-70. 'Finance and production: two strategies in New Guinea Highlands exchange systems', *Oceania*, vol. 40.

———— 1970-1. 'Cargo and inflation in Mount Hagen', *Oceania*, vol. 41.

———— 1971. *The Rope of Moka: big men and social change in Mount Hagen*. Cambridge.

———— 1972. *One Father, One Blood*. Canberra.

Strathern, A. J. and Strathern, M. 1969. 'Marriage in Melpa', in Glasse and Meggitt (eds), *Pigs, Pearlshells, and Women*.

Strathern, M. 1972. *Women In Between*. London.

Todd, J. A. 1934-5. 'Report on research work in S.W. New Britain', *Oceania*, vol. 5.

Uberoi, J. P. Singh 1962. *Politics of the Kula Ring*. Manchester.

Wagner, R. 1967. *The Curse of Souw*. Chicago.

—— 1969. 'Marriage among the Daribi', in Glasse and Meggitt (eds), *Pigs, Pearlshells, and Women*.

Watson, J. B. 1964. 'Anthropology in the New Guinea Highlands', *American Anthropologist*, vol. 66, special publication.

—— 1964-5. 'Loose structure loosely construed: groupless groupings in Gadsup?', *Oceania*, vol. 35.

—— 1965. 'The significance of a recent ecological change in the Central Highlands of New Guinea', *Journal of the Polynesian Society*, vol. 74.

Wedgwood, C. H. 1930-1. 'Some aspects of warfare in Melanesia', *Oceania*, vol. 1.

—— 1958-9. 'Manam kinship', *Oceania*, vol. 29.

Whiting, J. W. M. and Reed, S. W. 1938-9. 'Kwoma culture', *Oceania*, vol. 9.

Williams, F. E. 1930. *Orokaiva Society*. London.

—— 1936. *Papuans of the Trans-Fly*. Oxford.

—— 1940. *Drama of Orokolo*. Oxford.

Young, M. W. 1971. *Fighting with Food: leadership, values and social control in a Massim society*. Cambridge.

Child Rearing and Socialization

Ann Chowning

The first anthropologists to investigate child rearing in Papua New Guinea on a comparative basis—Mead, Hogbin and Wedgwood—were struck by the great diversity, and further work has confirmed the initial impression. Everywhere, so far as we know, babies are normally suckled for more than a year and girls are expected to assume adult responsibilities much earlier than boys. Apart from these, few generalizations can be made to which there are not conspicuous exceptions, even though there are not many detailed studies to compare. The fullest data come from a relatively limited area, notably the East Sepik District and islands north and east of the New Guinea mainland. Information on traditional systems is increasingly difficult to obtain because of the spread of Western attitudes and practices. Even where European contact is recent, the societies investigated are usually under government control. The removal of the constant threat of enemy attack allows children considerably more freedom than they enjoyed when warfare was endemic. The following description can give only a general impression of how children were, or are, brought up prior to the introduction and acceptance of alien theories about hygiene, discipline and education.

It should be remembered that even within a single society there is never absolute uniformity of opinion and behaviour. Children may be indulged in one family and neglected in another, parents may quarrel over questions of discipline, and the children of one family may receive differential treatment according to birth order, sex, individual personality, or simple favouritism. Diversity in such matters is not peculiar to Western civilization.

Child rearing

EARLY INFANCY

In most traditional societies the infantile death rate is high. Young babies are treated with the greatest care and surrounded by taboos until it seems clear that they will survive. If a baby dies within a few days of birth it is usually buried without ceremony and without mourning; the occurrence is too common. The mother often remains in seclusion with the child at least until the umbilical cord has dropped off and the skin begun to darken. Their emergence may be marked by a ritual welcoming of the baby into the community. His life is still precarious, however, and the parents must think constantly of his interests. The mother is usually forbidden sexual intercourse at least until the baby is well developed, a prohibition which prevents her becoming pregnant too soon and so depriving the child of a milk supply for which there is no substitute. Particularly in the Highlands, the post-partum taboo may last as long as three years; in most societies a mother who becomes pregnant again too quickly is strongly condemned. The mother must avoid exposing the child to the sun or taking him near places haunted by spirits, which are particularly likely to attack infants. It is often believed that the child's soul, sometimes localized in the fontanelle, is loosely attached at first, and that nothing, such as startling or striking the infant or permitting it to cry excessively, must be done to drive it away. Babies are almost always fed on demand for some months and distracted or lulled with jogging or songs if they cry for reasons other than hunger.

FEEDING

In some societies another woman feeds the baby until the mother's milk appears, and later he may be suckled by anyone who has milk if his mother is absent. Elsewhere the milk of other people is considered dangerous, or women feel that they have only enough for one child and none to share. If the mother alone can feed the child, she either stays at home for some time while relatives perform her garden work or carries him everywhere in a sling or net bag. The mother generally seems to enjoy suckling the infant, and it is a long, drawn-out process during which the child is fondled and talked to. In a few societies, such as the Mundugumor, babies are regarded as something of a nuisance to be fed and placated as quickly as possible and returned to their baskets. As the child grows older he is allowed to go for increasingly long periods without milk and the mother tends to be more casual about suckling, sometimes not holding or looking at the child. If a child is frightened or ill, however, the breast may be offered primarily for the sake of comfort, and both mother and child revert to the earlier pattern. The use of dummies is very rare, though the Mbowamb employ one soaked in salt. Where betelnut is chewed, babies are given the rind to suck as a mechanical pacifier and teething aid. But most commonly a child whose mother is absent is pacified with solid food. Malnutrition is occasionally seen if the mother's milk supply is inadequate or she has become pregnant too soon, or if the baby is an orphan.

Although babies are normally suckled at least until they are walking well, solid food is usually added to the diet in the first few months. In Kurtatchi, prechewed taro is given from the day of birth, but most peoples wait until the baby is three to five months old or has his first teeth. Prechewed starchy foods, water from sugarcane, and coconut milk are typically the first foods. These are supplemented as the child grows older and acquires more teeth. Most peoples forbid some foods to small children on the assumption that these will cause sickness or stunt growth. Children are always forbidden to eat any foods taboo to their kin groups but, unlike their elders, are not normally expected to abstain from staple foods in mourning for dead relatives. On the whole, there are relatively few distinctions between the diet of child and adult: a two-year-old usually has what the rest of the family eats, simply washing it down with mother's milk. Occasionally the chewing of betelnut is also introduced in infancy, though most societies discourage both chewing and smoking until at least six and often until adolescence.

CARING FOR THE BABY

In many societies contact with the blood shed in childbirth, the aura of which is thought to cling to the new-born child, or even contact with the infant himself, is considered dangerous to masculinity. Consequently, the father may avoid touching his child for periods that range from a few days or weeks to the extreme in Wogeo of one year. Men may also consider it degrading to be soiled by a baby or to be seen carrying one, or women may believe men incompetent to look after babies. It is not uncommon for the care of small infants to be entirely in the hands of women. Women may also specialize in treating childhood ailments, though men may be called in to perform growth magic or deal with serious diseases. But once the baby is a few months old he may spend almost as much time with his father as with his mother. Masculine attitudes vary from society to society but, in most, offspring are a source of pride. The father and grandfather care for the baby and play with him while the mother is working and usually draw the line only at cleaning up after him. Rarely are men reported to be sterner disciplinarians than women. Even where fathers spend relatively little time with their babies a man may be constantly mindful of his child—providing food, observing taboos and making sure that his wife does so as well, sponsoring ceremonies, and even arranging a betrothal. If the father has more than one wife, and the women are friendly, they are likely to share the baby-sitting.

In addition to the parents, aunts or grandmothers who live nearby normally help care for the baby; and so may older siblings. A child of eight or more is usually considered capable of minding an infant for hours at a time. The baby-sitter is likely to be female unless the baby has only brothers of the right age, but in many societies boys enjoy playing with babies as much as girls do. In some places, however, babies are not entrusted to the care of a child or even to that of adults other than the closest kin. Here babies grow up accustomed only to the narrow family circle. The observable consequences of these different attitudes are the older child's reactions to outsiders or strangers, though timidity also varies with age and personality. Sometimes parents deliberately teach children to fear strangers, who are equated with enemies. By contrast, the parents may teach the baby to extend kinship terms at an early age, and persuade him to accept strangers by identifying them as aunts, uncles, or other trusted relatives.

There are notable differences in the treatment accorded to children who are frightened or in pain. Older children are rarely coddled unless they are really ill. Among two- to three-year-olds prolonged crying fits and real temper tantrums are not only common but often are ignored. Furthermore, even among peoples who treat young babies with the greatest tenderness, adults may delight in teasing older ones to tears. In some areas, as among the Orokaiva, little boys are deliberately frightened so that they will eventually become courageous, and parents elsewhere may invoke bogey men to keep a small child out of dangerous places; but in many societies the teasing and false tales have no aim other than to amuse adults.

APPEARANCE AND ADORNMENT

Most groups have well defined standards of beauty, and even a new-born child may be appraised in such terms. Women may attempt to mould the infant's features by shaping the skull with the fingers, pinching up the bridge of the nose, or flattening the ears to the head. It is unlikely that the pressure is sufficiently great or continuous to have any effect. But in south-west New Britain, where a highly elongated skull is the ideal, babies have their heads bound with bark cloth immediately after birth and the binding is renewed every day for at least three months. The motive is purely aesthetic, and the results are permanent. In a few other areas, notably on Bougainville, the lobes of the ears and septum of the nose may be pierced and cicatrization begun in infancy on the assumption that these actions are less painful to a baby. Circumcision is only occasionally carried out in infancy. It is more often assumed that such mutilations should be delayed until the child is older and stronger.

In some regions neither children nor adults wash regularly, though a baby may be bathed for coolness on a hot day. On the coast babies are usually bathed frequently, and it has often been noted that people otherwise careful not to shock or upset a baby will douse him with cold water, ignoring his howls. They may be concerned only with appearance, but the motive is often hygienic, with older children being allowed to go dirty. Similarly, the oils and pigments sometimes rubbed on a baby's skin may be designed to strengthen it or to give protection against the sun rather than simply to improve its appearance, and the pendants and bracelets he wears may be intended primarily as amulets.

Adults often delight in adorning babies and even dressing them in miniature grown-ups' costume for special occasions. Though usually naked until they are about six, children may wear necklaces and armbands, and have designs painted on their faces and bodies, from earliest infancy. As the hair grows it may be trimmed, dyed, or adorned in various ways, though small children have their hair cut short to prevent severe louse infestation.

WALKING

During the suckling period the child learns to walk and talk. Walking is usually encouraged by adults who hold him erect, guide his first steps, and set up stakes on to which he can hold. Parents boast of the precocious walker and recite spells to speed up the retarded. Only the Wogeo are known to try to prevent crawling and to discourage walking until a child is old enough to look after himself—about two years. Elsewhere the parents are glad to be partially relieved of the burden of carrying.

Once the baby is able to move around freely, there are specific dangers to be avoided. Different groups are nervous about different things: the Sengseng are careless about letting babies get into fires and allow the smallest infants to play with sharp knives, but they guard constantly against falls. Some peoples teach babies to swim as soon as they can walk and others keep them away from the water. Manus babies are trained very young to be physically adept and then are left to their own devices; Wogeo babies are watched at all times.

TALKING

Speech seems to be encouraged in all societies. The mother in particular usually talks constantly to the baby, imitating and responding to his babbling and often saying words and simple phrases over and over again. As the child grows older he may be told to repeat the phrases. Sometimes the phrases are sung, and babies may learn to carry a tune before they can talk intelligibly. Baby talk, in the strict sense, is rarely used by adults, though many people teach babies special easy-to-pronounce terms for 'mother' and 'father'. The Kove pronounce words in a childish fashion, as by substituting *t* for *s*, in speaking to babies, but such behaviour is rare. Children often have difficulty in pronouncing all the sounds of their language correctly before the age of six or so, and usually adults ignore their mispronunciations, assuming that these will disappear with age. Mistakes in terminology are usually corrected at once, but grammatical errors may be tolerated. Whatever the attitude of adults, older children often mock mistakes and stammering, and small children are frequently reported to be shy about talking in front of strangers.

TOILET TRAINING

While caring for a young baby an adult may try to anticipate his intentions and place him aside to avoid being soiled by faeces. Serious toilet training does not usually take place until the child can walk and talk. He is simply expected to leave the house to urinate; but he may need an escort to the place set aside for defecation, especially if he goes after dark, and he may also need help in cleaning himself. He is expected to avoid soiling the house at some period between two and three, and toilet training is usually accomplished gradually and without noticeable difficulties. After a period of instruction and explanation the child may be scolded or slapped if he has an accident, especially if he dirties clothes or a sleeping mat or misbehaves in front of a visitor. Toilet training usually focuses on defecation; urine is often equated with water, and urination may be treated casually unless or until the child is taught to feel shame about exposing the genitals.

CEREMONIAL IN INFANCY

Throughout infancy the baby's parents are concerned with his health and development. Magical devices of various sorts—amulets, spells, the observation of taboos, the placation of spirits—may be used to ensure that he grows up normally, and each stage of development may be marked ceremonially. Often the full set of rites is carried out only for a first-born child, on the assumption that subsequent children will benefit as well. In those coastal areas where hereditary rank exists, upper-class children are usually the focus of more ceremonies than those of lower class. A man who is rich or powerful, or aspires to high status, often sponsors particularly numerous or elaborate ceremonies in honour of his child.

Many of these ceremonies are what Oliver calls 'introduction rites'. The *naven* ceremonies of the Iatmül are a famous example. These are carried out when the baby does something significant, or has something done to it, for the first time. In addition to emergence from seclusion, ceremonies may mark the first haircut, the appearance of the first tooth, the first trip to the gardens, the first visit to a strange village, and a variety of other occasions. They may also be held when a child has recovered from any illness. Occasionally, as in *naven* and the Siuai baptism, the ritual is most elaborate; but often it is simple, though the child is normally adorned and displayed and the ceremony is assumed to be of some direct benefit to him. These occasions also serve to cement relations between the child's various kinsmen and typically demand exchanges of wealth and a feast.

The bestowal of a name may also be marked by ceremonial. An outstanding example is found among the Mbowamb where naming marks the child's real acceptance into his clan. It is delayed until the members are sure that he will survive. In some other areas an adult names a child after himself (or herself) before or shortly after its birth; the same name may be used for either sex. This person then assumes certain responsibilities towards his namesake. The whole question of naming is complex: children are often given several names, sometimes commemorating their ancestors, and the child himself may be forbidden to speak his 'true' name. Names given in infancy are not necessarily permanent, and often a child receives a new one at a puberty ceremony.

WEANING

The child is usually considered ready for weaning at between eighteen months and three years of age, though he may occasionally be suckled for five years if the mother does not become pregnant.

Some older children are said simply to wean themselves, or the mother may be able to persuade the child that further sucking is babyish without having to employ forcible means. If the mother becomes pregnant when the child is between one and two she may have to use drastic measures, especially where continued suckling is thought to harm the older child or the foetus. She either puts a repulsive or bitter substance on her breasts, or the child is sent to stay with relatives for a week or two. Sometimes a child weaned forcibly may seem permanently alienated from his mother. Children being weaned appear particularly likely to have temper tantrums, but whether these are the result of weaning or simply tend to occur at the same age is uncertain. Thumb- and finger-sucking are rare and seem to bear no relation to age at weaning; they can be observed in unweaned babies when the mother is within reach. Nakanai parents punish thumb-sucking as a reflection on themselves, saying that onlookers will conclude that the child is underfed. Arapesh children play with their lips after weaning and throughout childhood in what may be a variant on thumb-sucking.

Weaning generally marks the transition from infancy to childhood. Unless the child is the last-born, it is also likely to produce a degree of separation from the mother, who turns her attention to the new baby. Jealousy of the baby, while often considered normal, is sometimes repressed by the parents' insistence that siblings must love one another; and sometimes, so long as it is only expressed verbally, is regarded as just amusing childish behaviour. The three-year-old is likely to spend more time with other children and less under the constant surveillance of his parents, although in some societies, such as Daribi, the father takes over the care of the child. Neglect and even abuse of children are reported of some societies; in Mount Hagen it is a recognized cause for divorce. Orphans and stepchildren are often expected to suffer some deprivation, but this is usually alleviated by the interference of other kinsmen or the practice of adoption.

Socialization

ATTITUDES TO EDUCATION

The absence of rigid discipline and identifiable schools has struck many commentators on village life, but it is incorrect to conclude that children automatically grow up conforming to the standards of the group. Some societies place a high value on formal instruction: the Wogeo, for example, believe that it is actually sinful not to teach a child the ways of the ancestors. By contrast, the Manus boy is taught only to observe a few restrictions and then is allowed to spend a carefree childhood bearing little relation to adulthood. Most societies fall between these extremes. Instruction is begun at various ages, depending on local theories about the development of intelligence. Some peoples feel that it is futile to expect rational behaviour or to impart moral instruction before the age of eight or nine. Younger children are not held responsible for offences, though their parents may be expected to keep an eye on them or to pay for damage. Elsewhere a seven-year-old may own property, have his opinions listened to solemnly by adults, and contribute to the work and food supply of the community. He might be severely punished for striking a sibling, refusing to share food, or stealing.

Similar kinds of things, however, are usually taught. At the earliest age, the child must know which objects, areas, and people are dangerous; whom he can trust; and whose food is safe to eat. He must learn to cope with his environment and handle simple tools, weapons and fire. He should know the properties of common plants and animals and be able to collect and prepare such food-stuffs as shellfish. He must be instructed to observe taboos. For the Madang District, Lawrence reports great stress on the learning of ritual and myths in childhood, yet neglect of formal instruction in technology. In other societies knowledge of the spirit world and of ritual on the part of children is often minimal; the parents are just concerned with protecting the child from supernatural dangers and with preserving the mysteries from non-initiates. Admission to full knowledge comes only with adulthood.

SOCIAL EDUCATION

The first social virtues inculcated often have to do with property, including food. Usually generosity is highly valued, and children may be urged or forced to share food almost from babyhood. Attitudes towards other sorts of property differ. In Manus, where children are not taught to be generous, they are so constantly warned and punished for touching goods belonging to others that all property is safe in their presence. Elsewhere the discipline is not so severe, and adults may have to hide valuables where children cannot see them. In Wogeo a small child is given any fragile object it cries for; in Sengseng wanton destruction of property, including garden crops, is tolerated even in six-year-olds. But generally speaking a child is told not to touch the property of others lest he damage it and so arouse anger or provoke a demand for payment, or lest he be called a thief. He may be told that people will condemn him or his parents or practise sorcery against him. Often only the fear of sorcery can prevent boys from stealing sugarcane or coconuts; it is a rare society that instils real respect for property in children.

Children are also taught property behaviour towards relatives and the duties they owe to the kin group as a whole. This is a slow process, and small children are often not expected to observe all the prohibitions that inhibit relations between certain categories of kin. Incest regulations are usually rigidly enforced from the beginning and children are strongly discouraged from engaging in anything approximating to sexual behaviour with forbidden kinsmen. Where infant betrothal is practised children may also have to avoid certain of their future affines. Children in societies in which kinship terminologies are normally used in address and reference learn these early, beginning with the expressions for mother and father. Parents concentrate on establishing favourable relations with people who will be the child's major sources of support later in life—such as his brothers, the members of his clan, or his closest neighbours—and may force him to refrain from quarrelling or fighting with any of these. On the other hand, striking a parent is often regarded with amusement rather than outrage.

Where warfare is endemic a certain amount of male aggressiveness must be tolerated if the people are to survive. Some Highlands groups seem to encourage boys to be bullies, ruthless even towards their kinsmen. Usually, however, they are allowed to display such traits only in dealing with members of other clans or residents of other villages. Within his own group a boy may be allowed to compete with others but not actually to fight. In some societies even competitiveness is discouraged lest the loser bear a grudge. It is noteworthy that rivalry rarely remains friendly in this part of the world, but adults do tend to compete with each other, more or less overtly, and the children often mimic the adult patterns without being taught them. The Arapesh and the Busama are virtually unique in trying to muffle all expressions of competitiveness and aggressiveness in boys as well as girls. In almost every other society boys are afforded considerable opportunities for developing initiative and independence in at least some spheres, even when they are not specifically trained for warfare. Adults typically allow boys plenty of freedom, cheer on their exploits against outsiders, offer no sympathy for minor injuries, and teach them to use weapons. In Iatmül little boys are helped to kill prisoners, but in most societies actual experience of killing and active participation in warfare is delayed until a man is fully grown. Boys simply play at fighting.

Juvenile tendencies to violence are almost always restricted by the demand that respect be shown to elders (usually excluding grandparents, who are treated with freedom) and, where an upper class exists, to its members. Older men are often adept at sorcery and the use of spears, and may have uncertain tempers. If they are powerful leaders, big-men, or hold hereditary high rank, their persons may actually be surrounded by taboos. Insistence on respect for those who possess special knowledge is intensified if there are secret societies, restricted men's houses, and rigorous initiation rites; children may be threatened with death at the hands of men or spirits if they trespass on the sacred areas. Older women, who are unlikely to be threatening figures, are rarely accorded the same respect as men, except in those few areas where they may be suspected of witchcraft. Children of both sexes must be careful not to antagonize the parents of potential spouses, and obedience to elders is a highly esteemed trait, as adults constantly remind their own children.

METHODS OF EDUCATION

As the foregoing statements indicate, different approaches are used to produce conformity to adult norms. Some peoples try never to strike a child and only do so when seriously provoked; others, like the Kwoma, subject them to constant cuffs and kicks and occasional beatings. The Wogeo reason even with a very small child, explaining just why he should behave correctly, and the Nakanai point out the probable consequences of his actions and expect him to react accordingly; but the Busama feel that small children are incapable of understanding, and they tend to employ force instead. Although bribery, in the form of food, is occasionally offered, a child who behaves correctly may get little reward but the knowledge of adult approval. The child who is particularly attentive to a parent or old person may be repaid with the teaching of special knowledge and with substantial gifts if the kinship system permits.

On the whole, children are more concerned to avoid censure than to acquire rewards. Good behaviour is induced by accounts of the probable retaliation of those offended, who may withdraw support and aid, refuse to consider the child as a possible affine, or actually attack him with physical weapons or sorcery. Often he realizes that the danger is in being caught, and may be prepared to evade the rules in secret. Through constant repetition, the parents may also inculcate a strong sense of shame at misbehaviour in a child. Sometimes the parents emphasize their own shame at the child's actions: In an area where shame frequently leads to suicide this can be a powerful sanction. Ridicule may be employed freely, though children may be warned not to ridicule others lest they alienate them. Parents may use standard epithets ('idiot!' 'bush demon!' 'hardhead!') with children, or may curse them and threaten mayhem. Since threats are not often carried out, and parents rarely consider it necessary to maintain a consistent attitude, many children simply run away to the bush or go to stay with a relative till the parent's anger has cooled.

Punishment is almost entirely in the hands of the parents and other senior kin, and they are likely to resent strongly anyone else striking the child. Sometimes the parents threaten to summon a village big-man or one of the masked figures which, in some societies, chase and beat non-initiates; but such threats are usually idle, as the child soon discovers. There are only a few societies in which adults believe that the spirits of the ancestors punish misbehaviour by bringing sickness to the child or to members of his family. Where such a belief is held, the threat of supernatural wrath may impress an older child who has seen the affliction of others explained in these terms.

When infants cry, adults seek to distract them; when older children lose their tempers, a diversion of attention may also be employed. The child is persuaded to attack things, as by chopping a tree rather than hitting people, and he grows up to be a man who chops down his house when he is offended. As an alternative, he may be permitted to scream and roll on the ground; Arapesh boys may do this even in adolescence. These devices are employed particularly in societies where violence within the group is deplored.

Where hereditary rank exists, an upper-class child may be pampered because people are reluctant to chastise him, and he may also have the right to order other children around. At the same time, such a child may be expected to be particularly well behaved and is constantly reminded to live up to his obligations. Wedgwood found upper-class children on Manam Island to be more courteous, generous and honest than others. The children of chiefs and important men may similarly be expected to provide examples.

Although most parents want their children to conform to community norms, the spoiled child is by no means unknown. Sometimes a recalcitrant youngster is regarded as simply unable, for one reason or another, to learn, but there are also parents who are amused by the stubbornness, independence or aggressiveness of their children and tolerate these traits at whatever cost to community relations. There also exist parents who cannot cope with a strong-minded child, and some who are blinded by affection to behaviour that may scandalize the neighbourhood. Occasionally other kinsmen intervene if the parents are unwilling or unable to discipline a young boy, but in some societies no one else would dare to usurp the parents' prerogatives, and the child grows up relatively free from restraint. Other adults find some relief in prophesying a bad end for him.

Apart from moral qualities, children must also learn such techniques as food production, house building, and the manufacture of various artefacts. Teaching is always the primary responsibility of the parent of the same sex, though an expert at such specialties as canoe manufacture or weather control may train a nephew or more remote relative, especially if he has no son of his own or is paid for the job. Much is learned by a child's simply trailing along, partly for amusement's sake, observing, and trying tasks for himself. Detailed instruction is sometimes given, however, with the adult demonstrating, explaining, and guiding the child's hands. Children are usually encouraged to help with small tasks, even when they may actually be a hindrance, on the assumption that they will only learn by doing.

General knowledge is usually passed on informally. Much information is volunteered, but parents usually encourage their children to ask questions and may test the fund of information by questioning them in turn. Knowledge is esteemed, and children are normally eager to learn and anxious to display their learning. A certain amount of information is imparted by story-telling, which is practised particularly at night and during the rainy season. Some of the stories are purely entertainment, though among the Massim it is believed that listening to stories aids growth. Many point a moral, teach the rules of traditional behaviour, describe the spirit world, explain the origin of natural features and human customs, and sometimes give the sacred history of the child's own clan. Among the Iatmül a spell is recited over a child to help him remember the clan legends. In Wogeo children are constantly enjoined to follow the example of the hero children described in the myths. Some myths may be too sacred to be revealed until the child is initiated, but otherwise there is usually no special category of children's tales or censorship for children's ears. The Manus are apparently peculiar in not telling stories to children, saying that they do not enjoy them.

PLAY

Childhood is by no means solely a time given to instruction: children, especially the younger ones, typically pass most of the day in play. The size and composition of the play group varies with the local residence patterns, but at least one companion is usually available, and ties of friendship may be forged that last into adulthood. In most areas a wide choice of diversions is available. Both the sea and the bush offer numerous amusements and, simultaneously, the opportunity to practise hunting, paddling canoes, and other useful skills. Formal and elaborate games, accompanied by rhymes, are often performed, particularly on moonlit nights. During the day children romp and scuffle, dance and sing, and imitate adult activities—playing house or pig-hunt, engaging in a ceremonial exchange, carrying out an elaborate mortuary rite. They may also pretend to be the evil spirits and witches whom they genuinely fear at night. Certain games and toys are particularly common: stilts of half-coconut shells, leaf whirligigs and puzzles, spinning tops made of a fruit pierced with a stick, swings of bark loops or vines, string figures (cat's cradle), contests in which darts are thrown at a rolling disc and, in a few coastal areas, surfboards. Perhaps because they usually have real babies to play with, little girls rarely own a doll, but girls too young to be trusted with an infant sometimes carry around an object such as a smooth stone or a stick and treat it as a baby.

Some games such a mock combat with miniature weapons and shooting at insects with toy bows, or preparing meals on improvised hearths, definitely train for adulthood. So, in different ways, do riddles and guessing games. The children, while amusing themselves, acquire physical skills and manual dexterity and may exercise their imaginations and develop social awareness. They are bound to learn standards of interpersonal behaviour: perhaps that the strong can bully the weak, perhaps that co-operation is necessary if the games and enterprises are to be successful and enjoyable. Boys typically continue to pass their days in play until adolescence, roaming in groups, while the growing girl gradually spends more time helping her mother with the work of the household and has less and less opportunity for diversions with her contemporaries.

SEX IN CHILDHOOD

Although babies are usually treated almost exactly alike regardless of sex, children begin to show appreciation of their separate roles by the age of about five. Adults may begin to tease small children about their marital prospects and often remind them of taboos on matters which would affect their sexual development. Emotional behaviour is gradually conditioned by expectations and demands. Whereas the Nakanai expect boys to be stoical and girls to be volatile, the Arapesh permit only boys to weep and indulge in fits of rage. The Wogeo and Siuai reproach girls for any display of violence, reserving such behaviour for boys, while the Sengseng teach baby girls to chase and beat boys in anticipation of the later courtship patterns. Children also impose some restrictions on themselves, identifying with adults of their sex and refusing to play inappropriate roles in games. If necessary, adults may forbid little girls to mimic men's ceremonies. Often by about six, boys begin to sleep apart from their mothers and sisters, though they are usually still forbidden to enter ceremonial structures. They may be impressed with the necessity for avoiding contamination by women, especially those who are menstruating. Even very small girls may be taught to observe taboos against behaviour which might eventually interfere with their ability to bear healthy babies.

It is rare for small children to be aware of sexual discrimination; most parents want children of both sexes and give them equal attention. As they grow older it is usually made clear to the girl that her life will be more restricted and drab than that of her brother. As children approach puberty they are likely to be held to standards of modesty in dress and behaviour and often seem to adopt these of their own accord. A few notably prudish societies like the Manus demand great modesty even of young children. Rigid standards are sometimes imposed even where adults wear no clothes: Kwoma girls, for example, are taught to sit with their legs together, and Kwoma boys are adjured not to stare at or react publicly to the sight of female genitals. Almost universally, children learn to seek privacy or darkness for defecation and sexual indulgence, and not infrequently for eating, which has complex connections with sex in many societies.

Attitudes towards childish sexual indulgence vary greatly. Because children usually go naked for years, are thoroughly aware of the facts of life at an early age, and are permitted to hear and use bawdy language, it is sometimes thought that they have complete sexual freedom, inhibited only by the incest taboos. In fact, children lead relatively free sex lives in only a few scattered coastal areas. Most people seem to believe that sexual indulgence in childhood will stunt growth, and a number of groups, especially in the Highlands, regard all contact with females as potentially dangerous to males. Adults in these societies often manage to frighten most boys out of attempting copulation prior to marriage. Masturbation in the young may be regarded tolerantly, but some condemn it lest it should lead to a precocious interest in sex. Especially along the Fly and Sepik Rivers a good deal of homosexuality occurs in the men's houses, often associated with ritual believed necessary to promote growth in boys. Active homosexuality between adolescents and children is rarely reported for other areas, even those in which boys are discouraged for many years from heterosexual relations. Among the Busama, who prohibit premarital intercourse, an old woman gives a girl sexual instruction after her first menstruation. In other societies the girl may be initiated by her husband. Constant chaperonage may ensure premarital chastity, especially where child betrothal is practised and a girl is supervised by her prospective parents-in-law.

Where premarital sexual relations are permitted, techniques are almost always learned from older children and from observation rather than from direct instruction by an adult. A parent may teach love magic to a growing son, or warn a daughter against it, but rarely do members of the same family discuss sex freely among themselves. Copulation between an adult and a child is usually strongly disapproved, and children, sometimes after a considerable period of experimentation, are typically initiated into intercourse by older and more experienced children. In some societies in the Milne Bay District girls are allowed to receive boys at night in their parents' house, and in parts of the Highlands free courtship is carried on for years in the boys' houses; but more often, young lovers must arrange a secret rendezvous in the bush and the girl is careful to preserve her reputation.

CEREMONIAL IN CHILDHOOD

Some societies hold no rituals for children between those marking birth and puberty, and a few, particularly in the Massim, do not even mark puberty formally. Other societies continue to perform introduction rites, especially for first-born children or children of high rank. These may mark such events as the first participation in a dance, first catch of game, and first harvesting of a crop planted by the child. Often the decorative mutilations, such as tattooing, tooth-blackening and ear-piercing, take place (or, in the case of tattooing, are begun) prior to puberty, and they may be the occasions for ceremonies honouring each child who undergoes them. The assumption of adult clothing may also be a formal occasion marking a step in the child's development to maturity. In some societies all children, or more often all boys, are caught up in a series of rituals that begins in childhood and culminates, years later, in initiation into adult society. Where such rituals demand seclusion, as in northern Bougainville, they may effectively remove the boys from contact with females for a long period. In most cases seclusion is relatively brief. Although the initiands are often exhorted to abide by the rules of the society, they seem rarely to receive any systematic instruction except in ritual matters: the nature and use of bullroarers or sacred flutes, the manufacture of masks, and myths.

Generalizing from his work in the Madang District, Lawrence stresses the enormous importance attached, especially in lowland societies, to the acquisition of religious knowledge by boys during and after initiation. It seems to be true, nevertheless, that in many such societies the teaching of ritual and myth is not stressed at the expense of secular skills, and even where their importance is recognized, they often are not taught to children.

ACHIEVING ADULTHOOD

Girls are usually considered marriageable after their first menstruation which, contrary to popular belief, tends to occur later among New Guineans than among Europeans. In the preceding period the girl has learned and become used to performing the task of an adult. Indeed, by the age of nine or ten she often is able at least to make leaf skirts, cook a meal, help in the gardens and plant a few crops, and care for a baby all day. By puberty she usually has a garden of her own and can manufacture all the standard woman's goods. She is urged to be industrious, obedient and good-tempered so that she will be sought in marriage. Infant betrothal is common, and the engaged girl usually spends part of the time with the groom's family, although marriage is rarely consummated before the girl is physically mature. She may, nevertheless, be expected to observe the decorum proper to a married woman. By contrast, unmarried girls in many societies are granted a great deal of freedom to travel around, dance, and conduct love affairs. This freedom ends at marriage, and consequently girls may try to extend the relatively carefree period as long as possible. Most marriages are arranged, and the girl often has little choice. Unless she is married very young she is usually well able to assume her adult role, though in some groups she may still need instruction about the processes of child-birth.

Boys tend to marry later than girls and, as has been noted, are not usually expected to settle down to steady work as soon. They are often adept at hunting and fishing long before they spend much time gardening. By late adolescence a boy should be able to perform all the everyday masculine tasks. He may still not control wealth, though he may be the nominal owner of a pig and some shell money, both of which are cared for by others. He too may be expected to marry at the desire of his parents, though he may have more choice than a girl. As a child he was taught a few simple spells—for example, to keep away rain, lure octopus, or attract a girl temporarily. Now he is admitted to the repertoire of garden and hunting magic, serious love magic, and spells to protect property and cure disease. Usually before he is ready to marry, the principal secrets of the men's house, if any, are revealed to him. Nevertheless, in many groups, learning continues well into adulthood. Only long after marriage does a man become a specialist at carving or curing; only in his forties, perhaps, is he admitted to the inner rites of a secret society; only when about to become a father himself is he taught the spells to ensure the growth of his children; and only when his own father is about to die is he instructed in the last of his special knowledge. In many societies fully grown and married men often announce 'I am but a child' in recognition of the fact that acquisition of knowledge and the gradual assumption of responsibility is a gradual process and that full maturity may come only with middle age.

Bibliography

Allen, M. R. 1967. *Male Cults and Secret Initiations in Melanesia*. Melbourne.

Bateson, G. 1936. *Naven*. Cambridge.

Blackwood, B. 1935. *Both Sides of Buka Passage*. Oxford.

Chowning, A. 1958. Lakalai Society. Ph.D. thesis, University of Pennsylvania.

Forge, A. 1970. 'Learning to see in New Guinea', in P. Mayer (ed.), *Socialization*, London.

Hogbin, H. I. 1963. *Kinship and Marriage in a New Guinea Village*. London.

—— 1971. 'A New Guinea infancy', *Oceania*, vol. 13, 1942-3. Republished in L. L. Langness and J. C. Weschler (eds), *Melanesia*, Scranton.

—— 1971. 'A New Guinea childhood', *Oceania*, vol. 16, 1945-6. Republished in L. L. Langness and J. C. Weschler (eds), *Melanesia*, Scranton.

Malinowski, B. 1929. *The Sexual Life of Savages in North-Western Melanesia*. London.

Mead, M. 1930. *Growing Up in New Guinea*. New York.

—— 1935. *Sex and Temperament in Three Primitive Societies*. London.

Oliver, D. L. 1955. *A Solomon Island Society*. Cambridge, Mass.

Powdermaker, H. 1933. *Life in Lesu*. London.

Strathern, M. 1972. *Women In Between*. London.

Vicedom, G. F. and Tischner, H. 1943-8. *Die Mbowamb*, vol. 2
(3 vols). Hamburg.
Wagner, R. 1967. *The Curse of Souw*. Chicago.
Wedgwood, C. 1938-9. 'The life of children in Manam', *Oceania*,
vol. 9.
Whiting, J. W. M. 1941. *Becoming a Kwoma*. New Haven.

Economy*

T. Scarlett Epstein

The quantitative and qualitative analysis of traditional economic systems is still in its infancy. The main reason is the absence of money as a generally accepted medium of exchange. Without such a common measure of value it is difficult to examine the rationality of choices or decisions. Time, the universally scarce factor, may be taken as a measuring rod. Salisbury did this successfully for the Siane. Yet to use time as a unit of measurement poses certain problems: it does not take into account the different amount of energies and skills invested on different occasions in the same unit of time. A further complicating variable in the study of under-developed societies is the entanglement of purely economic trans-actions with the social ties that often channel the movement of goods and services. Economic transactions no doubt pervade the social life of primitive peoples, and economic difficulties constantly face them. Yet hardly any of their activities or relationships are guided by purely economic considerations, i.e. the maximization of material gains; these form only one strand in the total nexus of socio-economic activities. Accordingly much information relevant to the study of isolated primitive economies can be extracted from general ethnographic and anthropological literature.

In discussing the operation of small economies in Papua New Guinea it is essential to distinguish between 'traditional' and 'modern' systems. The basic difference between the two is that the former were isolated and stagnant whereas the latter are integrated and geared to growth. One distinction is important particularly with reference to reports of large surplus production and shrewd indigenous entrepreneurs operating in the traditional economy. These reports may give the impression of a history of economic development even prior to European contact. A flexible socio-political system of rule by big-men certainly encouraged individual

* Entitled *Economy, Indigenous* in the *Encyclopaedia*.

thrift and enterprise, yet it simply meant a periodic re-allocation of control of a volume of productive resources that was in the long run stable and fixed. Life must have proceeded without any major economic or social changes. A limited mastery over the physical environment had been achieved and, with the knowledge and equipment available the standard of living could not have been improved. Moreover, there was no alien civilization near at hand to provide models for imitation.

Traditional

Most economic activities were associated with agriculture. Each area had its staple crop: in the Highlands this was mainly sweet potatoes, along the coast usually taro or yams. Shifting cultivation was practised with extensive periods of bush fallow. Coconuts, bananas, and other nuts, fruit and vegetables were grown wherever climate and soil permitted. Environmental conditions determined whether or not indigenes supplemented their cultivation with hunting and fishing. In the sphere of animal husbandry the people mainly concentrated on raising pigs. These, like human beings, feed largely on root crops, which in turn have to be cultivated. Crafts were, on the whole, developed only to a rudimentary level.

LAND

Agriculture formed the basis of most pre-contact economies. Accordingly, land tenure and inheritance were of vital importance. Rights to land were in most cases vested in social groups. A man could cultivate a certain plot of land by virtue of his membership of the particular kin-group that controlled it. Systems of land tenure and inheritance differed from area to area. In some places, for instance among the Wain of the Lae highlands, a man had rights not only in the land belonging to his paternal relatives but also in that belonging to his maternal relatives. Which rights he invoked depended on where he decided to live. If he settled patri-virilocally he rarely claimed his maternal land rights; on the other hand, he was at no disadvantage if he happened to live among his mother's kin. Other peoples, like the Chimbu of the Highlands who have been studied by Brookfield and Brown, placed greater emphasis on land inheritance in the patrilineal line of descent. But even among them there were several kin-groups to which a young man could attach himself, and so he had a choice as to where to exercise his claims to land. In many Melanesian societies descent and inheritance were matrilineal. But even in these it was often possible for a son to cultivate some of the land vested in his father's relatives if he gave a large feast for them or handed over valuables or distributed shell money at one of their important mortuary rites.

There was thus much flexibility in the traditional pattern of land rights. This was facilitated by the absence of population pressure on land. Salisbury suggests that it might be argued that the balance between population and available resources in any one area was the result of conscious planning. He cites one of the Siane clans, members of which in 1953 recognized that they had reached the maximum population density; consequently some of them were migrating, offering as excuse that lineage strips at home were too small and too few. The availability of large areas of uninhabited bushland made for frontier societies. In pre-contact days warfare was probably the most important means by which major areas of land were transferred between social groups. This enabled families who found that they had exhausted landed resources within their home area to shift to other places and exploit different ground. More often it was a case of the big-man trying to gather a following to help in the cultivation of land and increase the supply of available manpower rather than of men fighting over, or moving in search of, cultivable land.

PRODUCTION PLANNING

All creation of wealth started with the cultivation of crops. This was the first labour investment any young man had to make. He may have inherited one or more pigs or acted as custodian for some, but in order to feed his family and his animals he had to grow food. Much production was carried on for specific ends. The Trobriand Islanders, the Kapauku of Irian Jaya (West Irian), and other peoples, distinguished between certain kinds of yams as appropriate for ceremonials and others for normal food. Moreover, cultivators frequently allocated the produce of certain plots at the time of planting. A man might plan one plot to produce food to be given to his affines, another to his wife to dispose of as she thought fit, another to provide for his family's consumption, and yet another to feed the people he expected to help him build a house or a canoe or clear another area of bush. The beneficiaries were informed at the time of planting that the produce was destined for them. Thus within the limits set by climate and soil conditions the recipients were able to plan their own cultivation as well as the arrangements for large feasts. There was, indeed, a considerable element of planning in traditional agriculture, though it frequently went wrong. Pospisil relates how a number of dry years caused the Kapauku to relax their precautions and disregard the weather factor in their choice of new garden lots. They planted most of their sweet potatoes in the lowlands, expecting more dry weather. But the next year proved to be so wet that all the crops in the valley gardens rotted, and the people almost starved. This clearly indicates the extent to which agricultural output was subject to forces beyond the cultivator's control. It also emphasizes the necessity to plan for a surplus in normal years as protection against possible drought or flood.

LABOUR

Many of the subsistence crops required comparatively little labour, and there was thus much unused manpower. All societies in the area practised some division of labour based on sex. Men coped with most of the physically heavy and dangerous work such as clearing bush, making fences and boundaries, fighting, hunting, and so on; women concentrated on the lighter tasks such as weeding, harvesting and household duties. Children were trained at an early age to perform the tasks appropriate to their sex. Thus economic practices, probably the result of trial and error, were handed down from generation to generation. For instance, the Mount Hagen people discussed by Gitlow knew that land might be replanted when a certain kind of tree had reached a height of approximately three metres. Similarly, the Kapauku cultivated their valley gardens intensively by means of drainage ditches, composting, and crop rotation. Often they were able to take three or four harvests from one plot. By contrast, they took only a single harvest from their slope gardens, which they simply cleared by fire and cultivated without fertilizer. Many indigenes were aware of the advantages of rotating crops: greens were often followed by corn, taro or bananas and then by sweet potatoes. They seemed to have worked out the most effective system of cultivation within the limits of their environment and technology.

Traditionally most peoples organized their agricultural activities at the level of the primary household. Yet there was extensive reciprocal assistance at irregular intervals for tasks that required strenuous or tedious work, such as bush clearing, or those that had to be completed within a short period of time, such as harvesting or house building. The Busama, discussed by Hogbin, explained the need for mutual aid in preparing garden land by saying, 'Felling the bush alone is like trying to empty the sea with a canoe bailer—it never ends'. Siane men also had reciprocal labour arrangements: they usually visited their mother's brothers or sisters' sons during the *roi* (pandanus fruit) and nut seasons and helped in harvesting.

Such assistance was reciprocated when their own crop was due. These mutual-aid arrangements often gave rise to limited trade and exchanges. Siane owners of *roi* trees tended to visit kinsmen who owned nut trees, from whom they received nuts; subsequently the nut owners visited the *roi* owners and received oil.

In other societies master-client relationships were used to secure labour. Parkinson describes how the shrewd Tolai big-man encouraged his followers to plant large areas. He had to reward them with either shell money or food but made a handsome profit when he finally sold the total output for shell money. Among the Kapauku, labour was employed on a contract basis and paid in shell money. The customary price for making a *peka*-sized garden —one *peka* equals about nine hundred square metres—was two Kapauku cowries. In their contractual transactions the Kapauku always stated the price for the accomplishment of a specific task, never for a unit of working time. If, for instance, a man agreed to build a fence and it was destroyed by pigs before he had been paid he could not expect to receive payment.

A number of possibilities were thus exploited to organize labour. In all traditional Papua New Guinea societies some household members provided at least part of the workforce. Among many peoples additional labour was arranged reciprocally, among some in master-client relationships, and in a few by contract.

CAPITAL AND ENTREPRENEURSHIP

The indigenous capital asset that required most labour and materials was probably the canoe. Cultivators handled only very primitive tools: often only sharp pieces of bamboo, pointed sticks and stone axes or adzes. Stone axe-blades took about a week to make (a Siane could produce one in six days), chipped easily, were quickly abraded by sharpening, and had an average life of no more than eighteen months.

Owing to the low level of technology, capital requirements were limited. Consequently there was no annual net addition to the stock of assets; replacement of tools was practically the only investment in productive equipment. The lands, associated with comparatively little labour input for subsistence production and capital replacement, made entrepreneurship the main limiting factor in the supply of output. These are the conditions responsible for the existence of 'primitive affluence' as described by Fisk. Organizing ability and entrepreneurship must be regarded here as important factors of production. Most of the settlements had one or more big-men. Recognition as a leader depended on prominent participation in feasts and ceremonial exchanges as well as on the possession of other qualities of leadership. A flexible social system with emphasis on achieved as opposed to ascribed social status provided the background to the exercise of entrepreneurship by capable men. However, not all big-men were entirely self-made. In many societies the heir to a rich man was in a favoured position. But if he proved to be negligent or careless his fortunes were soon dissipated. In fact no leader was ever secure.

ECONOMICS AND POLITICS

The low level of technical knowledge made almost impossible the production of unusually elaborate items of food, clothing or shelter. Consequently big-men could hardly consume any different quality or quantity of goods from those of their followers, in spite of the fact that as leaders they controlled the economic resources of land, pigs and such valuables as feathers and shells. Hoarded wealth did not in itself carry prestige or attract a following. It was the distribution of wealth and the extension of credit that did this. A wealthy creditor not only became a political leader and legal authority, he was also regarded as among the most moral of individuals. This stress on egalitarian living was often reinforced by fears of magic. A big-man tempted by conspicuous consumption was afraid to arouse jealousy because of the possibility of sorcery being directed against him.

The lack of opportunity to acquire durable consumer goods or to invest in the creation of new and additional productive assets therefore led big-men to invest their wealth in scarce valuables and to build up a following by making loans to young people. The real skill of the traditional entrepreneur was expressed in his ability to strike the right balance between his accumulation of valuables and his redistribution of goods. If he spent too much on valuables he was bound to lose influence in his society; on the other hand, if he dissipated too much of his wealth he lost respect and went bankrupt. The Tolai big-man had to be a shrewd operator: he had to accumulate shell money and simultaneously display generosity towards his followers.

ECONOMICS AND RELIGION

Economic activities and religious beliefs were frequently interdependent. Among the Tolai, for instance, thrift was supported by supernatural sanctions. It was believed to provide the passport to a happy afterlife. On the other hand, the leader was also expected to finance and organize large ceremonials and religious festivals. He occupied a key economic position and translated this into the sphere of religion and rituals. Accordingly the Tolai big-man was also the master of his local group of the *Dukduk*, a male cult that represented the central theme in Tolai philosophy. Every man of ambition was an entrepreneur; ceremonial and its marked exchange character forced him to be. If a young man was about to be married, or if the death of an important elder was imminent, the nearest kin had to plan ahead by planting large food gardens so as to have sufficient crops not only to feed the necessary helpers in the performance of marriage or mortuary rites but also to offer lavish hospitality to a wide circle of visitors. Thus religious ceremonies provided some of the occasions for large-scale feasting and redistribution of wealth.

CONSUMPTION

In most traditional societies the consumption of the productive unit differed radically from that of the unit of consumption. The Kapauku had 'gardening units', composed of the simple or polygynous family of the landowner, which were responsible for productive activities, whereas the people who shared a common residence, often several families, planned consumption in common. They placed great emphasis on the intake of sweet potatoes, their staple diet. Hunger was the state of being without sweet potatoes in the stomach. Consequently eating pork, greens, or any other food did not in their eyes alleviate hunger; only a dish of sweet potatoes could do that. This emphasis on the consumption of the staple crop resulted in the size of the cultivated area being determined by the number of people who lived together rather than by the number making up the 'gardening unit'. The Kapauku were compelled by custom to share food with their friends and relatives. Therefore, to avoid extensive sharing, a man who had some delicacy usually tried to hide it and consume it secretly.

The stress of reciprocity was often sanctioned by religious beliefs. The Busama were convinced that illness would follow if they were to eat any meat from a pig they had themselves raised. Accordingly when a household slaughtered an animal the pork was given away. The distribution without expectation of immediate return was of paramount importance for nutrition. Fresh meat deteriorates quickly in the tropics. The owner had no way of preserving pork and therefore gave it away in the expectation of a countergift. This general method of exchange ensured that in time individuals obtained roughly equal shares. It necessarily implied the notion of credit.

SPECIALIZATION, BARTER AND TRADE

All barter or trade is based on some specialization unless for ritual reasons identical articles are exchanged. Often the natural resources of neighbouring areas differed. The Busama, for example, had more agricultural land than required for their immediate needs. The villagers therefore produced quantities of taro for export. Other villages in the area possessed large swamps where surplus sago was grown; yet others specialized in pottery or woodcarving. There were thus some economically interdependent regions within which the population exchanged products. In some places soil variations were so great that a certain variety of one crop flourished only in strictly limited localities, thereby encouraging barter or trade.

The pattern of exchange varied. At one extreme were highly personal relations between *kula* partners in the Trobriand Islands, at the other the largely impersonal and contractual market transactions of the Kapauku and the Tolai who have a system of shell currency almost equivalent to Western money.

It is difficult to analyse the price-formation process in traditional economies. The Siane had a relatively fixed equivalence of one salt cake to one pig. When a Siane clan had publicly received a presentation of *roi* oil it behoved them to return an equivalent value. If the initial donors regarded the amount as insufficient they expressed dissatisfaction. This usually led the initial recipients to add to what they had given rather than risk the loss of future supplies of *roi* oil. In some instances the return was expected immediately, but in others the settlement may have been delayed for years. Among the Suau all transactions were registered either as credits or debts, as also were the pigs speared and the portions distributed. At the periodic pig feast some men obtained payment for past credits, others incurred fresh debts to be settled at a future date, perhaps after five years. Accounts were memorized and return gifts always expected and usually effected. In this way barter was conducted to the mutual satisfaction of the parties. Return gifts were sometimes more valuable than the initial presents. In such cases the man's intention was to show off his wealth and stress his generosity.

In contrast with these personal economic exchanges the Kapauku, the Tolai, and other societies employing shell money, had largely impersonal economic dealings. Market exchange, with shell money as the medium, frequently occurred between strangers who met once to conclude a single transaction. Since ultimate social advantage and prestige could be achieved only through becoming wealthy, trading was largely profit-motivated with few other considerations. The Tolai had chains of markets linking the coastal settlements with the interior of the Gazelle Peninsula, where middle-men acted as intermediaries. At the Kapauku pig market, trading was often conducted by complete strangers. Men invested shell money in pigs and chickens with the hope of breeding from the animals and selling their offspring. At times when supply was good in relation to demand, and prices consequently low, shrewd businessmen bought commodities such as bundles of salt or pigs as a speculation. At Tolai markets, too, prices fluctuated in the short run as a result of changes in supply and demand. Besides, the closer the relationship between parties to a transaction the less profitable it was for the initiator. When a Busama acquired a string bag from a fellow villager he always gave twice what he paid to a more distant relative on the north coast. A rich Kapauku political leader was frequently offered commodities for prices lower than normal, either because the seller expected favours or because he was afraid the rich man might demand payment of a debt. Accordingly big-men were able to buy several pigs from followers, or even from outsiders, at less than the customary or even the market price. Though all traditional trade articles appear to have had a customary price, actual rates differed from the norm not only because of changes in supply and demand but also because of the social status of the parties. Nevertheless, the customary price remained an ideal, a moral and fair price that ought to be asked and paid. Paying the right price meant security for both parties to the contract. This security, however, was obtained at the expense of greater profit.

SHELL MONEY, CREDITS, SAVINGS, INVESTMENT AND INTEREST

In most of Papua New Guinea shells acted as valuables. Being highly desired, they were usually a liquid asset. Yet the exchange value differed according to age, size, texture, regularity of shape, and colouring. Among the Abelam some shells were kept as heir-looms and called by the name of the owners' totem. Fine specimens were stored with care and much admired for their smoothness and shape. Shells were given away at marriage, at the birth of a child, and at death; a small one was handed in compensation for adultery; and a man who wished to injure someone sent a shell to a sorcerer in another village to engage his services. Yet shells hardly ever facilitated everyday exchanges, nor were market values of other commodities expressed in them. Their significance was social and ceremonial rather than economic. In these circumstances the employment of shells in certain exchanges did not mean they were being used as money, i.e. as a medium of exchange and as a measure and store of value.

In contrast, societies such as the Kapauku, the Tolai, and the Rossel Islanders had highly monetized economies even in pre-contact days. The Kapauku cowrie money (*Cypraea* sp.) came in various denominations with a fixed equivalence between the different types of shells: one *tuanika mege* equalled five *kawane*, and one *dege bomoje* was equivalent to three *tuanika mege* or fifteen *kawane*. These shells were not found locally; all were acquired through trade from peoples on the coast. Consequently the amount in circulation was limited. Pospisil believes that in pre-contact days the number of cowries in circulation remained the same; those lost or destroyed through wear and tear about equalled importations. The value of the currency was generally stable and fixed by its scarcity. Similarly the Tolai used shells (*Nassarius callosa*) as money, called *tambu*, which were not available in their own area. Tolai from the eastern part of the Gazelle Peninsula had to undertake dangerous and costly trips three hundred kilometres along the coast to obtain shells through trading or fighting. This limited their supply. *Tambu* consisted of pierced shells threaded on string, and was counted in numbers of individual shells or in fathoms—measured from fingertip to fingertip when both arms were outstretched—or fractions thereof. It was durable and could easily be kept as small change for daily purchases. Larger quantities were stored as coils made by winding strings of *tambu* about one hundred to five hundred fathoms—around a circle of bamboo, these then being covered with pandanus leaves. The Tolai, like the Kapauku, paid shell money for most of the goods and services derived from outside the household. They clearly distinguished between purchase and barter—they had different words to denote the two—and the overwhelming exchange was through sales. Barter operated according to certain rules on spheres of exchange, which limited the free movement of goods. In contrast, shell money was accepted as a general means of settling transactions. Only money enabled a Kapauku or a Tolai to marry, to gain prestige, to become a political leader and legal authority, and to secure for himself a happy afterlife. Big-men often started their careers with borrowed shell money and subsequently became large-scale creditors themselves. Both peoples were familiar with the concept of interest; but they did not believe that time was money. Consequently, the amount of interest bore no relationship to the duration of the loan and was stipulated at the time the credit was given; among the Tolai it was usually twenty per cent. If a man refused to pay a debt he was marked, and no one would lend him anything in future. The Tolai big-man acted as banker for his followers by storing all their *tambu*, and thereby offered a place for safe deposit as well as channels for reinvestment. Bankers could utilize at least part of the deposits to finance such activities as planting large food gardens so as to sell the crop, or to invest in the distribution of articles with a view to collecting payment, including some profit, at a special function. In some instances the banker became too extravagant and used up too much of the stock of *tambu* in his care. If found out in his lifetime he was immediately discredited. More often his fraudulent activities remained undiscovered till after his death, when his kinsmen scrutinized his assets. In societies with shell currencies, savings were usually kept in this form. The Kapauku distinguished between two kinds of savings: shell money for requirements and tabooed shell money destined to be inherited by sons. The Tolai, on the other hand, placed more emphasis on redistributing the accumulated stock of a deceased man at the mortuary rites. The distribution of the hoarded *tambu* at rituals and ceremonies appears to have been the only way in which the vast majority of the accumulated Tolai wealth was actually used. The Kapauku invested a major part of their wealth in raising pigs, always with a view to holding a pig feast at which a large number of the total stock were slaughtered and consumed. Their economy passed through four-year pig cycles, starting and finishing with a pig feast and high monetary income, and with a period in between made up of two years of reinvestment and two years of breeding and fattening the growing animals, with occasional slaughter of male pigs and sales of piglets to outsiders.

Accounts of the operation of shell-money economies throw into relief the similarities with modern capitalism. At the same time they emphasize the basic difference. The development of capitalistic economies has been marked by trade cycles, yet throughout there has been a growth trend. In contrast, pig cycles have brought about hardly any economic expansion. Pre-literate peoples, even those who used money, were halted in their progress by limited technology. There was thus no net addition to the stock of capital assets and consequently no improvement in the standard of living.

Modern

First contact with the wider cash economy offered indigenes two new economic opportunities: they could sell their produce or their labour. The first European traders in the area sought mostly shell

—turtle, trochus, etc—and later coconuts. Recruitment for work on plantations in other Pacific areas, such as Samoa and Queensland, started almost simultaneously with external trade. The 'primitive affluence' of pre-contact days made many young men reluctant to volunteer for labour migration. In order to secure supplies of workers some blackbirders made deals with indigenous big-men, offering steel tools and other desired articles for permission to abduct young men. The attractiveness of the new goods induced many leaders to become parties to these unsavoury deals. In exchange for steel axes, knives, guns, ammunition and such-like articles, natives were prepared to give almost anything they had. The immediate effect of this external trade on the traditional economy was to induce a more efficient use of available resources; for instance, all fallen coconuts were carefully collected rather than left about, sometimes even to rot, as had been previous practice. The coastal people, the first to be approached, were quick to realize the strategic position they occupied. The possession of guns increased the power and influence of big-men, who were often also war leaders. This enlarged the size of political units by enabling a few men to wield greater power and influence over more people. The monopolistic big-men resented any attempts by traders or missionaries to establish direct contact with peoples from the interior.

For some years traditionally produced commodities—coconuts, sandalwood, turtle-shell—were the only items sold to the newcomers. Then the Europeans realized that large areas of land for plantations could be bought for only a few trade articles. Before long the local people began to regret these sales.

The new plantations needed labour. Most were situated in coastal regions where the people had alternative opportunities to acquire trade goods and were therefore reluctant to accept employment. Consequently workers had to be recruited from further afield and fed by their new employers. This created an additional demand for locally produced food. The foreign cash-crop ventures also set an example to the indigenes, who soon expanded their cultivation for the purpose of selling the surplus. Colonial administrators in the area actively sponsored and encouraged them to plant more coconuts. New economic opportunities were thus extended over a wider range of activities as well as over a greater number of people.

European planters not only produced copra but also experimented with several other crops such as cotton, coffee, cocoa and rice. The local people did not have the necessary expertise to copy these experiments. Accordingly coconuts were practically their only cash crop until after World War II, when the Australian authorities organized large-scale extension programmes and instructed and supervised the cultivation of a variety of crops.

LAND

Most of the country's increasing cash produce is derived from perennial tree crops. Allocation of a continuously increasing area to long-term tree cultivation is necessary and hence land tenure plays a vital part in economic expansion. Among many peoples, owner- ship of land is vested in groups. Corporate control is suitable for traditional shifting cultivation and facilitates the pooling of financial resources to invest in costly capital items; but in the long term it presents an obstacle to economic growth. The overlapping claims of various clans and sub-clans often cause uncertainty as to the rights of each, particularly with respect to lands planted with cash crops. Perennial trees tend to freeze land titles and so eliminate the flexibility of traditional land tenure. But as long as there is ample land available, the allocation of titles presents little problem.

However, the extension of cash cropping in districts where there has been considerable land alienation and where the population is growing rapidly has already produced pressure on land resources, and in the most developed regions disputes have become frequent and often insoluble. Cash cropping has not only introduced additional strains in the large kin units by creating a profit motive for individual members, but it has also strengthened the tie between fathers and sons, who usually operate their cash ventures jointly. This is particularly apparent in matrilineal societies with patri- virilocal residence. Many Tolai men would like to leave their property to their sons, who assist in accumulating it, rather than to their sisters' sons, who frequently grow up in another parish and never offer any help. Yet according to customary law the nearest uterine relative, rather than the son, has the right to inherit all wealth. As a result there is much unofficial cultivation by young men, encouraged by the father, of cocoa and coconuts on the father's lands. They sell the crops secretly to Chinese traders and deposit the cash received in their own savings bank accounts. As soon as the present elders die it is likely, therefore, that strife will occur between the sons on the one hand and the uterine kin on the other. Previously a Tolai who wanted to stake a claim to some of his father's property had to help his paternal kin arrange a lavish mortuary feast at which he generously distributed shell money to all and sundry. Attacks by missionaries on feasting and traditional exchanges may have serious social and economic consequences.

The hindrances to economic growth caused by the system of corporate land-holding, particularly by a matrilineal descent group, will become more and more apparent as land shortage becomes acute. The Australian Administration has attempted some reform of indigenous land tenure by legalizing conversion of holdings to individual titles, and by offering long-term leases to some individuals under secure conditions of tenure on resettlement schemes. Neither of these attempts has yet gone far enough to offer any great relief to the problem of land tenure. By 31 March 1967 only 17113 hectares had been allocated for resettlement, of which no more than 1717 blocks totalling 15041 hectares had been taken up by leaseholders. The resettlement projects occupy less than 0·1 per cent of the total area of unalienated lands. Yet these new possibilities for cultivators indicate the trend of change. At Silanga mission-sponsored resettlement scheme the cultivators decided jointly to make their cash crops subject to patrilineal inheritance rather than continue their traditional matrilineal system; each son is to get an equal share of his father's property. Settlers say that 'there are two ways for working at Silanga: one for the gardens where they all work together, and one for the cocoa, each one for himself. This is the new way because they get money for cocoa and each one takes his own money'. Enterprising men want to be able to realize the full value of their work. However, conversion to individual titles necessitates the agreement of all members of the group which by custom has a claim to the land. This probably accounts for the slow process of land reform: since December 1964 when the Land (Tenure Conversion) Ordinance came into operation only 153 titles and approximately 2000 hectares have been officially granted to individuals.

Shortage of land in some of the most developed parts, as for instance the Gazelle Peninsula, acts as an obstacle to young potential big-men in asserting their influence; it results in serious intra-tribal political tensions and is one of the most important contributing factors to the rise of political movements such as the Mataungans.

LABOUR

The introduced steel axes have in a very brief period almost entirely replaced those of stone. The latter, once carried habitually by most male adults, have been relegated to display in men's houses. Steel tools have considerably reduced male labour requirements for cultivation. One Siane group was estimated to have spent 1000 man-days on land improvements when working with stone tools as compared with only 620 man-days when using steel equipment. In earlier times Siane men spent as much as eighty per cent of their time on subsistence work; the new steel technology has reduced this proportion to half. By contrast, female labour remained unaffected by the introduction of new tools; Siane women still devote eighty-two per cent of their days to subsistence activities. Remoteness prevented Siane men from reinvesting the saved time by producing for the market. Instead they spent longer on ceremonials and political manoeuvrings.

However, some of the more accessible peoples began cash cropping soon after first contact. Copra, the first indigenous cash crop and still the country's major export—in 1964-5 it contributed about twenty-five per cent of the total produce sold abroad—requires little labour. It is in fact a lazy man's produce. Other tree crops, such as cocoa, coffee and rubber, are only slightly more time consuming. Hence the resistance to growing one-season crops, like grain or millets, which require periodic digging up of soils. Cultivators normally like to clear the ground and inter-plant subsistence crops with perennial trees until the latter provide too much shade. This practice facilitates a steady extension of production by indigenes for sale in open markets. Traditional labour organization still provides the bulk of work required on small holdings, though there is an increasing emphasis on contract labour. Some Tolai now employ men from more backward areas and pay them pitifully low wages.

CAPITAL AND INVESTMENT

The few tools normally needed for small-scale primary production are easily acquired. A Siane man has to work only twelve days to secure one steel axe, which lasts for about twelve years. The acquisition of more expensive capital items such as tractors was at first facilitated by the traditional corporate ownership of assets. An example was the Erap Mechanical Farming Project, where 426 people contributed to raise $1841.40 for their first tractor. Similarly, many large Tolai trucks were bought by most members of a matrilineage pooling their savings. However, they soon discovered that joint ownership of capital assets was a different matter from joint ownership of land. In subsistence cultivation it was easy for each partner to exercise his rights to land without his interests clashing with those of the others. This is not so in the case of vehicles, where continuous maintenance and periodic overhauls are necessary. Consequently many a truck was stranded waiting until the owners could pool more money to pay for necessary repairs.

There is now a trend towards individual ownership of capital items. This in turn creates a financial problem. Few individuals have sufficient resources to acquire a costly asset themselves. Most people distrust intra-societal loans because they suspect that the borrower will rely on kinship obligations when the creditor wants repayment of the loan. Therefore there is a need to familiarize them with new forms of economic organization, such as fixed shareholding and limited liability.

Many tree crops, like cocoa, coffee, copra and rubber, have to be processed before they can be exported. The more elaborate the processing, the more costly the machinery. The Tolai Cocoa Project, one of the biggest indigene-owned and controlled enterprises, was started in 1955 and is vested in the Gazelle Local Government Council. It operates eighteen fermentaries for which a total outlay of $544000 was necessary. A commercial bank made this amount available under guarantee from the Administration. Almost seventy-five per cent of this loan was repaid within twelve years. The project board of management is now composed of seven men, six Tolai council members and a European agricultural officer. Although it was started by active Administration participation it is now largely under indigenous control. Similarly the Kerema Bay Rubber Project was at first actively sponsored by the authorities, who provided a factory costing about $5000, but the production of latex has now been handed over to indigenous control. Such large-scale indigenous ventures are still few and far between, probably because of organization and management problems.

Most indigenes prefer to invest their money in small trade stores. As many as 5849 licences to operate shops had been issued by 1966, and others were operating without official recognition. The traditional system of trade exchanges with delayed reciprocity provided the basis for modern shop trade. But as most supplies have to be obtained from external sources and require immediate cash payment many a small store gets into financial difficulties. The social ties between an indigenous shopkeeper and his customers are responsible for the high proportion of credit sales. In turn this accounts for the mushroom growth and decline of trade stores in villages.

So far, all indigenous investment has been in agricultural, and processing and servicing industries. The very nature of these ventures protects them from foreign competition, though they are still subject to competition from local Europeans. In contrast, manufactured articles would have to compete with imports from advanced industrial economies.

ENTREPRENEURSHIP AND POLITICS

Europeans provided an example for indigenous enterprises. The higher an indigene's degree of education, and the longer his period in employment, the more ready he is to accept innovations. This vanguard sets an example to fellow villagers. Such men are also a channel for the redistribution of wealth among those who continue their traditional work. In many cases men who make their wealth through modern trade spend some of it on pigs for feasts and heirlooms for exchange. This expenditure on traditional items provides income for others not directly concerned with modern business. In Ware, discussed by Belshaw, many enterprising men are among the most active in trade exchanges and the most wealthy in heirlooms. Success in new cash ventures is also tied up with traditional social status. Not all Tolai who were in employment blossomed out as modern entrepreneurs; only those who on their return home managed to get themselves accepted as lineage elders have in fact become rich. These elder-entrepreneurs translated their strategic political position into economic advantage for themselves, while simultaneously redistributing part of their accumulated wealth along traditional channels. This throws into relief the interaction between forces of social continuity and of change in the process of economic development.

Traditional big-men were leaders not only in the economic but also in the political sphere. Similarly, indigenous entrepreneurs, the modern big-men, take an active part in formal politics. Most indigenous members of the present House of Assembly are comparatively wealthy business men. This is true also of members of the local government councils. But not all entrepreneurs compete for political positions. Some are too busy making money; others act as powers behind the throne rather than occupy it themselves.

EXPENDITURE AND SAVINGS

The availability of new consumer goods, together with ready cash derived from the sale of labour or crops, resulted in a widening of the indigenous expenditure pattern. The more urban the population the greater the quantity of purchased articles, though twist tobacco, cheap tinned fish or meat, and rice appear to have reached even the remotest peoples. Yet native produce is so readily available that bought food is regarded by most as a luxury. Prior to contact, the people were only scantily dressed. Now most possess at least a few items of introduced clothing; women wear loin cloth and blouse, men dress in shirt and loin cloth or shorts. Some of the wealthier indigenes dress like Europeans. Housing also is changing:

fibro-cement houses with corrugated-iron roofs are replacing the old huts with thatched roofs. The new bungalows are rare in the more remote areas but are beginning to be common in developed regions such as the Gazelle Peninsula. Household chattels are still rare. Only the most sophisticated villagers have much furniture and household equipment. Fear of sorcery and witchcraft militates against extreme economic differentiation expressed in terms of varying standards of living. The richer may have small luxuries, but they refrain from being ostentatious in order not to arouse the jealousy of others. Similarly, young Siane men, who in the 1950s returned from spells of plantation labour, distributed more than half their accumulated acquisitions to their kin and friends. This emphasis on egalitarian living has important economic consequences. It results in a high elasticity of demand for most purchased articles and leads to a continuous redistribution of incomes from the rich to the poor. Furthermore, it encourages a high rate of savings, which provide finance for investment and in turn can be employed to speed up economic growth.

In June 1966 total indigenous bank savings amounted to about \$9 200 000. This means average savings over the whole population of approximately \$7.50 per adult. The uneven distribution of wealth necessarily means a considerable range in the amount of cash saved. Some men also have cash hoards. There is thus a reasonably large fund available for profitable investment.

MARKETS AND TRADE

In most areas indigenes were quick to respond to the increased demand for their food crops, and many markets have been set up. Most commodities are over-supplied, and sellers have to take back at least part of their produce. Villagers could supply considerably greater quantities of fresh vegetables, particularly their staple crops of taro and sweet potatoes, if the demand could be increased. In spite of this, surplus prices are uniform and rarely change in reply to changes in demand. There is very little competition among vendors. Many sellers are women, who regard market trade as a social occasion as well as an economic enterprise. They are frequently satisfied to cover just the expense of visiting the market-place and regard any extra as windfall profit. 'Primitive affluence' accompanied by socially integrated sellers may explain the lack of competition apparent in the local markets. New Guineans are not accustomed to seeking out the highest bidder even in their sales of cash crops to expatriates. Ware people prefer a standardized relationship with one firm for selling their copra rather than moving from one buyer to another. They prefer security in trade to greater risk, possibly associated with higher gains.

Cash is now widely used, not only in inter-racial trade but also in exchanges between New Guineans. In many areas it has supplanted such valuables as cowrie shells and feathers. Some people, like the Tolai, cling to their traditional shell currency. *Tambu* is still used for payment in intra-Tolai trade and circulates freely at Rabaul market.

The flexible social systems of the pre-contact peoples provided a fertile field for economic improvements. Big-men constituted the prototype for modern entrepreneurs. Capital formation was at first facilitated by the traditional pattern of corporate ownership of assets. In turn capital formation is undermining the very system that helped to create it. As the pace of economic growth increases it is likely to have a revolutionary impact on social organization.

Bibliography

Armstrong, W. E. 1922. 'Report on the Suau-Tawala', *Territory of Papua, Anthropology Report*, no. 1. Port Moresby.

Belshaw, C. S. 1955. *In Search of Wealth*. American Anthropological Association Memoir no. 80. Menasha.

Brookfield, H. C. and Brown, P. 1963. *Struggle for Land*. Melbourne.

Crocombe, R. G. and Hogbin, G. R. 1963. *The Erap Mechanical Farming Project*. New Guinea Research Unit Bulletin no. 1. Canberra.

Epstein, A. L. 1962-3. 'The economy of modern Matupit', *Oceania*, vol. 33.

────── 1969. *Matupit: land, politics and change among the Tolai of New Britain*. Canberra.

Epstein, T. S. 1968. *Capitalism, Primitive and Modern: some aspects of Tolai economic growth*. Canberra.

────── 1969-70. 'The Mataungan affair', *New Guinea and Australia, the Pacific and South-East Asia*, vol. 4.

Fisk, E. K. (ed.) 1966. *New Guinea on the Threshold*. Canberra.

Gitlow, A. L. 1947. *Economics of the Mt Hagen Tribes*. New York.

Hogbin, G. R. 1964. *A Survey of Indigenous Rubber Producers in the Kerema Bay Area*. New Guinea Research Unit Bulletin no. 5. Canberra.

Hogbin, H. I. 1951. *Transformation Scene*. London.

Hogbin, H. I. and Lawrence, P. 1967. *Studies in New Guinea Land Tenure*. Sydney.

Jackson, G. 1965. *Cattle, Coffee and Land among the Wain*. New Guinea Research Unit Bulletin no. 8. Canberra.

Kaberry, P. M. 1940-1. 'The Abelam tribe, Sepik District, New Guinea', *Oceania*, vol. 11.

Kleintitschen, A. 1906. *Die Küstenbewohner der Gazelle-Halbinsel . . . ihre Sitten und Gebräuche*. Hiltrup bei Münster.

Malinowski, B. 1922. *Argonauts of the Western Pacific*. London.

——— 1935. *Coral Gardens and their Magic*. 2 vols. London.

Parkinson, R. 1887. *Im Bismarck Archipel*. Leipzig.

——— 1907. *Dreissig Jahre in der Südsee*. Stuttgart.

Pospisil, L. 1963. *Kapauku Papuan Economy*. New Haven.

Salisbury, R. F. 1962. *From Stone to Steel*. Melbourne.

——— 1970. *Vunamami: economic transformation in a traditional society*. Melbourne.

van Rijswijk, O. 1966. *The Silanga Resettlement Project*. New Guinea Research Unit Bulletin no. 10. Canberra.

Hiri

Murray Groves

Until recently an overseas trading expedition known as *hiri* significantly shaped the lives of the Motu people who live on the coast near Port Moresby. Each year in October or November, before the south-east trade winds faded, Motu seamen sailed vessels called *lagatoi*, specially built for the occasion, north-west for several hundred kilometres across the Gulf of Papua, sometimes beyond sight of land, to exchange pottery manufactured by Motu women for sago produced in the west. In late December or January they sailed home on the north-west monsoon. These voyages were part of a larger cycle of activities that linked the people of many different villages and several different linguistic groups in a network of ceremonial and economic exchanges. At the same time they conferred differential prestige within their own communities upon the entrepreneurs who participated. In scale and complexity the *hiri* rivalled the Trobriand Islanders' *kula,* which in some ways it resembled.

The *hiri* was a conspicuous feature when the first English missionary settled at Port Moresby in 1874. Barton, who published a detailed account of it in 1910, suggested that the institution had existed 'for many generations'. It continued to flourish until 1941, when World War II disrupted traditional customs. Motu from villages close to Port Moresby did not resume the *hiri,* but the people of Manumanu, the Motu village furthest west from Port Moresby, sailed regularly each year until 1958 when they built their last *lagatoi,* and several other Motu villages sponsored *hiri* sporadically after the war. In 1957 two communities, Boera and Porebada, conducted a modernized version of the *hiri* in chartered motor vessels. It appears that no Motu village has sent any vessel westward on a *hiri* since 1961 when some people at Porebada organized a traditional voyage.

The following account is based upon observation of three

expeditions from Manumanu: in 1954, when two vessels known as *hakona*, smaller than true *lagatoi*, sailed west; in 1957, when again two *hakona* sailed; and in 1958, when the people of Manumanu built a true *lagatoi* with all the many ritual appurtenances, ceremonies and restrictions traditionally required. Despite the change of time and place, these expeditions were identical in almost every detail with those described by Barton fifty years earlier.

A man who intends to sponsor a *hiri* must start planning at least a year in advance, but he keeps the information to himself and his closest associates. One of these is normally his partner. During the year he and his family plant larger gardens than usual to provide food both for the feasts that accompany each stage in the *lagatoi*'s construction and for the voyage itself. At harvest time in April or May, if his gardens are successful, he finally decides to proceed. From now onwards he must observe certain ritual restrictions, such as avoiding his wife, so that he may keep himself *helaga*, 'sacred', 'charged with ritual potency', and thus 'set apart'. When ready to begin construction of the vessel the sponsor (*baditauna*), who has control of the forward half of the vessel, is expected to open the enterprise with a small ceremony in the village street. At this point, first his partner (*doritauna*), who has control of the stern half of the vessel, and then all those who wish to sail as crew under either man, smoke a pipe together.

It takes many weeks to build a *lagatoi*. First the sponsor must assemble the required number of large dug-out hulls. He may use old hulls brought back from the west in previous *lagatoi*, as Barton described, but at Manumanu several additional hulls were shaped from trees felled in the rain forest on the banks of the Vanapa River and floated downstream to the river mouth. Otherwise, the completion of the vessel followed exactly the stages described by Barton: floating the hulls in the water, lashing them together, and constructing the deck, with accompanying magic; building the deckhouses; cutting the mast from a mangrove tree; stepping the mast; hoisting the sail; and finally testing the craft in a trial run. At each stage before the last a small feast was held for those who participated. Meanwhile, the women of the village spent all their spare hours making earthenware pottery, each one firing five or six pots at a time in an open fire of fast-burning dry softwood.

Every member of the crew takes his own consignment of pots. In addition to those made by women of his household, he customarily volunteers to take one for each of his female kin in other households, to whom ultimately he returns a package of sago. This practice provides a means of maintaining exchange relationships with female kin and their households. On the day set aside for loading the pots each man lays his consignment out on the ground in front of the house and brushes the whole collection with a bunch of leaves in a magical rite to ensure the success of his overseas exchanges. The women then carry the pots to the beach from where they are ferried to the *lagatoi* which lies at anchor some distance off shore. The crew load the pots in the *lagatoi* hulls with dry banana-leaf packing to prevent breakage on the voyage.

On the day of departure women and children take tearful fare-well of their men on the beach. The men are then paddled out to the *lagatoi* in small canoes, the sail is set, and the anchor raised. With a good wind and no mishap the party can reach the nearer villages on the far side of the Gulf within two or three days.

Upon arrival at their destination the crew pole the *lagatoi* into a sheltered river mouth near the host village and drop anchor. The senior hosts then lead a ceremonial visit to the *lagatoi*. The *badi-tauna* greets his exchange partner, with whom he has usually made arrangements on a previous *hiri*, announces that he has brought the *lagatoi* for him, and makes him a gift of armshell ornaments. Other men then seek out old exchange partners, or solicit new ones, and each gives his partner an armshell. A day or so later each man lays out the pots intended for his partner. Together they make a count, using tally sticks.

For every item, the Motu man expects a fixed return. In 'present-ing the *lagatoi*' to his partner, the *baditauna* is in fact presenting neither the vessel itself nor its contents, but the social role of principal entrepreneur among the men of the host village for that particular *hiri*. In return for this honour the partner presents a pig to the crew. For certain large armshells the fixed return is a log from which the recipient shapes a *lagatoi hull*. For other armshells and ornaments the return is a large conical package of sago which has special ceremonial value in Motu villages. For each pot the return is a smaller package of sago. Exchange rates are fixed and have remained constant for half a century.

It takes many weeks for the hosts to prepare the sago. During this time the Motu dismantle their *lagatoi*, fell and shape a number of new dug-out hulls, and then rebuild the craft with sufficient additional hulls to carry the return cargo of sago, which is heavier than pottery and therefore requires a larger vessel. During their stay in the west the Motu also fish and sometimes supply fish to their partners for other food. They also engage in 'hidden' barter trade, exchanging additional pots which they have concealed from their exchange partners, tobacco, and other trade goods, for sago or betel-nut at the best rates they can get by bargaining. All this time they camp on the beach a short distance from the village, maintain a formal relationship with the local men, and scrupulously avoid any undue familiarity with the women. When all the sago is ready the regular bundles are packed in the hulls and the conical cere-monial bundles lashed between the beams so that the top half of each stands some thirty centimetres above the deck.

When the weather seems favourable the *lagatoi* sets sail for home. The return journey is more hazardous than the forward voyage, for with a heavier cargo the vessel has less freeboard, and the north-west monsoon is less reliable than the south-east trade wind, often giving way to sudden violent squalls. One of the two vessels that went on the *hiri* from Manumanu in 1954 broke up in heavy seas during a fierce northerly squall, with the loss of one life, all the cargo, and all the personal possessions of the men.

Once the *lagatoi* has safely crossed the Gulf it drops anchor inshore at a point some distance west of its home village. Here the men adorn themselves with perfumed leaves, facial paints, and various items of festive apparel. Then some of the crew pole the vessel slowly towards its home anchorage while others sing special *hiri* songs to the accompaniment of a bamboo percussion instru-ment. At the approach of the vessel the wives, sisters and daughters of the crew, wearing brightly coloured grass skirts and other adorn-ments, dance on the beach in welcome. The day is then given over to festive reunion.

Between 1954 and 1958 Doura and Gabadi people from inland and Koita from villages along the coast gathered at Manumanu. They came to receive sago in return for gifts of food made to the people left behind while the breadwinners were away. Formerly, at Motu villages in the Port Moresby area, Hula men assembled in the same way to receive payment for fish supplied to the women while their men were away and for armshells given to members of the crew before departure. At Manumanu the sponsor of a *lagatoi* invited his Gabadi or Doura exchange partners to bring a party of dancers, and then the *hiri* terminated in a large-scale feast with dancing. In payment for the dance the exchange partners received one or more large conical sago packages, each equivalent to a pig in the currency of ceremonial exchange.

Traditionally the *hiri* was a major link in a maritime trading network extending along the coast from the Vailala River, just west of Kerema, in the west to the eastern extremity of the mainland and even further to the Trobriand Islands and the other islands of the *kula* ring. The *hiri* at the western extremity and the *kula* at the eastern extremity were the two most spectacular institutions in this system. Armshells and other ornaments were the major item of ceremonial currency. The centre of manufacture lay in the villages of the Hula, Aroma and Mailu peoples east of Port Moresby. The *kula* carried these armshells into the eastern archipelagoes; the *hiri* carried them west to the head of the Gulf of Papua, from where they were taken along inland trade routes into the mountains.

A major function of the *hiri*, Motu themselves insist, was economic. Without it they could not have subsisted, for in the frequent poor seasons neither their gardens nor their inland exchanges of fish for bananas and tubers yielded sufficient staple food to tide them over the months immediately preceding the annual harvest. Yet they valued the institution for other reasons also. It sustained their links with regular exchange partners among their immediate neighbours. It provided one of the two great festive occasions of the year, when for days or even weeks they gave themselves up entirely, as the early missionaries indignantly complained, to feasting and dancing. Finally, it conferred prestige upon those who participated. Acquiring prestige, or as the Motu put it, having a 'name' (*mai ladana*), was traditionally the major objective of almost all Motu householders. Each man strove to gain advantage over others in a continual battle for prestige. The heads of village sections competed at the highest level, but lesser men competed also at lower levels, all attempting to outshine their rivals in certain public enterprises that particularly conferred prestige: small-scale distributions of food at various stages in the cycle of mortuary rites; bride-price payments; the *hiri*; and the great feast with dancing that closed the cycle of mortuary rites.

It was ultimately in political disputes and debates that prestige became most important to the Motu, for discussions of relative prestige constituted the major form of political discourse. A man of higher prestige could usually silence a lesser man completely, causing him to withdraw in shame, by referring to their relative performances in those enterprises that particularly confer prestige. Ultimately, most serious public issues were traditionally settled by consensus among the two or three men of highest prestige.

Each man valued his reputation, not because in itself it gave him political power but because it directly reflected his command of those resources upon which political power rested. These happened to be the same as those required for economic enterprises carrying high prestige: a large personal following—comprising his family, his village section, and the kin and affines who were his clients in reciprocal exchange relationships; character, physical strength and managerial skill; and wealth in the form of capital assets, such as land, canoes, nets, armshells and armshell credits, rather than perishable foodstuffs which he gave away when possible. A large personal following gave a man the numbers to win a political struggle; character, strength and skill gave him influence; and wealth provided him with economic sanctions to ensure the continued political support of his followers.

The *hiri* was one of the two major enterprises—the other was the feast with dancing known as *turia*—in which Motu entrepreneurs at all social levels publicly displayed the cards they held in the power game.

Bibliography

Barton, F. R. 1910. 'The annual trading expedition to the Papuan Gulf', ch. 8 in C. G. Seligman, *The Melanesians of British New Guinea*, Cambridge.

Williams, F. E. 1932-3. 'Trading voyages from the Gulf of Papua', *Oceania*, vol. 3.

Land Tenure

Thomas G. Harding

For the peoples of Papua New Guinea, who are subsistence cultivators and now, in some areas, producers of cash crops for world markets, the importance of land and land tenure needs no emphasis. Anthropologists concerned with the material basis of community life agree on one main point: the difficulty of reducing the subject of land tenure to manageable proportions. As all who have investigated the problems have discovered, examination of the various rights to land reveals their connection not only with agriculture and technology but also with kinship, political, economic and religious institutions. One ethnographer has said, 'No adequate account of the system of land tenure of any native community can be given without first carrying out a detailed anthropological analysis of its culture'. Conversely, a focus on land tenure provides a useful point of departure for undertaking such an analysis. In addition to its practical and economic significance, then, land tenure has engaged considerable interest as a part of the general anthropological study of social institutions.

In defining the scope of the subject in substantive terms, it should be noted that a variety of things have been treated under the heading of land tenure. In addition to arable land, dwelling sites, burial and ceremonial grounds, and non-agricultural land utilized for hunting and collecting, the following should be mentioned: paths and rights-of-way; strategic locations for trade or defence; streams, wells, springs and fords; stone quarries, salt wells, and deposits of clay and rare earths; off-shore and fringing reefs; bird rookeries; economic trees of all types—coconut, sago, *Areca*, Java almond (*Canarium indicum*), pandanus, breadfruit and so on; and such natural features as caves, rocky outcrops, and groves that may be significant to particular social groups by reason of their mythological associations. The justification for such inclusiveness is that these are all fixed and relatively permanent features of the cultural-geographic landscape, and the property rights of which they are the objects are similar, at least in some major respects, to rights in land. This article will be concerned primarily with the most important of these fixed resources—arable land.

Our own notions of private ownership have frequently been a stumbling block to a proper understanding of the traditional concepts of land tenure. In Anglo-American society ownership confers a number of definite rights: principally the right to use the land; the right to exclude others from its use and enjoyment; the right to transfer it by sale, lease or gift; and, perhaps most notably, the right to receive income from the property independent of use. This particular combination of rights—use, exclusion, alienation and income—does not occur in any Papua New Guinea society. Ownership of land confers rights of exclusion—temporary at least—and of use; rarely, however, are individuals empowered to alienate on their own initiative any part of a group estate. In any case, it is more common for people to transfer themselves than their land— that is, by affiliating themselves with different estate-holding kin groups, people acquire rights to new lands while relinquishing or suspending their rights to the estates of their former groups. Finally, the right to claim income independent of use is virtually non-existent; there was no landlord class in the pre-contact societies of Papua New Guinea. Occasionally gifts or payments are made in consideration of grants to temporary usufruct but, even if regarded as income, such payments are not generally significant in economic terms.

From the point of view of the community, land and other fixed resources form a territorial domain. Territorial rights are vested in the community as a whole and are maintained, by force of arms if necessary, against infringement by neighbouring communities. From the point of view of kin groups—the component parts or sub-groups of the community—land and other items of value form a series of estates. Normally each kin group defends its claim to an estate not by force but rather through a custom-dictated machinery which provides reasonably orderly procedures for detecting infringements and resolving disputes. For the individual or, more properly, the household, it is the garden plot—some parcel of a group estate— that is of chief interest. Individual rights to garden plots are assured through membership of an estate-holding kin group to which a person looks for defence of his rights against outsiders. Membership of such groups is normally conferred by descent or filiation.

So for community, kin group, and household, land assumes the forms of territorial domain, estate and garden plot respectively. Land regarded as a territory leads to a consideration of land tenure in relation to boundaries, politics and warfare. Once the territory is viewed in terms of its component estates, attention shifts to land tenure as an aspect of community social structure. Finally, a consideration of land in the form of usable plots or sites, as instruments of production under the temporary control of households, turns discussion to the economic aspects of land tenure. It is, therefore, under these three headings—land and community, land and kin groups, land and households—that some attempt will be made to generalize about the hundreds of distinctive local systems of land tenure. A final section, land tenure and change, assesses the implications of recent events for indigenous systems of landholding.

LAND AND COMMUNITY

In pre-European times local communities ranged in size from less than a hundred to a few hundred persons. A number of local communities made up a large cultural-linguistic unit, distinguished from neighbouring units by a number of shared customs and a common language or dialect. But it was the local community, whatever its characteristic form of settlement, which formed an autonomous political unit. Within the local community peace was enjoined, or rather there were accepted procedures for resolving conflict, while dealings with neighbouring communities were in the nature of 'international' relations. Such relations included warfare and feud, trade and intermarriage.

The interests of the community include the territory that it occupies and habitually uses. In former times the maintenance of territorial rights ultimately depended on the community's ability to defend its domain from encroachment by others, though traditional warfare was seldom aimed at acquisition of territory. Only in a rather loose sense, however, can the occupancy and defence of group territory be regarded as community land tenure. For though the community may be organized as a whole for some purposes, generally it is not specifically organized to govern the allocation of rights to land. The Sio, to take one example, hold that anyone of Sio ancestry, whether or not he was born or had resided in the community, is entitled to claim land in the Sio domain. Yet there is no mechanism by which the community as such can bestow rights to land. In all cases such rights would have to be obtained from an individual owner or set of individuals, typically the senior men of a particular landholding kin group.

Understandably, the proprietary interest of the cultural-linguistic group is expressed less precisely than that of the local community. A, a member of group X, may refer to X's territory as 'our land' or 'my land' vis-a-vis an outsider. But A's effective rights include only a minute fraction of the domain. In post-European times, however, the identification of cultural-linguistic groups and territorial domains has emerged with greater force and clarity. A tendency towards the development of a concept of group tenure among Bougainville peoples was observed by Oliver prior to World War II. Workers, thrown together in labour compounds and on plantations, aggregated on the bases of language and area of origin, and they thus developed a sense of group consciousness. Such ethnic labels as 'Orokaiva', 'Siuai' and 'Chimbu' have a reality today that was lacking in pre-European times. More recent developments will doubtless contribute to concepts of 'tribal' land tenure. Surveys of language boundaries have the effect of fixing territorial domains and hence making them more apparent. From another side, modern elections are important in that they lead to bloc support of ethnic candidates who take, as a major plank of their election manifesto, the preservation of territorial land claims.

LAND AND KIN GROUPS

Papua New Guinea societies are family- or kin-based. They lack the highly specialized land use, market system, and formal politico-legal institutions that give form and substance to property in land characteristic of Western society. Both economic and political processes may be said to be embedded in social relationships, usually of a kinship or quasi-kinship kind. Property relations in general, and those concerning land in particular, are attributes of these social relationships. It is accurate to say that 'principles of land tenure grow out of the social relations of the people who use the land'. The social system determines land tenure; or rather, the latter is a part of the former. Since principles of land tenure are not codified, and since in disputes there was formerly no agency charged with preserving and interpreting principles that was independent of and superior to the litigants themselves, customary rules are subject, to a marked degree, to the pressure of circumstance and dominant interests.

The actual types of land that are the objects of proprietary interest are determined largely by patterns of land use, and these flow from the relationship between technology and environment. As this varies—between, let us say, sago processing, taro growing in lowland rain forest, yam cultivation in savannah, or fishing—forms of tenure will vary also.

Even so, social systems impinge on land use: for example, it frequently happens that the various blocks of land making up the estates of kin groups are dispersed within the territorial domain of the community. Such dispersal results from social processes (e.g. inheritance) and may even run counter to the technical interests of production. Or again, there is nothing in techniques of agricultural production *per se* that dictates continuity of land rights. The land rights of the people of a village might be re-allocated annually, every ten years or at longer intervals. But continuity in claims to land—by means of inheritance—serves the interests of social relationships and groups. In this sense the various rights to land are not only symbolic of social relations, they are components of these relationships. Often they are the most important components because, in general, the significant attribute of membership in corporate kin groups is that a person is caught up with other members in activities concerning the land.

Kin groups may be constituted in a number of distinctive ways. Patrilineal groups accord membership to people who trace descent from a single ancestor exclusively through males. Matrilineal groups, on the other hand, are composed of men and women who share common descent through a line of females. Cognatic descent groups, a third type, allow individual choice among two or more groups in which descent from the founding ancestor can be claimed through males or females indifferently. Patrilineal descent is perhaps the most common basis of group affiliation in Papua New Guinea.

Membership of kin groups defines some, but not all, of a person's important interests and obligations. These groups are protective associations, defending their members from physical harm and loss of property and reputation, and seeking vengeance or compensation when any member suffers such harm or loss. They secure spouses for their junior members by exchanging women with other groups. Frequently many of the members of a group live together and co-operate extensively in economic activities. And typically the group claims an estate which, of course, includes land. Thus rights to land are but one aspect of membership of such a group.

A person's interests are not completely or even largely circumscribed by his belonging to lineage or clan. Everyone possesses a circle of kinsmen—people who are members of his own descent group and those who are not—and neighbours and friends who are treated like kin. This circle of kin or kindred is as concerned with the individual's welfare as he is with theirs, and it is not surprising to find that relations within the kindred are expressed in the allocation of rights to use land.

In addition to kin groups and kindred men had, in pre-European times, membership status in political factions—the followings of local big-men or leaders. In some cases political factions might be made up largely of members of a single kin group, but more often they were heterogeneous. Relationships between leaders and followers entailed, ideally at least, a reciprocal flow of goods and services, which sometimes included land. A prominent big-man who won the right to adjudicate land disputes was in a position to benefit members of his own faction. Or, to take another example, men might be recruited to a big-man's faction in consideration of a grant of rights to good gardening land.

Thus, while people count on benefiting most from the estate in land of their natal kin group, claims to the estates of other groups regularly develop from important extra-group kinship and political relationships. Relationships created by membership of kin group, kindred, and political faction are the real substance of land tenure.

An ethnographic example will serve to document some of these general observations. Among the Sio, gardening land is viewed much as Europeans view real estate. Part of the Sio domain, the lands closest to the villages and most used, is divided into named blocks more or less rectangular in outline. A number of these blocks, ranging in size from a few hundred square metres to several hectares, and dispersed over the territory, make up the estate of a patrilineal lineage. This division of lands results partly from the method of tillage. The Sio cultivate yams in a grassland environment. The grass is burned off and the ground worked up; stones, ash and debris are swept to the margin. In time low mounds are formed at the borders, and these serve as land boundaries. The formation of bounded plots, in this case, stems from land utilization (compare the acre, the traditional English land measure, originally the area a yoke of oxen could plough in a day). Beyond the bounded land are much larger blocks which are more loosely claimed by the patrilineal landowning groups. Here individuals may stake out restricted claims by cultivation, but such rights tend to lapse if continued use is not made of the land by the original cultivator and his heirs.

The patrilineage is headed by the senior male descendant of the group founder. He is referred to as *tono tama*, 'father of the land', and he serves as the principal administrator or trustee of the land blocks making up the group's estate. Lineage members may garden at will or plant trees on any part of the estate. Non-members, such as sisters' sons of the men of the lineage, and also other relatives, are granted rights of temporary usufruct. They are supposed to seek the *tono tama's* permission beforehand but, as this would rarely be refused, a simple declaration of intent to garden on such and such a block is normally sufficient. Frequently, however, a number of people having primary land rights in different groups make joint gardens on land belonging to one of them.

The *tono tama* does not necessarily direct the activities of his fellows, nor does he assign garden plots to his junior kinsmen. His role as administrator and spokesman is important mainly in the event of disputes over ownership or boundaries, and here he relies on his reputed superior knowledge of genealogy and of land boundaries and blocks to validate his group's claims. Part of his role is to impart this knowledge to his successor, often a younger brother or the eldest son.

The land rights of lineage members and certain classes of non-members overlap in some respects but are clearly distinguished in others. Non-members readily acquire usufructuary rights, but unlike members they may not extend use privileges to others. The lineage reserves certain rights exclusively to itself. Alienation of a part of the estate, a rare occurrence, requires the unanimous consent of the senior male members. Disputes, similarly, are entirely the affair of the lineage.

In addition to a consideration of rules or principles of tenure, the study of land tenure involves plotting the distribution of different kinds of rights among distinct classes of persons. If by 'communal ownership' one means that group members enjoy equal rights, or that resources are somehow pooled, then the phrase is misleading with reference to land tenure in Papua New Guinea. 'Corporate' is a more appropriate term, for just as in modern corporations there is a differentiation of rights and prerogatives among directors, employees, and large and small stockholders, so there is among members of landholding kin groups. Unity in some contexts gives way to a diversity of interests and claims in others. Differentiation is apparent, for example, when one examines the rights of adults as opposed to children, for the latter are usually regarded only as potential landowners. The Siuai of Bougainville say that 'children possess only their appetites; land is man's affair'. The roles of men and women in activities and decisions affecting land vary both within and between societies. The distinctions depend on such factors as the type of crops, division of labour, and whether property rights are transmitted matrilineally or through both males and females. Differentiation is also evident when one compares senior and junior members of kin groups, natal members as opposed to naturalized or in-marrying members, and leaders or big-men and non-leaders. Thus, one describes tenure in terms of corporate ownership with the understanding that the individual's rights to land and to participate in land-related activities vary considerably with age or seniority, sex, political status, and other social attributes.

Since land tenure, as usually conceived, is an aspect of social structure—it consists of the social relationships governing the allocation of particular rights to land—it is reasonable to suppose that the availability of land in relation to need will influence these social relationships and through them social structure as a whole. We have to consider, then, the possible sociological impact of variable supplies of land. A number of anthropologists have suggested that this relates even to the basic constitution of the corporate units or kin groups that have landholding as a main function. Consideration of some social correlates of relative scarcity, absolute scarcity, and abundance will be valuable.

Even where the total man to land ratio is favourable, relative scarcity often results from the differential population growth and decline of the landowning kin groups. Expanding groups may find themselves short of good arable land as their numbers increase, while smaller units may have more than they need. In a situation such as this, which appears with modest frequency, open recruitment of members to the proprietary kin groups, allowing people of land-poor groups to enter those better endowed, effectively alleviates relative scarcity. This is achieved, for example, by a cognatic descent scheme in which individuals, as young adults, are afforded a choice between affiliating with two or more descent groups—that of the father, mother, mother's father and so on.

Transfer of group membership, entitling new members to full rights to group property, is one way of adjusting man to land ratios. There are other possibilities. (1) In a situation of relative scarcity it is often easier simply to transfer land rights among members of different landholding units. The Garia may typify this situation: 'In central Garialand pressure of population has induced a need for security in land and has led to a type of transaction whereby individuals can acquire personal rights (hunting, fishing, cultivation and arboriculture) on strips of patrilineages to which they are closely affiliated. In the peripheral areas . . . where the population is less dense, the practice is not so frequent'. The exchange of such 'personal' rights, as opposed to the 'guardian' rights retained by the lineage, takes place mainly among maternal uncles and nephews. (2) Land-poor groups may acquire additional land by opening up frontier territory for cultivation or by forcibly seizing adjoining territory. (3) Land-poor groups may reduce or stabilize their

numbers by means of population-limiting techniques or by migration. (4) Land might be periodically redistributed among the various
landowning units, perhaps by a formal agreement on repatriation
among leading representatives of the various groups. Periodic
redistribution is practised by some tribal peoples, for example in
the Middle East, and by traditional peasant communities in different
parts of the world, but it does not appear in Papua New Guinea.
The reason for its absence here may be that serious shortage of the
largely undifferentiated agricultural land used for root-crop cultivation is not a problem over most of the area. It should be noted also
that formal deliberative bodies of tribal leaders—the social
mechanism of redistribution—are not well developed in Papua New
Guinea societies.

Absolute scarcity—general land shortage affecting all the groups
of society—presents a different problem and requires different
responses. Where, as in some areas of the Highlands, scarcity
approaches an absolute shortage, one would expect a general
tightening up of recruitment to landholding groups, perhaps even a
policy restricting membership to agnatic descendants of the founding
ancestors. Meggitt suggests that given the prior bias toward patrilineality, acute land shortage will result in a strong emphasis on
patrilineal recruitment and ideology. Correspondingly, as one moves
to areas where land is less scarce, landholding kin groups may be
more willing to accept non-agnatic descendants as members. Thus,
the importance of the social distinctions between agnatic and non-
agnatic kinsmen may be related to the variable needs of maintaining
rights of exclusion (but see Allen).

If, on the other hand, land is abundant, one may again expect
landowning kin groups to exhibit a relatively open or cognatic
structure, especially if control of land is the main or sole function of
the kin groups in question. The patrilineages of the Sio, for example,
are almost exclusively landholding units; land is abundant, and we
find that the land rights of sisters' sons and other non-lineage
relatives are insisted upon both in theory and in practice. A kin
group's estate, however, may include other than agricultural land.
Among the western Motu, scarce assets such as house sites and
fishing nets are held exclusively by agnates and are passed on to
patrilineal descendants. But land, as in Sio, is abundant, and we
find that claims to it on the part of non-agnatic descendants are
clearly recognized. It may be added that in Sio also, house sites,
especially important and valuable by reason of the great amount of
labour required to drive post holes through solid rock and coral,

were formerly inherited along more strictly patrilineal lines than was agricultural land.

All this assumes a relatively static technology and a fixed level of productivity per unit of land. This assumption is justified for the earlier period but not for post-European times which have witnessed increased productivity afforded by the introduction of new crops and steel tools.

LAND AND HOUSEHOLDS

Most phases of agricultural production in Papua New Guinea communities are carried out by individual households. A familial mode of production means, among other things, that the various factors of production are under the control of households. In addition to implements, requisite skills, and seed or planting stock, these factors obviously include land. To the household as producing unit, what is most important is unimpeded access to land in the amount and of the types required to earn a livelihood. In Papua New Guinea no communities of which there is record have sought to deprive any households of the material basis of livelihood. However, even though each household has land and supplies most of the labour needed in food production, certain phases of gardening are regularly associated with collaboration on a wider scale. Frequently a number of households join in making gardens, or they co-operate during such phases as clearing or tillage. In pre-European times technology, considerations of defence, and social sentiments required or were conducive to co-operative forms of labour, and a preference for co-operative work and team effort is still evident on the contemporary scene.

Husbands and wives share the produce of the land in providing for themselves and their children, and similarly they share in the use of the land. In patrilineal societies women are treated, to a large extent, as members of the husband's kin group—particularly after they bear children—and they therefore develop strong identifications with the husbands' land. Under matriliny, with uxorilocal residence, a husband moves to his wife's village or hamlet and is found gardening, for the most part on land belonging to her kin group. Yet these husbands are seldom as fully assimilated to membership of the wife's kin group as are women in a patrilineal system. Even so, as long as a man maintains good relations with his in-laws, his claims to use their land are generally effective.

Annually, households cultivate more than one garden or plot, not all of which need be situated on land in which a member of the household has primary rights, i.e. through membership of a land-owning kin group. Probably in most communities a large part of the land utilized by a family during its lifetime consists of plots owned, in a primary sense, by others. Of course, people's relationships with others are manifold, and many of these varied relationships entail actual or potential claims to land. Thus, a person seldom needs to rely on his natal kin group's estate: indeed, as intermarriage extends kinship relations far and wide, he may claim rights to land in neighbouring communities, even in areas belonging to linguistic groups different from his own. In sum, the rights of a typical villager are multiple, complex, and highly differentiated in terms of type of right—e.g. primary ownership *v.* actual or potential use privileges; the manner in which rights are acquired—by cultivation, inheritance, gift, loan, purchase; and the extent to which the various claims are actually exercised.

The relationship of households to the land is conditioned by labour requirements and arrangements: labour including skills, technical knowledge, and magical expertise. In most instances labour is a more costly factor than land. That is to say, such considerations as the prestige or skill of the leader of a gardening party, or who one's workmates are going to be, are more important than the nature of one's rights, if any, to the land being cultivated. Collaborative effort in gardening, or some phases of it such as clearing, tillage, fencing and harvesting, is often technically advantageous as well as being preferred from a social standpoint. Production teams of some sort appear to be universal, but they vary a great deal in structure or composition, depending on technology, the nature of the tasks, available leadership, and other factors. In some cases they are homogeneous, that is, composed of members of a single kin group which utilizes its own resources. In Sio the digging-stick teams of a half-dozen men formerly tended to be of this type. More often teams are heterogeneous and may include people who are related in some way to a team leader but who are not all related among themselves. Understandably, repeated participation in particular teams engenders a sense of ownership or identification. Team members who are not primary owners of the land in question may come to view their claims as something more than secondary-use privileges, even though their rights are apt to remain conditional and terminable.

Because of the prevalent system of shifting cultivation, a household's interest in particular plots of land is short-term, extending for the life of the garden which is a year or two unless economic trees are also planted. In many communities temporary usufruct for the purpose of subsistence gardening—which may rule out planting trees, collecting wild products or removing valuable timber—is granted freely by the kin group claiming guardian rights. Through farming activities alone, households can often acquire use rights sufficient to meet their needs. Joining in a gardening team, even when the man has no rights in the land being cleared, still gives him the right to cultivate a plot.

LAND TENURE AND CHANGE

In Papua New Guinea, unlike many former colonial areas, relatively little land has come under the control of settlers from outside. Currently, ninety-seven per cent of the total land area remains subject to traditional forms of tenure. Of the alienated land, much of it is used by or for the benefit of indigenous peoples; only a small fraction is freehold controlled privately by Europeans.

One should not be misled by aggregate figures on landholding, for alienation, conversion from customary to Western tenures, and localized land shortage, pose serious economic and political problems. Before World War I, native lands were purchased by Europeans. Alienation tended to be concentrated in certain areas such as the Madang coast and the Gazelle Peninsula around Rabaul. In these regions, European plantation development caused severe dislocation of social and economic life. In the Gazelle, in particular, extensive land alienation combined with rapid population growth has produced a situation which many of the indigenous Tolai people find intolerable. Nearly half of their lands have been alienated, leaving them with less than a hectare per capita for gardening and cash-crop production. Since 1969 the Mataungan Association, formed originally to oppose the establishment of a multi-racial local government council but later focusing attention on the land-shortage issue, has been responsible for mass demonstrations, confrontations with police, and attacks on traditional leaders. Thus a shortage of land induced by alienation has been a continuing source of civil disorder and violence in the area.

One of the most important questions facing New Guineans generally, and particularly leaders who will be guiding programmes of economic development, is the relationship of traditional and modified systems of land tenure to commercial production. In part, this involves consideration of the distinctive patterns of land use associated with such diverse crops as cocoa, coconut, coffee, rubber, peanuts and tea, and also livestock management. Also of importance is the probable relationship of institutional changes in landholding patterns to individual and community performance in cash cropping.

For example, should one encourage the transformation of traditional land tenure into individual freehold tenure, on the assumption that this is necessary to motivate and sustain satisfactory levels of economic activity? Such questions require empirical investigation. If the answers are in the affirmative, one then has the task of selecting from the alternative ways of effecting such changes. Local government councils, because their action involves maximal participation of the people themselves, are especially appealing in this regard. Most people now live in council areas—by 1970 there were 146 councils encompassing more than two million people—and the councils can, if they so choose, impose rates and taxes on land. Thus land-tax policies, devised by local government councils and adjusted to local conditions, could be directed to implementing freehold tenure. In coastal areas relying on coconuts as the main cash crop, the objective might be to encourage the establishment of individual- or household-operated plantations of two to six hectares. Established plantings of six hectares can be managed by a household which in addition has to plant food gardens, and such holdings would produce annual gross incomes of $600.

In some areas—the central Highlands and small islands—increasing pressure on available land will necessitate resettlement in the near future. As schemes are devised, it will be well for the people and their leaders and advisers to realize the opportunity that shifts to new areas afford for the introduction of innovations in land tenure. Individual freehold tenure, in particular, might be most easily established in such situations. On the other hand, recent comparative evidence shows the necessity of thorough investigation prior to the implementation of land-tenure reforms. In the case of the Micronesian communities recently resettled in the Solomons and other island areas, the plan for equal allotment of freehold, by ignoring Micronesian cultural principles and values related to land, has proved a failure. The costs in time and money of anthropological studies of land tenure are comparatively small, and such studies can often help to prevent problems that administrators or the people themselves cannot readily foresee.

While pressure towards individual land tenure is evident in areas where cash cropping is of increasing importance, it is by no means clear that it is either a desirable or necessary development. The contrary view of some economic planners is probably based in part on the questionable assumption that corporate kin groups and group control of resources necessarily restrict or stifle initiative in the economic sphere. In certain parts of Africa traditional kin groups have converted themselves into corporations aggregate under modern law—the Yoruba lineage group or *ebi* is a case in point—and a similar development in Papua New Guinea would seem to be inevitable. Landholding kin groups, in their traditional forms, exhibit company-like characteristics. Legally recognized as land-holding corporations, they might well perform as effective proprietary and producing units in modern commercial agriculture. Kin-group organization has already served as the basis of successful commercial enterprise in a number of areas of Papua New Guinea.

Bibliography

Allen, M. R. 1971. 'Descent groups and ecology amongst the Nduindui, New Hebrides', in L. R. Hiatt and C. Jayawardena (eds), *Anthropology in Oceania: essays presented to Ian Hogbin*, Sydney.

Barrau, J. 1958. *Subsistence Agriculture in Melanesia*. Honolulu.

Bell, F. L. S. 1953-4. 'Land tenure in Tanga', *Oceania*, vol. 24.

Brookfield, H. C. and Brown, P. 1963. *Struggle for Land*. Melbourne.

Brown, P. and Brookfield, H. C. 1959-60. 'Chimbu land and society', *Oceania*, vol. 30.

Crocombe, R. G. 1964. 'Land tenure in Papua-New Guinea', *Réalités du Pacifique*.

Crocombe, R. and Hide, R. 1971. 'New Guinea, unity in diversity', in Crocombe (ed.), *Land Tenure in the Pacific*. Melbourne.

Epstein, A. L. 1969. *Matupit: land, politics and change among the Tolai of New Britain*. Canberra.

Frake, C. O. 1956. 'Malayo-Polynesian land tenure', *American Anthropologist*, vol. 58.

Galis, K. W., de Bruyn, J. V., Pouwer, J., Schoorl, J. W. and Verschueren, J. 1970. *Land Tenure in West Irian*. New Guinea Research Unit Bulletin no. 38. Canberra.

Goodenough, W. H. 1955. 'A problem in Malayo-Polynesian social organization', *American Anthropologist*, vol. 57.

Groves, M. 1963. 'Western Motu descent groups', *Ethnology*, vol. 2.

Hogbin, H. I. and Lawrence, P. 1967. *Studies in New Guinea Land Tenure*. Sydney.

Howlett, D. R. 1965. *The European Land Settlement Scheme at Popondetta*. New Guinea Research Unit Bulletin no. 6. Canberra.

International Bank for Reconstruction and Development. 1965. 'Agriculture, livestock, forestry and fisheries', in *The Economic Development of the Territory of Papua and New Guinea*. Baltimore.

Kelly, R. C. 1968-9. 'Demographic pressure and descent group structure in the New Guinea Highlands', *Oceania*, vol. 39.

[Kohler, J.] 1960-1. 'Land tenure in Papua and New Guinea', *Australian Territories*, vol. 1.

McGrath, W. A. 1964. *A Select Annotated Bibliography on Land Tenure in the Territory of Papua and New Guinea*. Port Moresby.

Meggitt, M. J. 1965. *The Lineage System of the Mae-Enga of New Guinea*. Edinburgh.

Morawetz, D. 1967. *Land Tenure Conversion in the Northern District of Papua*. New Guinea Research Unit Bulletin no. 17. Canberra.

Ogan, E. 1971-2. 'Nasioi land tenure: an extended case study', *Oceania*, vol. 42.

Oliver, D. L. 1949. *Land Tenure in Northeast Siuai, Southern Bougainville, Solomon Islands*. Papers of the Peabody Museum, Harvard University, vol. 29.

Panoff, M. 1969-70. 'Land tenure among the Maenge of New Britain', *Oceania*, vol. 40.

Ploeg, A. 1971. *The Situm and Gobari Ex-servicemen's Settlements*. New Guinea Research Unit Bulletin no. 39. Canberra.

Pospisil, L. 1958. *Kapauku Papuans and their Law*. Yale University Publications in Anthropology no. 54. New Haven.

Reay, M. 1959. 'Individual ownership and transfer of land among the Kuma', *Man*, vol. 59.

―――― 1967-70. 'Structural co-variants of land shortage among patrilineal peoples', *Anthropological Forum*, vol. 2.

Rimoldi, M. 1966. *Land Tenure and Land Use among the Mount Lamington Orokaiva*. New Guinea Research Unit Bulletin no. 11. Canberra.

Salisbury, R. F. 1964. 'Changes in land use and tenure among the Siane of the New Guinea Highlands, 1952-1961', *Pacific Viewpoint*, vol. 5.

Simpson, S. R., Hide, R. L., Healy, A. M. and Kinyanjui, J. K. 1970. *Land Tenure and Economic Development: problems and policies in Papua-New Guinea and Kenya*. New Guinea Research Unit Bulletin no. 38. Canberra.

Singh, S. 1967. *A Benefit Cost Analysis of Resettlement in the Gazelle Peninsula*. New Guinea Research Unit Bulletin, no. 19. Canberra.

Spinks, G. R., Langton, T. W. and Gray, E. C. G. 1964. 'Appraisal of two land settlement schemes in the Gazelle Peninsula, New Britain', *Papua and New Guinea Agricultural Journal*, vol. 16.

Verschueren, J. 1958. 'Rechten op grond bij de Marind-Anim, (Zuid-Nieuw-Guinea)' [Land rights among the Marind-Anim], *Nieuw-Guinea Studiën*, vol. 2.

Marriage

D'Arcy Ryan

Papua New Guinea culture is not homogeneous. The area includes a number of separate societies differing in their structure, beliefs and practices, descent and kinship systems, patterns of affiliation and residence, and in the organization of their social institutions. The ecology—geographic, topographical and climatic—also varies. High mountains, river flats, coastal plains, swamps, and islands large and small each support populations that have adapted themselves to life at a more or less subsistence level. To a large extent, culture is a response to environment, and in a broad sense it might be feasible to categorize Papua New Guinea culture ecologically. But even within a virtually identical environment such cultural divergences are found that it does not seem possible to type any single institution, such as marriage, by this criterion.

There are, however, some features that seem to be common to all traditional Papua New Guinea societies, and these provide a general framework for the forms of marriage. The first is the fragmented pattern of small politically autonomous groups organized on a basis of kinship and characterized, with a few exceptions, by the absence of hereditary or self-perpetuating leadership. Moreover, the fertile areas support fairly heavy populations, and when a considerable number of kin-oriented and politically discrete groups occupy contiguous territories it is usual to find that the institution of marriage is an important means of linking them together by political alliances. Therefore marriage is perhaps best examined in this context.

A second striking characteristic of Papua New Guinea societies is their preoccupation with various forms of economic exchange. Such exchanges are a common way of creating, marking or preserving social relationships and are a distinctive feature of many marriage arrangements. Marriage payments, or bride price, reach a high degree of ceremonial elaboration in many societies, and

122

although in others they are less emphasized, few instances of marriage unaccompanied by some exchange of wealth between the contracting sets of affines have so far been reported.

Although monogamy has always been enjoined by the Christian missions, and societies with more than a generation of contact actively enforce it, polygyny was the traditional norm and is still practised in the more remote areas. Unlimited polygyny was the ideal, and a man's status was related to the number of wives he could acquire, the wealth he could amass to offer for them, the number of children they bore him, and the gardens and pigs they could tend for him. In the Trobriand Islands, one of the few places where differential status was formalized into rank, polygyny was restricted to 'chiefs', according to Malinowski (p. 113); yet in neighbouring Dobu, which was culturally similar, Fortune reported that polygyny was rare. In practice, however, the number of wives a man could hope to marry was limited by several factors, mainly economic and demographic: economic because each wife usually represented a considerable financial outlay, so that only a wealthy man could afford several; demographic because the populations do not have a preponderance of females. In contrast with the Australian Aborigines, the peoples of Papua New Guinea do not practise the custom of allowing the older men to monopolize the women. On the contrary, elders encourage the young men to marry and settle down at an early age. Few remain unmarried. A high rate of polygyny, together with former female infanticide, was reported from the Eastern Highlands by Langness (p. 178), but this is unusual and is not explained demographically.

In all polygynous marriages, relations between co-wives are a potential source of conflict which, in matrilineal Bougainville, could even drive a husband to suicide (Oliver p. 224). More commonly, a husband's neglect of one wife in favour of another causes jealousy and unhappiness (Read pp. 65–70), and the hostility of a senior wife can break her husband's relationship with an unwelcome newcomer. According to Held (p. 117), the Waropen of Geelvink Bay in Irian Jaya (West Irian) do not usually take a second wife without the consent of the first. A common way of avoiding conflict is to establish each wife and her family in her own house separated as far as possible from those of her co-wives. In the Western and Southern Highlands, where patterns of settlement are dispersed, co-wives often live kilometres apart; thus tension, from this source at least, is minimized.

Courtship practices, modes of arranging marriages, and patterns of marital relations, are influenced by a complex of factors that can, to some extent, be correlated with certain culture areas. In the Highlands, male-female relations are coloured by a strong belief in the impurity of women, expressed in many places by bachelor cults that ensure the ritual protection of young men from the dangerous effects of female contact. Although exclusive male cults and secret societies are found in many other areas, they do not have the predominant tone of conflict found in the Highlands, where relations between the sexes are characterized by tension and aggression. Although female impurity, as a specific ritual concept, is typical of the Highlands, sexual relations elsewhere are often fraught with strain, especially in the matrilineal areas where a husband may be at some social and economic disadvantage vis-a-vis his wife's kin.

Ideally, most people marry, and although some individuals with pronounced physical or mental defects are forced to remain single, few do so voluntarily.

People marry for one or more of the universal reasons: personal attraction, desire for children, achievement of full adult status, and economic advantage. This question has been solemnly discussed by many ethnographers, but the main reason is simple. People marry because few societies at this cultural level have recognized roles for bachelors or spinsters. Not to want to marry is almost unthinkable.

The Sengseng of southern New Britain are exceptional in that marriage is normally instigated by the women, while the men display a marked resistance to their approaches and usually postpone the union till middle age. Many remain single (Chowning 1968).

The marrying age varies so considerably that it is not possible to generalize beyond saying that most men are married by twenty-five and most girls by twenty. When a man delays marriage beyond this age there is usually some special reason such as absence from home, defeat in warfare with a consequent disruption of status, or difficulty in assembling bride payments. In the Eastern Highlands —Bena Bena, Gahuku-Gama, Kamano, Yagaria—all members of the same male age-grade are betrothed simultaneously and, ideally, married at about the same period, although this is often impossible to arrange in fact (Langness, p. 178; Read, p. 143). In Busama, brothers are expected to marry in order of seniority (Hogbin 1963, p. 103). In all these societies, sibling seniority ranking is emphasized in other ways also.

Young people are never entirely free to arrange their own unions, but the degree of restriction varies. To begin with, every society recognizes, and for the most part observes, incest and exogamy prohibitions. In those societies with a pronounced unilinear bias the lineage is invariably exogamous—with one possible exception in northern New Britain (Chowning 1963-6, p. 478)—the clan nearly always so, and the phratry usually. In addition, some degree of locality exogamy is common in the east (Capell; Corlette; Belshaw; Hogbin 1963), and the feeling that marriage is not proper between people who were reared and live together is general even when it is not made explicit. In non-unilinear societies marriage is forbidden with specified categories of cognates and affines. People of the same totem may not marry (Oliver, p. 117; Malinowski, p. 70), and moieties are also exogamous (Hogbin 1944–5, p. 324). Rank affects these restrictions. Statistics show that the marriage rules are more carefully observed in some societies than others, but even in the strictest communities men of high status can sometimes defy them with impunity (Read, p. 66; Held, p. 122).

Besides general proscriptive rules, the choice of spouse is further circumscribed in some areas by positive injunctions or preferences. Thus a patrilateral cross-cousin is the preferred wife in parts of the Eastern Highlands (Salisbury 1962, p. 103) and in the Trobriands (Malinowski, p. 66), but she is forbidden as a spouse in Dobu. Bilateral cross-cousin marriage is common in some of the islands (Oliver, p. 81; Chowning 1963–6, p. 485), but in at least one district of Bougainville a recent trend to matrilateral cross-cousin preference is reported (Ogan, p. 185). Preference for marriage between children of cross-cousins is found in areas as disparate as Wogeo (Hogbin 1944–5, p. 328), Manus (Mead 1933–4, p. 228), and the Star Mountains of Irian Jaya (Pouwer, p. 142). The examples of cross-cousin marriage observed in Papua New Guinea have certain correlative features. The societies that favour it are specifically concerned with a balanced alternating exchange of women and land rights between descent groups. This can be achieved by patrilateral cross-cousin marriage (Malinowski, pp. 81 ff.); and cross-cousin marriage of either kind can be used to organize alliances for the raising of economic or political status (Ogan). It should be emphasized that such marriages are preferred and never prescribed; and, moreover, there appear to be such difficulties in arranging them that in all societies for which we have adequate figures the majority of marriages do not follow the expressed ideal.

Whether actually achieved or not the presence of formalized marriage preferences always implies that young people have relatively little say in the selection of their marriage partners. And even without preferences this is probably true to some extent in most areas. A young couple's first marriage is usually arranged by the parents, the lineage, or the corporate cognatic kin group, some-times through the agency of a chief or headman. Child betrothal is common, for example in Bougainville, the Trobriands, Manus, and Geelvink Bay (Irian Jaya). The sanctions here are mainly economic. As marriage usually involves the exchange of wealth between the kin groups of the contracting parties, it is obvious that a young man is dependent for his bride payment on his kinsmen. These men thus have the power, which they frequently exercise, to influence his choice. Nevertheless, the relationship between dependence on kin in securing a spouse and freedom of choice is not the same every-where, and in many places young couples are allowed considerable latitude within the general marriage rules. In many coastal areas a good deal of pre-marital sexual licence is allowed, or at least tolerated, and the courtship of young couples takes place in this setting. In the Highland cultures pre-marital intercourse tends to be disapproved, an attitude deriving from the notion of dangerous female impurity. Yet many Highland societies allow the greatest freedom of choice of spouse.

Where choice is permitted, the coastal pattern encourages the narrowing down of a series of casual affairs to one steady liaison leading at last to permanency. Such relationships are publicly known but ostensibly clandestine, and the final step is sometimes pre-cipitated by the couple arranging to have themselves caught in compromising circumstances. Where this is the practice—in the Trobriands, Dobu, Wogeo and Geelvink Bay—it may be accom-panied by elopement. Courting ceremonies in the Highlands are more formally conducted. In the Southern Highlands a girl of marriage-able age, chaperoned by mother, brother or married sister, receives several nightly callers in her house simultaneously. Over a period of time she establishes an understanding with a particular young man who then approaches her kinsmen (Ryan). In the Eastern Highlands each village with nubile girls holds a nightly courting party, known in Pidgin as *kariem leg*, in a selected house where the girls together receive their male visitors. There is much erotic petting which may lead to brief love affairs formally allowed, for a consideration, by the girl's kin. These affairs do not normally lead directly to marriage, which is arranged without the girl's consent, but they may be regarded as a preparation for it (Reay 1959).

Even in such relative freedom, parental or other pressures may be exerted. Two men may, for economic and political reasons, favour an alliance between their children despite the fact that this may be contrary to the wishes of the young people. The outcome of such conflict is usually determined by the relative strength of the individuals concerned. It can be said that resistance to unwanted arranged marriages can and does occur. Boys can resist more readily than girls. Where a man's first marriage is always arranged by his parents or seniors, rejection of his intended bride may mean forfeiture of their economic assistance in his bride price. But since European contact began, a young man has been able to earn his own bride price as a labourer. A frequent ploy to overcome opposition is deliberate pregnancy. Even where pre-marital intercourse is relatively free, as in the Trobriands, illegitimacy seems to be rare in Melanesia. It is generally condemned, and the child is usually reared as the mother's sibling or clan-brother. The lover is often expected to marry the girl. When forced marriages do take place they tend to be unstable. It seems reasonable to infer that although Papua New Guinea marriage is circumscribed with a great many rules and prohibitions that could be onerously restrictive, freedom to choose the spouse is far greater in practice than might at first appear. It should be noted that the above discussion has been confined to a man's first marriage. For subsequent marriages he must observe the rules of exogamy, but the arrangements and payments now become largely, or even entirely, his own responsibility.

Marriage by capture occurred in earlier times in Bougainville, Wogeo, Manus, Fore and elsewhere. It was once common in the Northern District (Williams 1930, pp. 130 ff.). Elsewhere it was more usual for enemy females to be killed.

The form, scale and importance of marriage payments show a wide and apparently random diversity; and it seems that they do not have the same function and are not viewed in the same way in every society. Europeans, whether administrators, traders or missionaries, at first believed that the associated payments meant the outright purchase of a woman as a chattel. Repugnance to this idea was at the bottom of missionary disapproval of the practice and of the persistent, but only moderately successful, attempts to discourage it. In a few places the Administration banned it, but this was not the general policy. Most anthropologists do not accept the interpretation of bride payments as purchase, and where the custom has been investigated it has been found that married women retain personal rights, however limited, that distinguish them clearly from livestock. By far the commonest rationale of bride price by peoples who practise it is that any marriage means the loss by the woman's family or kin or local group of a useful and valuable member and a potential bearer of children, with a corresponding gain by the man's group. It is therefore thought just to restore the balance by the gainers compensating the losers, in conformity with general principles of economic reciprocity. Throughout Papua New Guinea, indeed, most societies explain their marriage payments quite reasonably in this way. But there are several anomalies. Armstrong, after stating that wives in Rossel Island were bought, reported that 'a man may be punished by the killing of the woman who cooks his food' (p. 98). He interpreted this fact as an illustration of complete purchase. But he did not make clear how this could be possible in a matrilineal society where wives live with, or at least close to, their own kin; nor did he indicate the consequences. More recently, Langness (p. 179) said that 'Bena brides . . . are bought and sold' because 'bride price does not result in an equivalent exchange'. But an imbalance in the material part of the transaction is, as we shall see, typical of marriage exchanges even in societies where purchase is specifically denied.

This view that marriage payments are compensation to the woman's kin for economic and social services would make sense for societies with patri-virilocal residence, where wives move always in theory, and usually in practice, to the husband's group. It should logically follow that no payments would be necessary in societies with matri-uxorilocal residence, where the woman's group retains her services or has controlling rights over her children. But this is not so. In New Ireland, one of the rare examples of matri-uxorilocal residence, bride price is paid, as it is in the matrilineal societies with avunculo-virilocal residence. Indeed, the only society in which it has been positively said that there is no bride price is Wogeo (Hogbin 1963, p. 121) where there is double-unilineal descent and virilocal residence. Yet even here marriage is sometimes accompanied by an exchange of food, and if there is a formal betrothal the groom's kin should contribute lavishly to the girl's coming-of-age feast.

Underlying the marriage arrangements of many societies, though with no regular regional distribution, is the principle of exchange of women. This is sometimes formalized by a strong preference for the exchange of sisters, real or classificatory; in other places it is merely implied in a general concept of reciprocity between the marriage-organizing units, whether they may be family, lineage, cognatic group or whatever. Where the principle is strictly applied a man gives his daughter to a group from whom he expects a bride for his son, while in other societies there may be nothing more than a general feeling that a group tends to seek wives from other groups to which it has previously given women. Where strict exchange is the norm, one would expect this to satisfy the desire for reciprocity and that no further payments would be required. But this is not generally true, although the Keveri of the Central District are reported by Williams (1944–5) to be an exception. The principle of woman-exchange was carried to unique extremes among the Keraki of the Western District: a man who lacked a woman of his own group to exchange for a bride, purchased and adopted a 'sister' from a neighbouring group and then exchanged her for a wife in the approved fashion. Such marriages were apparently not accompanied by further exchanges of wealth (Williams 1936).

Elopement or seduction may be used by ardent couples to force a marriage and to avoid or minimize bride price, and in some places the groom is required to compensate his wife's parents with labour; but this is regarded as an inferior kind of arrangement according to Held (p. 102).

The question here seems to be, what precisely is bride price and what distinguishes the practice from marriage exchange? It has been customary to speak of bride price when a significantly large and valuable payment is negotiated beforehand and transferred from the groom's side to the bride's. The payments are invariably met by a formal counter payment, incorrectly described by some writers as dowry, from bride's kin to groom's. The question of whether these payments are, or are not, bride price arises when gift and counter-gift are comparatively small, when their value is more or less arbitrary, and when they approach the parity of reciprocal gift exchange.

It may be more illuminating to consider bride price in the general context of economics. In most cases a woman's services are exchanged either for a large quantity of valuables or for a lesser quantity of valuables plus the implied promise of another woman some time later. There is always a counter payment, and in many societies, notably in the Highlands, gift and counter-gift must continue between the two sets of affines for the duration of the union. In Papua New Guinea, social relationships of all kinds tend to be established and maintained by the exchange of material goods; it would be surprising if marriages, which always imply new relationships between separate sets of kin, were not so celebrated. Any distinction between bride price and marriage exchange would seem, therefore, to be a matter of scale, formalization and local cultural emphasis.

Traditionally, the goods in marriage exchange comprise all the valuables of the particular locality. They include such European commodities as steel axes, where these are plentiful, and in the more sophisticated areas the payments are now made partly, or even wholly, in cash. On the northern coast of Irian Jaya, antique

Chinese pots of the Sung and Ming periods are family heirlooms that change hands at marriages (Held, p. 96).

The size of the payment is influenced by the desirability of the bride and the status of the contracting parties. It is often a matter of pride to both sides that the highest possible price should be paid. In recent times marriage payments have been affected by inflation. The quantity of goods exchanged in the Highlands has increased noticeably in the last decade (Salisbury 1962, p. 116; Reay 1966, pp. 169 ff.), and in Hanuabada, near Port Moresby, bride payments of $3000 have been reported.

Apart from the myth of purchase, another common misconception about bride price is that it is motivated by the desire for profit. Analysis of the contributions to, and distributions of, these payments show that in almost all cases payments are made by a kin group to a kin group. For his first marriage at least, a man is assisted financially by his family or close relatives and perhaps also by age mates or trading partners outside his immediate kindred. But assistance of any kind is always reciprocal, and all these persons must sooner or later be repaid. A man meets this obligation when one of his close female relatives is given in marriage and he himself is a recipient of some of her bride payment. These goods he uses to repay those kinsmen who had already contributed at his own marriage. For his subsequent marriages he usually finds most of the payment himself, for by that time he is usually of an age to maintain numerous economic credit relationships that he can tap when he needs liquid assets. Thus in the course of his economic lifetime a man contributes just about as much to other people's marriage payments as he receives from those of his own kinswomen. This means that those who receive the payments for any bride are roughly the same people who would have contributed to her marriage had she been a man. The motivating factor is not profit but prestige, for it is characteristic of Papua New Guinea that the ability to act as a channel for the flow of wealth in the form of food distribution feasts or of contributions to intergroup exchanges is everywhere an important means of achieving high status.

Except in cases of capture, and in some elopements, cohabitation is marked by ceremony—most commonly the formal delivery of the bride to her husband's people or the symbolic sharing of food by the newly-wed couple. The Keraki celebrate direct sister exchange at a wedding with the two bridegrooms who are exchanging women standing at opposite ends of the settlement and, simultaneously, each firing an arrow in the direction in which he is about to send his sister. The flight of the arrow 'shows her the path', and the exchange is symbolized as the arrows pass in mid-air (Williams 1936, p. 144). Among the Siane there are rituals to retain a departing bride's soul in her own village (Salisbury 1965, p. 74), but such religious implications are rare and most weddings are entirely secular.

The status of a married woman varies from one society to another. In personal relations she is nearly always subordinate to her husband and rarely owns or handles much property of her own. She bears her husband's children and tends his pigs and gardens. There is everywhere a marked sexual division of labour; even most artefacts are the exclusive responsibility of one sex or the other. Women play a minor role in the religious life, although in a few societies they are active as magicians and witches. Although it is usually accepted that a provoked husband will occasionally strike his wife, consistent cruelty is the exception, and the brutal female subjugation and slavery reported from Buin in Bougainville by Thurnwald seems to be unique. Generally, a good deal of affection and companionship exists between married couples, and a sensible woman of strong character can achieve a position of considerable respect in the community.

There is also much variation in the rights claimed over a married woman by her husband and the kin group that helped pay for her. Although she is nowhere thought to have been bought like a piece of livestock, she is in some areas expected to transfer her allegiance completely to her husband's people who may even go so far as to provide her with surrogate brothers to take over the protective obligations of her own blood kin (Langness, p. 178); but even then she still retains latent rights of membership of her natal kin group. As a corollary of his transfer of allegiance, a number of societies practise widow inheritance, according to which a widow must marry one of her late husband's real or classificatory brothers (Thomas; Oliver; Held; Belshaw; Berndt; O'Brien). In the Trobriands a chief inherits his predecessor's wives (Malinowski, p. 114). In other societies a married woman remains unequivocally a member of her own kin group and visits them regularly, symbolizing her constant relationship with them in many ceremonial contexts. In such societies widow inheritance is specifically forbidden (Ryan).

Isolated examples of a man's having a claim to his wife's sisters have been reported. In the Western District this institution is associated with the practice of woman exchange, so that if a new young wife dies her husband can claim a replacement from her kin group. Actual cases of this are rare (Williams 1936, p. 156).

Papua New Guinea men are usually jealous of their wives, and the hospitable practice of wife-lending, so common among Australian Aborigines, seems to be confined to the south-western coast. Among the Keraki, wives were lent, or preferably exchanged, to visitors on certain ceremonial occasions, though the rules of exogamy were still observed (Williams 1936, p. 159). Serpenti (p. 183) reported that the Kiman allowed a considerable amount of licence on special occasions, but only to married persons, and 'in the western villages . . . all the women and head-hunters used to take part in promiscuous sexual intercourse before and after head-hunting expeditions. . . . In these cases kinship was the only restriction'.

Relations with close affines are usually marked by some degree of formality ranging from polite constraint to total avoidance, and it is commonly considered offensive to utter the personal name of a close affine within his or her hearing. Some writers hold that affines in such fragmented societies as those of Papua New Guinea are always potential enemies (Brown, P. 335), and that marriage forms an important bridge between autonomous political units that might otherwise be hostile. The expression 'We marry those whom we fight' is reported to have wide currency in both Africa (Mayer, p. 123) and Papua New Guinea (Cook, p. 115); and formalized behaviour between sets of kin related by marriage may thus be considered as a means of cushioning potential hostility between them. On the other hand, some Papua New Guinea societies assert categorically that affines are *ipso facto* friends, and that mutual respect prevents friction and helps to preserve a desirable alliance (Ryan, p. 171).

Residence after marriage is influenced by the prevailing local custom. Usually patrilineal societies have virilocal residence as the norm, but in matrilineal societies, uxorilocal residence is uncommon. In the latter it is more usual for a youth at puberty to move to the locality of his mother's brother, from whom he inherits his land. On marriage his wife joins him there; this is avunculo-virilocal residence. It is important to remember, however, that rules of residence are nowhere followed with absolute rigidity. They should perhaps be described as ideological preferences whose observance is encouraged by more or less persuasive economic and political sanctions. Thus we find that in most societies there is in fact some flexibility, and there are always individuals whose choice is determined by availability of land and the complexity of their personal relationships, regardless of the prevailing mode. In most cases the majority follow the rule, but there are always exceptions, and some societies are noticeably more permissive than are others.

It is not possible to estimate the stability of marriages in any realistic sense because of wide regional variation, lack of reliable figures for comparison, and because the term itself is relative. As a broad generalization it might be suggested that marriages tend to be stable in societies where they are the focus of economically significant exchanges of material goods, as in the Highlands, or where the reciprocity of woman exchange is explicit, short-term and strict, as in the Western District. In such circumstances marriage concerns the economic or social interests of many people besides the couple themselves. These people have an investment in the union and often exert considerable pressure to preserve it.

Arranged marriages tend to be unstable, though the Busama are an exception (Hogbin 1963). Young girls forced into an unwelcome union, especially with an older man, frequently run away, sometimes to a lover but usually back to their own kin group or village. The situation is handled in a variety of ways. To begin with, the girl's kin are naturally reluctant to return the payments or the incoming bride received in exchange for her, and try to send her back to her husband. Should she persist in her refusal, her kinsmen may relent and permit an annulment with appropriate exchange adjustments. In other societies she is forced to go back to her husband by various punitive sanctions: rejection by her own kin, thrashing by brothers or husband, group rape by the husband's brothers or, in rare cases, public execution by the husband. There are instances of unhappy young wives committing suicide. The outcome is also influenced by imponderable factors such as the consensus about a married woman's rights and the girl's own personal relations with her father and brothers. Thus, in areas where a woman is considered to remain a member of her natal group rather than to transfer to that of her husband, her kinsmen continue to protect her interests and look after her welfare; this means that she has a refuge should her marriage become intolerable, while at the same time her husband, being aware of this, is induced to treat her well and give her less cause to leave him. In such circumstances, marriage payments function as a kind of indemnity or assurance of good treatment.

Desertion, the more important factors of which have just been summarized, is probably the major cause of divorce. Apart from distaste for a forced marriage, other reasons for desertion are a husband's cruelty, bullying by co-wives, or the husband's failure to meet his marriage payments.

Divorce can generally be instigated by either party, and a husband may dismiss a wife because she is shrewish, neglects her domestic duties, or is barren. The last is a common cause in the Eastern Highlands and is another manifestation of the prevailing sexual hostility, for when a man divorces a barren woman he thereby alleges that, by secret contraception, she deliberately refused to bear him children (Read, p. 100). Most divorces are brought about by the wife. This is understandable when we remember that usually a man has an economic stake in his marriage, and that an unsatisfactory union does not cause him nearly as much physical or mental suffering as it does a woman. He is even more reluctant to divorce when he has only one wife and lacks the means to acquire another.

Adultery, although nearly everywhere the occasion of serious conflict, does not seem to be a major cause of divorce. A woman can do relatively little about adultery by her husband. With the support of powerful kin she may be able to leave him, and wronged wives have been known to resort to actual violence. Usually, however, women have no weapon but their tongue. By airing their grievance and public vituperation they invoke the powerful sanction of public shame against the adulterous party (Held). This sanction can be strong enough to force an accused adulterer to commit suicide (Serpenti, p. 180). In some societies women lack even this degree of independence, and the wife of an adulterer can enlist public sympathy only by threatened or actual suicide.

In all but a few matrilineal areas men are in a much stronger position. A husband catching his wife in adultery often has the right to kill both wife and lover if he can; so an adulteress often defends herself by pleading rape, or a woman who knows she has aroused her husband's suspicions may anticipate his charge by so accusing her lover. The exercise of the husband's rights may, however, be modified by a number of factors. His status and strength and the support he can muster may be insufficient for him to exact physical redress; hence an adulterer of high status enjoys some degree of immunity. Moreover, if the adulterer belongs to the same kin or local group as the husband, the kinsmen usually persuade the injured party to control his indignation and accept material compensation. Some societies do not take too grave a view of occasional infidelity, although they may punish severely a flagrant and promiscuous adulteress. It seems probable that a husband does not usually exercise his right to kill his errant wife but satisfies his honour rather by thrashing her or, less commonly, divorcing her.

When a divorce has been instigated, and before marriage can be finally dissolved, two further matters must be decided: the future of the children and the winding up of marriage payments. These questions are not separable.

The prevailing rule of descent implies not only affiliation but also rights and obligations. In patrilineal societies, marriage payments establish rights not only over the wife but also over her children. When a marriage terminates, the children remain members of the father's descent group and he retains rights over them. They look to him for their land and all the other privileges of group membership. However, if at the time of divorce they are too young to be deprived of a mother's care, she takes them with her on the understanding that they can, when old enough, make a choice as to whether to return to their father's people or remain with their mother's. The choice is sometimes irrevocable, sometimes not. The question is bound up with such factors as the relationships between the paternal and maternal kin groups, and the supply of land. In territories where land is plentiful, children in this situation are permitted theoretically to maintain joint affiliation; in practice they tend to align themselves with the group in which personal ties are strongest. In matrilineal societies, even those in which there are substantial marriage payments, the children go with the mother since their future security depends on identification with her kin group (Malinowski, p. 125). Two exceptions are southern Bougainville, where they remain with the father (Oliver, p. 198), and southern New Britain, where they are divided equally between the parents with any odd child going to the mother (Chowning 1963–6, p. 493). In cognatic societies they normally stay with their father's local group.

Divorce usually implies some economic adjustment. It is here that the interdependence of marriage payments and the bearing of children becomes most apparent. When the husband initiates the divorce there is usually no claim for refund of bride payment unless he can establish that his wife flagrantly neglected her duties or was otherwise in error. Even then his status must be such that he can enforce his demands. Should his wife leave him, and this is more common, he and his group endeavour to recoup their expenditure. This is a frequent cause of litigation both at an informal local level and in the Administration courts. In the traditional situation, negotiations take place within a framework of certain broadly accepted principles which are, however, influenced by various *ad hoc* personal and political factors. It is generally conceded that as services and children are the main considerations for bride payment the fulfilment of these obligations relieves a woman and, by implication, her supporting kin, of her commitment in a marriage. Hence cohabitation over an appreciable period, and the bearing of children, are considered an adequate recompense to the husband and his group for any payment they have made. Two children, among the Nakanai and the Siane, or three, among the Mendi, are enough to cancel out a marriage payment. When the community considers that a deserting wife has not fully discharged her obligations, then the precise amount of the refund often becomes a matter for protracted haggling, and it is at this point that the relative status of the negotiating parties is a significant factor. At the same time it should be noted that the birth of children often acts as a stabilizing influence on marriage. In Wogeo at least it is asserted that as no woman would willingly leave her children, divorce does not occur at all after children have been born; although some 20 per cent of marriages break up before that time (Hogbin 1944–5, p. 351).

A woman who is properly divorced—that is, one whose husband has no longer any legitimate claim on her—is free to marry again. In a subsequent marriage her kin demand and receive whatever bride payment is appropriate to her present age and status.

Among most peoples a widow goes into mourning for as long as two or three years, during which period she usually stays with her late husband's people and wears clothing considered sexually unattractive. When the widow has discharged her mourning obligations she is free to remarry.

The future of widows seems to be related yet again to the general question of the allegiance of married women. Where women are considered to have joined their husband's people, it is the latter who negotiate the widow's next marriage either within their own group or elsewhere; they conduct her marriage exchanges, with perhaps a small payment to her natal group in recognition of former affinal ties. In other areas, such as the Southern Highlands, where all the practices of marriage are based on the assumption that a woman maintains her original kin affiliations, any future marriage is organized by her own people who make a token compensation to the sons or brothers of her late husband.

Subsequent marriage payments diminish with age, and in the Eastern Highlands a widow's kin can claim no payment until she has borne her new husband a child (Read, p. 68).

In southern New Britain it was formerly the custom for widows to be strangled at their request by their own kinsmen (Chinnery), who paid compensation to those of the widow's kin who had not taken part in the act (Chowning 1968); Todd records this treatment for 'widows of rank'. The rationale of the practice is the belief that marriage should be permanent, even to the extent of a wife accompanying her husband to the afterlife. An obvious corollary is that divorce is not recognized, and an intolerable marriage can be broken only by the wife running away. This is an uncommon pattern.

Some salient factors will now be clear. The economic implications are obvious. In most, but not all, areas marriage is based on the direct or delayed exchange of women between kin or local groups and, with very few exceptions, is accompanied by some exchange of wealth, the universal method of marking social relationships. Thus, even where considerable freedom of choice is allowed, marriage is primarily a group transaction, and among the networks of politically-fragmented kin-based societies it is the most important means of creating links between the small autonomous units. In former times, when warfare was more or less constant, marriage created economically cemented affinal ties that could when necessary be translated into military alliances important for group survival. This situation was complicated by a widespread hostility between the sexes, often religiously sanctioned, so that marriage usually brought about a relationship of potential conflict between two sets of affines who distrusted but also needed each other. This often precarious balance of alliance was probably an accurate summary of the traditional political picture.

The question now arises as to how far the people themselves are aware of these functional implications: to what extent do they arrange marriages in the conscious pursuit of political advantage? Although it is impossible to answer precisely, reports from many different areas afford instances of marriages arranged for this reason, and it is probable that in most cases where parental pressure enforces a marriage it is because the alliance is considered politically or economically desirable. Even where the negotiating parties do not have particular benefits in mind, it is generally agreed that the rules of exogamy are reinforced by people's desire to maximize socially useful relationships by expanding their personal kin networks. More explicit is the Mendi marriage rule forbidding more than one marriage between any two patrilineages for about five generations (Ryan, p. 163). In Dobu 'marriage of two or three matrilineal kindred into the same village is discouraged' (Fortune, p. 28). In these and similar cases expansion of affinal ties is not only desirable but enforced. On the other hand, sister exchange and the various forms of marriage preference mentioned above tend to have the reverse effect. They concentrate marriages by causing each kin group to seek its wives from groups to which it has previously given women. Thus, while many societies undoubtedly contract useful alliances by marriage, and may or may not manipulate their marriages to do so, others have marriage rules that expressly prevent them from doing so (Barnes; Langness, pp. 177 ff.).

On the level of individual politics, in the sense of the enhancement of personal power, there is in all parts of Papua New Guinea a clear relationship between marriage and status. Rarely is there a stable or hereditary leadership, and even in the Trobriands it has been shown that the role of the chief is by no means as strictly defined as Malinowski's statements suggest (Uberoi). Power is achieved by headmen who may have much influence but little formal authority. Their position is relatively insecure and must constantly be reinforced by the same economic and social manoeuvring that originally established it. Of these activities one of the most important is marriage. In the discussion of polygyny it was pointed out that a plurality of wives is the aim of an ambitious man who uses the resultant kin or locality ties to expand his sphere of political influence.

Status is everywhere dependent also on the ability to contribute generously to community feasts and important inter-group gift exchanges, and in this general nexus of exchange and status, marriage payments play an essential part. Prestige accrues not to the married couple but to their kinsmen who negotiate and mount the marriage exchanges. Thus in many areas a leader not only disposes of his own children in marriages advantageous to himself but seeks also to have some say in organizing the marriages of all people within his sphere of influence (Ogan). Waropen marriage payments are so caught up with all other prestige exchanges that childless couples adopt children in order to be able to take part in them and so secure their future status (Held, p. 117).

The indigenous cultures of Papua New Guinea have undergone marked change under European influence, the degree varying with length of contact. The Australian government has, in the last decade or so, accelerated the process. Although many remote communities in the hinterland have been as yet little affected, social institutions like marriage have to some extent modified their functions in others. In places like the Highlands where marriages were frequently arranged with an eye to military alliance, the diminution of inter-clan warfare has obviated this.

The Christian missions have exerted considerable influence on such practices as polygyny, sister exchange, forced marriages, divorce and bride price. Polygyny is no longer found among people who have had any effective degree of European influence. Probably it is the first important marriage practice to disappear.

Preferred or arranged marriages, while still common, are now less easily enforced. The economic independence of young men and the sympathetic attitude of government courts to the wishes of a reluctant bride tend to weaken the authority of parents and kin group.

Missionary disapproval of divorce is often sanctioned by the threat of suspension from church membership. This is a serious punishment in some of the coastal communities. Whether the result has been the stabilization of marriage or an increase in covert adultery is debatable.

Attempts to interfere with bride price have had unexpected effects. There is now a growing tendency for marriage payments to be made partly or wholly in cash, and their increasing size reflects the affluence of the new cash economy. Reay (1966, p. 168) suggests that the notion of marriage as outright purchase is coming to supersede old ideas of exchange:

> the idea of a 'bride-price' as the valuation of a bride and her sub-sequent purchase is modern, not traditional, custom among people who used to barter bride for bride and pay not for a woman herself but for rights over her offspring. Being modern, however, it makes it no less valid as custom when European acceptance has frozen it in this form.

She then outlines a number of problems at present causing concern.

Despite shifts in emphasis, there is no indication that marriage payments will be abolished within the present generation, and while they remain, marriage will retain much of its traditional character.

Bibliography

Armstrong, W. E. 1928. *Rossel Island*. Cambridge.

Barnes, J. A. 1966. 'African models in the New Guinea Highlands', *Man*, vol. 62, 1962. Republished in H. I. Hogbin and L. R. Hiatt (eds), *Readings in Australian and Pacific Anthropology*, Melbourne.

Belshaw, C. S. 1957. *The Great Village*. London.

Berndt, R. M. 1962. *Excess and Restraint*. Chicago.

Brown, P. 1964. 'Enemies and affines', *Ethnology*, vol. 3.

Capell, A. 1943-4. 'Notes on the islands of Choiseul and New Georgia, Solomon Islands', *Oceania*, vol. 14.

Chinnery, E. W. P. 1928. 'Certain natives of south New Britain and Dampier Straits', *Territory of New Guinea Anthropological Report* no. 3, Melbourne.

Chowning, A. 1963-6. 'Lakalai kinship', *Anthropological Forum*, vol. 1.

———— 1968. Personal communication.

Cook, E. A. 1969. 'Marriage among the Manga', in Glasse and Meggitt (eds), *Pigs, Pearlshells, and Women*.

Corlette, E. A. C. 1934-5. 'Notes on the natives of the New Hebrides', *Oceania*, vol. 5.

Fortune, R. F. 1932. *Sorcerers of Dobu: social anthropology of the Dobu Islanders*. Revised ed., London, 1963.

Glasse, R. M. and Meggitt, M. J. (eds) 1969. *Pigs, Pearlshells, and Women: marriage in the New Guinea Highlands*. Englewood Cliffs.

Held, G. J. 1957. *The Papuans of Waropen*. The Hague.

Hogbin, H. I. 1944-5. 'Marriage in Wogeo, New Guinea', *Oceania*, vol. 15.

———— 1963. *Kinship and Marriage in a New Guinea Village*. London.

Langness, L. L. 1966. 'Some problems in the conceptualization of Highlands social structures', *American Anthropologist*, vol. 66, special publication, 1964. Republished in H. I. Hogbin and L. R. Hiatt (eds), *Readings in Australian and Pacific Anthropology*, Melbourne.

Malinowski, B. 1932. *The Sexual Life of Savages in North-Western Melanesia*. 3rd ed., London.

Mayer, P. 1950. 'Privileged obstruction of marriage rites among the Gusii', *Africa*, vol. 20.

Mead, M. 1933-4. *Kinship in the Admiralty Islands*. Anthropological Papers of the American Museum of Natural History, vol. 34.

———— 1965. *New Lives for Old*. London.

Meggitt, M. J. 1964. 'Male-female relationships in the Highlands of Australian New Guinea', *American Anthropologist*, vol. 66, special publication.

O'Brien, D. 1969. 'Marriage among the Konda Valley Dani', in Glasse and Meggitt (eds), *Pigs, Pearlshells, and Women*.

Ogan, E. 1966. 'Nasioi marriage', *Southwestern Journal of Anthropology*, vol. 22.

Oliver, D. L. 1955. *A Solomon Island Society*. Cambridge, Mass.

Pouwer, J. 1964. 'A social system in the Star Mountains', *American Anthropologist*, vol. 66, special publication.

Read, K. E. 1966. *The High Valley*. London.

Reay, M. 1959. *The Kuma*. Melbourne.

—— 1966. 'Women in transitional society', in E. K. Fisk (ed.), *New Guinea on the Threshold*, Canberra.

Ryan, D. J. 1969. 'Marriage in Mendi', in Glasse and Meggitt (eds), *Pigs, Pearlshells, and Women*.

Salisbury, R. F. 1962. *From Stone to Steel*. Melbourne.

—— 1965. 'The Siane of the Eastern Highlands', in P. Lawrence and M. J. Meggitt (eds), *Gods, Ghosts and Men in Melanesia*, Melbourne.

Serpenti, L. M. 1965. *Cultivators in the Swamps*. Assen.

Strathern, M. 1972. *Women In Between*. London.

Thomas, K. H. 1941-2. 'Notes on the natives of the Vanimo Coast, New Guinea', *Oceania*, vol. 12.

Thurnwald, H. 1934-5. 'Woman's status in Buin society', *Oceania*, vol. 5.

Todd, J. A. 1934-5. 'Report on research work in S.W. New Britain', *Oceania*, vol. 5.

Uberoi, J. P. Singh 1962. *Politics of the Kula Ring*. Manchester.

Williams, F. E. 1930. *Orokaiva Society*. London.

—— 1936. *Papuans of the Trans-Fly*. Oxford.

—— 1944-5. 'Mission influence amongst the Keveri of south-east Papua', *Oceania*, vol. 15.

Traditional Political Organization[*]

L. L. Langness

Generally when people speak of government, administration and politics they have in mind industrialized nations and problems of international law. We are familiar with the sophisticated procedures developed over the long course of human history whereby the affairs of men in the modern world are decided and regulated. When for some reason the political machinery fails to operate, or one or more groups violate the canons of international agreement, hostilities ensue either within or between nations; and eventually out of the holocaust new forms and techniques of government emerge that again attempt to maintain harmonious relations between large units with different regional, national and international interests. Where small non-literate societies came into this picture, it was usually as wards of some modern nation. 'Primitives' were assumed to be without government, politics, administrative machinery, judges, and courts of law; and they were therefore incorporated into some more developed system. But in fact all men everywhere, and in all circumstances, have affairs to manage. Even among small groups there are conflicts of interest, boundary disputes, decisions to be made that affect the society as a whole. And as anthropologists have evinced the most interest in isolated small-scale societies, it is anthropology that provides information about how such groups organize themselves politically.

Contemporary interest in non-literate or traditional political systems can be traced to the book *African Political Systems* edited by Fortes and Evans-Pritchard, although the main lines of enquiry were outlined much earlier by Maine and Morgan who were in fact preceded by Montesquieu, Machiavelli and Aristotle (Balandier).

The subject of traditional political organization has been approached from many points of view (Balandier; Cohen; Easton;

* Entitled *Political Organization* in the *Encyclopaedia*.

142

Gluckman 1965; Mair; Middleton and Tait; Swartz, Turner and Tuden). But until recently (Berndt and Lawrence), however much the various approaches differed, all were developed primarily from African studies. Thus our limited knowledge of Melanesian societies led us to place many of them tentatively according to typologies developed in Africa, and to discuss them in terms of conceptual schemes also developed from that continent. It is increasingly apparent that modifications must be introduced to accommodate distinctive features of Melanesian social and political organizations. This task cannot be performed here, although as a beginning some terminological innovations are suggested. Definitions of 'politics' and related terms vary widely, and such innovations should not cause difficulty.

The term 'political' refers fundamentally to public affairs. The extent of the community concerned—the public—and its organization must be empirically determined. As political activity occurs between groups of all kinds as well as within them, the community, or public, is usually, though not always, itself a corporate group and is made up of a number of such groups that are its political units. Australia, for example, is from some points of view a political unit within the public of the British Commonwealth, even the United Nations. Traditionally, a Papua New Guinea clan or village is a political unit in a much smaller public, the boundaries of which must be determined in each case from the point of view of the participants.

The units making up a public are termed 'polities'. Polities can vary in size and number, in functions, in internal organization, and in the processes employed to manage internal and external affairs. By polity is meant not simply the largest unit of social structure that can be defined as a corporate group but rather any unit of social structure that at times and for some purpose acts as a group. A tribe might be considered a polity for some purpose, one of its constituent clans a polity for others, a sub-clan or lineage for still others, and so on down to the level of families. Likewise, a village can constitute a polity, as can a secret society or an age grade. Polities can be joined in various combinations, forming larger or smaller groups of people, and act with greater or lesser degrees of cohesiveness and efficiency. They need not be permanent and may emerge at certain times for certain purposes and then remain dormant or even disband entirely. Each polity has its own political system that is always part of a larger system, either the political system of a larger polity or of the wider public. A polity that is not part of a larger polity is the largest political unit within the public.

It is possible but not necessary for a public to be composed of units having identical political systems; but the political system of the public is never identical with the political system of any one of its constituent parts. Ordinarily political systems of publics are systems of power relations, whereas political systems of polities are always characterized by systems of authority that distinguish a polity. Groups cannot exist and act without authority relations of some kind.

Public affairs are always managed within a framework of power and authority relations which, as Smith has made clear, are the elementary forms of political relations. Power is the ability to impose one's will on others in spite of opposition. Authority is limited power. It is the legitimate right to influence, to make binding decisions, and to direct the affairs of polities within the rules recognized by the members of those polities. There is variation in the extent to which the use of power is permitted, as also in the kinds of power relations allowed. In some systems a great deal of compulsion is tolerated, in others very little. In some the use of violence and physical coercion is legitimate, and in some it is not.

Political organization through the use of power and authority facilitates, influences and regulates public affairs. Comparative studies of political organization must specify the particular publics being investigated, their political systems, the distribution and types of polities found within that public, their political systems, the ways in which numbers of polities characteristically join together into larger units, the particular affairs that are of concern to and are managed by the various polities, and the manner in which they allocate authority and recognize and legitimate the use of power.

Power and authority are also aspects of many social relations not in themselves political but which may influence public affairs. A man may have the authority to use economic sanctions for influencing group action, but he may or may not exercise it. Or he may have the supernatural power to cause rain but not use it to influence public affairs. Comparative studies of political systems must also, then, take cognizance of the relations between other institutions and those that are political; indeed, in some cases such studies may reveal that political activity is so embedded in social relations of other kinds that specific political institutions do not exist.

Before describing Melanesian political organization it is necessary to describe briefly segmentary lineage systems. This so-called African model has influenced much of the Papua New Guinea literature, particularly that on the Highlands, and made the task of analysis more difficult. The major features of the African model can be stated as follows: (1) there must be unilineal descent, and members must be recruited on that basis (Smith); (2) there must be a dogma of descent and a concern for lineage solidarity (Barnes; Langness 1964); (3) the lineage must be corporate in that it has continuity in time and a single jural personality (Fortes) (4) it must be corporate in function by acting as a unit for some purpose (Radcliffe-Brown; Smith); (5) the lineage must therefore have its own leadership and authority to maintain its internal organization and co-ordinate its common action (Langness 1964; Smith); and, most important, (6) it must discharge specifically political functions —as Smith writes, 'the fundamental concepts of segmentary theory centre about the definition of a system of political relations, and on the basis of this, differentiate lineages from other kinship groupings in terms of segmentary principles and structures which reflect and discharge political functions'.

Unilineal groups if they do not form units for political competition lack segmentary structure—except in genealogy—and hence do not conform to the African model. The principle of unilineal descent is the ideological base of lineage organization and defines the lineage as a corporate perpetual group with governmental functions. According to Smith,

> The lineage is an ideological conception of governmental character in some societies, just as the nation, the class, or the party is among ourselves. In lineage systems the principle of unilineal descent is redefined, reinterpreted, followed, or deviated from as the conditions of governmental organization make necessary or convenient. The lineage principle of itself does not entail organization in terms of lineage corporations, just as the democratic principle of itself does not entail democratic states, while the dictatorial principle is one thing, and dictatorship is another. The problem of lineage development, its form and formation, is therefore a problem of the governmental significance of lineage structures in any society.

Ideally, then, in a system of this kind the polities are permanent corporate groups in which the members are jurally equal, they are recruited following the principle of unilineal descent, great emphasis is placed upon descent, and there is a system of authority based upon lineage and clan seniority. Such societies have usually been described with little or no regard to the larger communities or publics of which they are a part, and thus, spuriously, they are seen to be an example of a community or public in which the political system is the same at all levels. Minimal lineages predictably oppose like units for certain purposes; these join in larger combinations, always following the same principles, for other tasks, until the level of the total community is reached, usually described as a tribe.

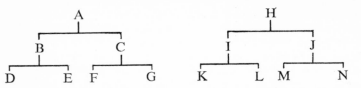

In the above diagram group D, which is a minimal lineage segment, opposes group E for certain activities, perhaps to exchange dead bodies for cannibalistic purposes. Groups D and E together, now designated as a major segment B, oppose the similarly constituted group C for some other purpose, for example to settle a dispute over a case of adultery. So all members of B, to which the wrong husband belongs, act together as one to oppose all members of C, among whom is the guilty man. Groups B and C, now designated A in turn, are a maximal lineage that opposes a similarly constituted group like H for certain purposes. In this case, perhaps, A and H are the largest units within which warfare cannot occur but between which it typically takes place. Again, all members are jurally equal, all must have the same interest, must come to the aid of one another, and are, in that sense, corporate. The various lineages—D, B, A, etc.—are groups of people related by bonds of common descent. When such societies are viewed in a larger perspective, that is, as part of a larger public, as Sahlins has done, it is seen that they can be more efficient than other forms of political organization for some purposes and may have adaptive advantages. Although segmentary lineage principles have relevance for studies of Papua New Guinea politics, their widespread application to date, particularly in the Highlands, is open to question on each of the six points listed above.

Generally speaking, the largest polities in the Highlands have been defined as tribes by Brown (1960, 1962, 1972), Langness (1964, 1971), Read (1952–3), A. Strathern (1972) and M. Strathern; as districts by Berndt (1962) and phratries by Meggitt (1962, 1965); as parishes by Reay (1959) and Glasse and Lindenbaum; and as clan parishes by Bulmer (1965), following a terminology suggested by Hogbin and Wedgwood. In coastal and other areas they have been defined in even greater variety: as villages by Kaberry (1963–6); territories by Chowning and Goodenough; neighbourhoods by Burridge; security circles (1963–6) or bush groups (1965) by Lawrence; phratries (1967) or super-clans (1969) by Wagner; clan clusters by Rappaport (1967a); and in other ways as well. The difference in terminology reflects in part real differences in social structure and political organization, but it also reflects difficulties in the conceptualization of Papua New Guinea societies by various investigators. Groups have sometimes been defined by linguistic or cultural similarities, or on a territorial basis, rather than by corporate functions. In some instances what authors have called a group or a people is what is here meant by a public or community; and, although a public can be a number of persons sharing a common language and/or culture, it does not have to be. Read (1952–3) speaks of the Gahuku-Gama in one context as a people and in another as a group, and although he specifies that tribes are the largest political units, he attributes behaviours to the population as a whole that can only have been true for specific tribes. Warfare, he says, occurred only between groups of Gahuku-Gama, his designation of a linguistically and culturally similar number of people. But this can only have been true for tribes that were situated in the centre of the language area because Gahuku-Gama on the eastern periphery are known to have fought and interacted with Bena Bena speakers. Gahuku-Gama on the western, northern and southern peripheries must also have interacted with others. Thus a specific tribe surrounded by other Gahuku-Gama speakers was part of a series sharing a common language and culture. If it was on the periphery of the language area the series would not have been linguistically or even culturally homogeneous. This situation was clearly perceived by Lawrence (1963–6) when he was working with the Garia in the Bagasin area: 'Indeed, a marked feature of the social system as a whole is that Garia living on the borders have exactly the same types of relationship with members of other linguistic groups as they have with other Garia further inland. In this way, the Garia social system can be said to be part of the wider social system of the Bagasin Area'.

Kaberry (1963–6), studying the northern Abelam, comments in similar fashion: 'This network of intervillage relations may be regarded as constituting a political system, and its extent can be defined only in relation to the village which, for purposes of this analysis, is taken as a focal point'.

Probably this situation obtained over the whole of Papua New Guinea and, prior to European control which allowed greater mobility, each autonomous group was a unit from their point of view in a finite and small public within which there was a known system of power relations but always an absence of overriding authority. Salisbury (1962) writes that 'In this situation no person can travel far, and ten miles [16 km] from one's own village is the normal limit. Few people have more than a sketchy knowledge of groups farther away. The Siane picture is of an entire world being composed of clan-villages, loosely linked into tribes, and each clan surrounded by latently hostile enemy clans'.

Although most investigators have not hesitated to define the largest political units found in the areas where they have worked, there has been much controversy over the nature of these units. In the Highlands in particular there has been a tendency to use terminology and concepts developed in Africa, so that words like 'clan', 'lineage', 'segmentary society', 'unilineal descent group', and the like regularly appear in the accounts. The difficulties in fitting Papua New Guinea societies into these patterns can be seen in their continual modification—in recent years such terms as 'loosely structured', 'structurally flexible' and 'quasi-unilineal' have been invented with increasing frequency.

Some have also found it necessary to speak of sub-clans, sub-sub-clans, sub-clan sections and men's house groups rather than of minimal, major and maximal lineages. This is the kind of thing that led Leach (1961) to speak of 'anthropological butterfly collecting' and Barnes to remark, 'it has become clear that Highland societies fit awkwardly in African moulds'. The complexities of the area as a whole were perceived earlier and led to the attempt by Hogbin and Wedgwood to construct an entirely new terminology.

The problem is, of course, not that recognizable units with political functions are lacking, but that they appear to be unlike units of social structure reported elsewhere with respect to their recruitment, internal constitution, functions, and the relations between and within them. The fact that there are some ideological similarities between these and African groups has helped to obscure the underlying differences in conduct, and the further fact that there appear to be significant variations in behaviour across the country itself makes the problem even more complex. Thus workers in Africa have reported a unilineal descent group with a known common ancestor, extensive genealogical depth and knowledge, and smaller segments with known genealogical connections between them which act and oppose each other predictably for certain purposes. But in the Papua New Guinea Highlands we find a group that, at its maximum size, may or may not have a common ancestor —who may or may not be known even if imputed—and at its maximal level may not even claim unilineal descent. But whether the largest unit does or does not claim unilineal descent, the lesser units that comprise it at some level usually do claim common descent although they cannot trace their genealogical connections except at the most minimal level and even there seldom for more than three or four generations. Recruitment to such groups should ideally be on the basis of agnatic descent; but there are frequently large numbers of non-agnates, and the position of female agnates is not clear. Individuals have a great deal of choice in group membership, and the corporate character of the groups is not yet fully understood. There is, as Barnes has stated, 'a considerable degree of optation'.

The public affair most widely used by anthropologists to define the largest polities has been warfare. No Papua New Guinea scholar has ignored this criterion, but while some have employed it alone, others have added further factors. Read (1952–3) defines the Gahuku-Gama tribe as the largest political unit because warfare did not take place within it; but Brown (1967) defines the Chimbu tribe as the largest unit in terms of territory, co-ordination of ceremonies, and warfare. Salisbury (1962) reports that although the Siane recognize the tribe as important in social structure, the largest unit within which warfare does not occur is the phratry. Newman suggests that for Gururumba the largest such unit may be a tribe, but that some phratries are not joined into tribes and thus can themselves constitute similar units in this respect. Reay (1967) says that for the Kuma the largest political unit, both on the basis of its being the largest unit within which warfare did not occur and of its having some kind of law and order, is the clan.

The criterion of warfare has also been employed by scholars working with coastal peoples. Kaberry (1963–6) reports that among the Abelam the traditional autonomous political unit is the village, which functions as a peace group and within which 'fighting should never be carried to a point where it involves loss of life'. Chowning and Goodenough report that for the Nakanai the largest political units are territories, again defined as the units between which relations were traditionally hostile. Maher reports that the Purari tribe, consisting of a number of villages, was the unit within which relations were supposed traditionally to be friendly. A similar situation seems to have obtained for the Ngarawapum in the Markham Valley, although in this instance Read (1946–7) prefers to call the allied villages districts rather than tribes.

If by politics is meant public affairs, it is obvious that defining political units simply on the basis of whether or not warfare occurs is inadequate, unless this is the only affair that is of public concern.

One of the problems in discussions of the country's political and social organization has been that the largest units that make war do not always coincide with the largest units that act for other public purposes. Furthermore, there is some doubt as to what is meant by acting as a single unit for warfare. Among Siane, according to Salisbury (1962), warfare is forbidden within the phratry, but the clans of a phratry do not combine to wage war. The only thing one clan in a phratry can be certain of is that the other clans in the same phratry will remain neutral. But Siane clans are units in a larger polity, the phratry; and phratries are units in a still larger unit, the tribe; and the tribe can be seen as a corporate and thus political unit in that it possesses a common territory. A similar situation occurs in the neighbouring Gururumba, noted by Newman, where phratries are the units within which warfare does not occur, and are also units within a tribe; but clans of the same phratries apparently join to wage war and can be assured of the neutrality of their paired phratry in the same tribe. It appears that, like the Siane, the tribe possesses a common territory. In the adjacent Gahuku-Gama the tribe is defined by Read (1952–3) as the largest unit within which warfare does not occur; the tribe is composed of two sub-tribes, which could just as easily have been termed phratries; but it does not possess a common territory. The Gahuku-Gama tribe is a corporate group, however, not only because of warfare being prohibited within it, but also because it performs as a group the *idza nama* festivals. Clearly tribes, phratries and clans are political units in all these cases in that they act as corporate groups for some public purpose; yet they cannot be so defined by the single criterion of warfare.

Although the prominence given to warfare as a criterion for defining political units has been out of proportion to its importance, limitations of space make it necessary in the remainder of this discussion to use warfare as the only example of political action.

One question of singular importance but seldom explicit in the literature is the problem of alliances and the permanence of groups making up larger units. Again using the Highlands as an example, it is clear that the unit Read (1952–3) calls a sub-tribe is similar in composition to that which Newman calls a phratry in Gururumba, Langness (1964) calls a tribe in Bena Bena, and Berndt (1962) calls a district among Kamano, Fore, Usurufa and Jate. It is equally clear that in general the groups in these four cases are for many similar purposes autonomous, their internal composition is similar, and they are functionally equivalent. The term 'tribe' is used by both Read and Newman to refer to a larger political unit that results from the permanent alliance of two such units. Both authors also distinguish such alliances from those that are temporary. Similar alliances are found in Bena Bena and Kamano, except that there they are always temporary. In terms of actual behaviour, involving in all cases pig exchanges and warfare, the largest groups formed are similar except for the expectation of permanence. Permanence is a factor of interest when analysing the political activity of these groups, but it does not establish a political unit in one case and not in another. The significant thing is not permanence but the fact that within the political system of the respective publics there is an existing known and formal machinery in all cases for establishing and breaking such alliances. The purposes for which this can readily be done are likewise known and, at the moment of action at least, the groups, however formed, act as one and constitute a single political unit in which there is a recognized if ill-defined and diffuse structure of authority. The relative permanence of groups in different publics is a factor of great importance for students of political systems, but it seems to have been neglected.

Among the Bena Bena it would be misleading to say that the largest group that went to war or performed as a single entity for a pig exchange or an initiation was the tribe or a group formed by an alliance, either temporary or permanent, of two tribes. This occasionally happened, but it was more usual for one or more sub-group of one tribe to ally itself with one or more sub-group of another tribe to wage war against, or exchange pigs with, still a third group similarly composed. The composition of the particular groups depended upon the ties of affinity and friendship between them, obligations, self-interest, and the presence of a leader or leaders who could effectively mobilize them. Here is a situation in which units in a larger polity that ought, on the surface at least, to act in concert do not always do so. The political unit the investigator sees localized on a common territory, or perceives in a genealogy, does not always constitute the unit of political action. It would be tempting to say that the sub-groups in this example are clans, but the problem of permanence and alliance is not restricted only to the larger segments of the societies, nor is it restricted to the Highlands. Impermanence of membership at almost all levels including the clan, and rapidly fluctuating alliances of both individuals and groups, appear to be among the distinguishing features of Melanesian political organization; provided, of course, the question is not begged by defining political units in terms of permanence in the first place. It is this, among other things, that has led to the modifications of terminology mentioned earlier, and especially to Lawrence's (1963–6) conception of the security circle:

> The organization through which political action is carried out is a system of interpersonal relationships, which collectively can be called the security circle. The people who belong to a man's security circle are neither a distinct social nor a distinct local group. They are merely those individuals—close kinsmen, affines, and persons tied to him in other special ways—with whom he has safe relationships and toward whom he should observe certain rules of behaviour.

The important thing here is that from the point of view of the investigator there are no permanent political groups from which to build a conception of Garia political structure and organization: the groups that form to decide public affairs depend upon who the principals are in the particular enterprise. Although the Garia may be an extreme case, the same thing appears to be true in a general way of other areas. Similarly, when discussing the formation of larger from smaller groups, the units that ultimately act as one can be different from time to time depending upon the circumstances. From the observer's point of view the people appear to form relatively permanent bodies of clan, sub-clan, phratry, tribal, village or hamlet size, but the groups that are in fact acting are of a different internal composition. Their build-up and break-down in accordance with the issues and activities is not according to segmentary lineage principles but in terms of self-interest and past obligations. Thus to suggest in the Bena Bena example above that clans behave as corporate groups is as misleading as to say that tribes do. Individuals and even lineages within clans may not act in concert with the others and may refrain from participating at all. The problem is one of defining corporate groups.

It has been common policy on the part of field workers to accept the notion, carried over from the classical African literature on descent systems, that when individuals act they do so as representatives of their clan or sub-clan conceived of as a corporate entity— the African notion of jural equality. But there is good reason to believe that in Papua New Guinea, in spite of an individual's being always identified as a member of a certain group, his actions do not necessarily represent the corporate interest of that group. The impermanence of groups is the result, in part at least, of the haphazard collections of people which the investigator actually observes on the ground or isolates in his genealogies. As Barnes and others have argued, in many of the societies there is a remarkable openness that permits recruitment, individual choice as to membership, mobility, shifting loyalties and a turnover of personnel. In many groups, in spite of the ideology of agnatic descent, large numbers of non-agnates are found. They may be there by virtue of matrilineal ties or bonds of affinity, or they may be refugees from defeated groups. In any case they often retain links with their original group —which may or may not be widely scattered—with other groups of past allies, and with trade partners. Such bonds can conflict with the interest of their host group, and thus individuals and lineages are sometimes permitted to remain neutral or to opt out of various enterprises should they so choose. The individuals who make up the host group itself may have multiple ties of kinship, affinity, friendship and trade elsewhere, and are likewise permitted individual choice as to whether they engage in warfare and other undertakings. The effect is flexibility and emphasis on individualism. This is so characteristic of some Highland groups that one investigator has recently suggested we think of such societies in terms of 'organized flow' (Watson 1970) rather than the more static terms previously employed. Although such a situation extends the network of interpersonal relationships in an infinitely expanding circle, it inhibits the formation of durable political units and authority— especially centralized authority—and promotes instead the principles of self-help, self-interest and self-regulation.

Exaggerated statements have been made with respect to leadership in earlier times. According to Brown (1963) and Salisbury (1964) either anarchy or despotism prevailed. But, along with the impermanence of viable political units, a relative lack of authority and a virtually universal lack of centralized authority were characteristic. Such authority as does exist is most often based on personal ability, not on inheritance, descent or supernatural sanction. Leadership is usually achieved, almost never ascribed (but see Hogbin 1969–70; Mead; Rappaport 1967a; Uberoi; Wedgwood; and Williams 1941, for apparent or real exceptions), but being the son of a big-man, the eldest of a number of brothers or some other such thing can confer advantages (Harding; Read 1959). Leadership is achieved through personal charisma, by accumulating wealth in the form of pigs and other material goods that can be used to aid others thus placing them under an obligation, sometimes by the possession of specialized knowledge, or through sheer physical power and the ability to direct warfare. And although Read (1959) has shown that leaders who attain prominence through physical strength and coercion are not generally as successful as more temperate men with the ability to manipulate wealth and people, it remains true that many societies allocate authority on the basis of raw physical power. Physical power, both in individuals and groups, is respected, valued and admired (Langness 1972; Watson 1971). There is no notion of an underdog and no concept of fair play. If a group is strong it is also good. People respect it and are eager to join and be identified with it. Conversely, if a group—or a person—is weak it is not good. The expectation is to be dominated, if not destroyed, by the strong.

A leader remains a leader only for so long as he can successfully dominate others, either through his ability to help them or to maintain their respect. If he fails in an undertaking his followers are quick to shift their loyalties to others. There are always competitors for power and influence. In so far as leaders do not control land, water supplies or other natural resources; cannot call on supernatural sanctions to back up their authority; do not regulate subsistence; and have little in the way of special skills or knowledge, their followers are never very numerous. There is a limit to how many people, over time and in space, can be recruited and satisfied simply through personal strength, charisma and limited material donations. The pattern of leadership and authority is related to the small size of the political groups that act and to the impermanence of membership. The respect for successful men jumps clan, subclan, and at times even tribal boundaries; and individuals change their membership for this reason. The limits imposed by personal life-span and ability, and the constant competition between men for followers, also prevents the growth of centralized authority and administration. Activities take place either because they are a natural part of the round of life or because a particular leader has the prestige to bring them about. But he must be careful not to command too much, or at the wrong time, and not to make mistakes, for his followers can desert him. This pattern of authority—that of the big-man or 'man with a name'—is widespread in Melanesia.

There is authority apart from that of the big-men in that it is also allocated on the basis of age. Generally speaking, in lineage, clan, village and age-grade affairs the eldest male acts as spokesman. But even this is tempered by strength, personal ability and actions. For a man to be accepted as spokesman he must be not only of a certain age but also still fit and active. Truly old men—men who can no longer work or move around—may be consulted on certain matters but are seldom of great importance. Likewise a man is not automatically the spokesman for his clan or sub-clan or lineage just because of his seniority: a younger brother who is more highly regarded may usurp the authority. The principle of age is a general one. Older people, provided they are active, have authority over younger ones. This extends from the most senior to the most junior. Infants and children have no authority at all, and females of any age typically very little. But matters of public interest, whether they concern permanent or impermanent groups, are decided by discussion and consensus and not by the authority of either elders or leaders. Lawrence (1963–6) has described the situation as follows:

> Yet the authority of these 'big men' is limited. In the first place, it is restricted almost entirely to setting in motion the . . . routine activities. The leaders direct the stages by which gardens are made. They impose food and sex taboos on novices during initiation. They supervise young men in sorcery training. But they are not hereditary or titular office bearers and they are unable to adjudicate or coerce. Although they use their influence in disputes as far as they dare, they cannot give binding decisions or judgments, and their only guarantee of obedience from their followers is the willingness of the latter to cooperate. They cannot inflict real and formal punishments on the insubordinate.

Given the flexibility of Papua New Guinea societies, the diffuse allocation of authority, the emphasis on individualism, and the ever-expanding networks of social ties and obligations, it perhaps makes sense to revise our thinking on the units variously described as clans, phratries, tribes, villages, and so on. Rather than truly corporate units with common, permanent, recurrent concerns, they are parameters within which activities are instigated and points of reference fixed to identify individuals and sub-groups within publics. Likewise it is more reasonable to think of leaders as those who instigate activities rather than those who command and administer. The distinction between power and authority so prominent in recent political anthropology, particularly as expressed in Smith's definitions of politics and administration, is difficult to perceive in Papua New Guinea and has been rejected by at least one worker in the area (Reay 1967).

This, paradoxically, is not to say that the units of social structure most usually mentioned—tribes, sub-tribes, clans, sub-clans, lineages etc.—are without any corporate functions and never act as corporate groups, or that they have few if any public affairs to manage. It is to insist, rather, that as groups they do not manage all public affairs. A complete analysis of the country's political behaviour cannot be made by concentrating exclusively on such bodies of people. There are times, to be sure, when the component localized clans of a particular phratry or tribe do have a common interest in defence or attack, or in an exchange with another group. But at other times these and other activities do not concern these particular units and instead are handled by units that come into existence for the occasion. Political organization is neither exclusively linked to permanent units of social structure, nor does it operate solely according to the principles of lineage segmentation and opposition. It is a flexible organization with, as Lawrence (1963–6) has pointed out, the frequent interplay of security circles, a great amount of individual freedom, and the operation of lineage and clan principles. In the classic segmentary systems all public affairs are managed by permanent units of social structure based on the lineage; indeed, as Smith has shown, these are the distinguishing features of such systems. The members of such groups are always conceived of as jurally equal and the segments that form and oppose are predictable. In Papua New Guinea only some public affairs are managed in this way. The emphasis on individualism is in fact incompatible with the concept of jural equality and, to a lesser extent perhaps, with the corporate nature of groups, although this seems never to have been made clear.

The best example is in the general area of law and order, including feud; although often feuding is difficult to distinguish from warfare. When a man is wronged by another it is up to him, along with those he can enlist to help him, to settle his grievance. This is clearly a public affair in that if the matter is not settled the lives of many more people than just the principals will be disrupted; but there is no automatic alignment of clan, sub-clan or even lineage behind him. In such situations the security circles comes into operation, and membership overrides clan and lineage affiliations. In many areas it is a man's age-mates who come to his aid rather than his true brothers. Usually affines also help, and sometimes friends and trade partners. Action groups that are specific to the situation are formed, and a public affair is settled. There is no interplay of lineages or clans as such, and still less is the individual looked upon as the jural representative of his lineage or clan.

Similarly, although transactions are sometimes phrased as occurring between groups, basically they are between individuals. Bena Bena marriages, for example, are said to be relations between clans, and most of the clansmen of the bride and groom do attend the ceremony. But the majority are spectators. The principals are actually a small number of persons on both sides who have agreed to exchange pork, live pigs, shells and other goods. They do not necessarily constitute a lineage or sub-clan. And although it could be said that a tie is formed between two clans, it would be wrong to assume that the bond is equally binding on all the clansmen. A man would not take refuge in any clan from which his own clan had received a bride. He would expect such aid only from those clans with which he had established an active relationship by being personally concerned in the exchange (Langness 1971). According to Salisbury (1958) the same thing appears to be true of the Siane:

> The tribe never acts as a single unit in economic activities, although when individual members of different tribes interact the relationship is phrased as one between whole corporate groups. This is true of all relationships involving members of different tribes, and, for example, a marriage involving members of two tribes is spoken of as taking place between one tribe and a sister of the other tribe.

Aid in warfare also is given on an individual rather than a corporate basis.

Individual transactions and flexibility of this kind, even though they may be phrased as occurring between groups, cast considerable doubt on the utility of speaking in the traditional sense of corporate groups.

The extent to which segmentary principles come into play appears to vary. Probably they are more characteristic of the Western Highlands than elsewhere (Meggitt; Langness 1964). Meggitt details the most important functions of lineage and clan for the Mae Enga and suggests several fruitful hypotheses which have yet to be tested in other areas. Sahlins, as was mentioned, argues in a different context that segmentary lineage systems may be more efficient for certain purposes than other forms of social organization. The work of both of these writers has relevance for further studies. It is obvious that most activities, although similar in outward appearance, are conducted on a much larger scale in the Western Highlands. Exchanges of pig and shell demand months of planning, a staggering amount of concerted action on the part of hundreds if not thousands of people, the raising and killing of extensive herds of pigs, the production of tons of surplus vegetable food, and the construction of enormous guest houses for use during the ceremonies. Certainly such activities take place in the Eastern Highlands, but on a smaller scale. Even so, there is little in the literature to suggest that patterns of leadership and authority are significantly different in the two areas, nor has it been widely argued that there may be variations in political organization associated with differing patterns of exchange. Variations that might exist can be seen more clearly, of course, by considering the exchange systems of non-

Highland peoples as well as those of the Highlanders. The political aspects of exchange systems have been recognized for some time (Bulmer 1960–1; Read 1954; Uberoi), but recent work on the subject will make for much greater understanding (Harding; Hogbin 1969–70; Rappaport 1967a; A. Strathern 1971; M. Strathern; Young).

The lack of any major differences in leadership related to exchange systems, if indeed there should prove to be one, would pose some interesting questions for students of politics. It is clear that much more careful consideration needs to be given to comparative studies of the various regions. It may be that entrepreneurship is more significant in one area, and physical power and success in war in another. It may be that emphasis on lineage and clan is more closely related to power and authority in one place than in another. Likewise the inheritance of magic or other knowledge may or may not be of importance in determining leadership.

Although Barnes and others have commented on the emphasis on violence, and although warfare is said to have been endemic in most parts, few details are known about Papua New Guinea warfare and not many attempts have been made to link it to aspects of social structure. Langness (1964) has argued that it may be warfare that brings about the flexibility of some of the societies and gives them their distinctive non-lineage character; but the literature has generally assumed that warfare, in the Highlands at least, was essentially similar and of a distinctive kind. It has been characterized as an 'athletic match' by Vicedom and Tischner, and 'antagonistic game' by Berndt (1962), and 'expected, recurrent, and coordinated activity between opposing groups' by Read (1954) and Berndt (1962). Brown and Brookfield, Ryan (1961) and Elkin see it as similar to economic exchanges, and Read (1952–3) as a kind of balanced opposition between equivalent groups. Other such phrases imply the maintenance of equilibrium. In some cases such characterization seems to represent a sociological bias stemming from British social anthropology—especially Gluckman (1956)—rather than a careful consideration of the facts. This is unfortunate because much insight into Papua New Guinea politics, including the questions of flexibility, alliance and impermanence, could be gained from a more careful analysis of warfare. Ryan (1958–9) has written:

> Until the establishment of control by the Australian Government in 1950, inter-clan fighting would seem to have been almost chronic; and clans that were not actually engaged in fights of their own helped other clans in theirs. Apart from formal open battles,

which were probably not very frequent, there was a constant series of sporadic guerrilla raids. The result of all this activity was that many clans were almost exterminated and the survivors driven off their land. It was the habit of the victors to lay waste the territory of the defeated, uprooting gardens, burning houses, felling trees, so that even had the survivors been able to remain, their devastated land would no longer have supported them. It is apparent, then, that the maintenance of places of potential refuge was a matter of vital importance, for even the strongest and most secure clan could be defeated by a sudden rearrangement of alliances against it. It is perhaps too much to say that the flexibility of residence-patterns was a direct consequence of Mendi's style of warfare; but certainly, it did offer a solution to problems of refuge raised by warfare. It was warfare that made it necessary; and it was warfare, too, that, as a major factor in limiting the population, made such flexibility possible.

Similarly Glasse writes:

My central thesis is a simple one. It is that in order to exact vengeance the small local groups of the Huli form temporary alliances; but these alliances are unstable because once the act of vengeance is completed, hostility develops between the allied groups due to the working of the system of redress. Revenge defines enemies and allies, but when the fight is over, the principles of redress divide the allies who fought as one. The result is that powerful factions are never able to fully develop. Revenge and redress ally and oppose different combinations of groups over a period of time and thereby promote an uneasy integration and a kind of balance within the wider social order.

Young, reporting on the Goodenough Islanders, says:

Certainly, raids rather than prearranged battles, ambushes rather than open attacks, were the norm. Even so, there can be no doubt that safety lay in numbers and that a large community was better equipped for survival than a small one.

But contrast this with Kaberry's account of the Northern Abelam (1963-7):

Sometimes a village would send a message, through a neutral village, challenging its *mama* (enemies) to battle in an area midway between its own settlement and that of the *mama*. The big men, elders and warriors of reputation consulted and, if they accepted the challenge, sent a shell ring with a leaf twisted through it to their own ally with a request for assistance. The challengers then cleared half the proposed battle arena, and on a different day when the place was deserted the recipients of the challenge cleared the rest of the arena. On an appointed day . . . all the able-bodied males . . . met for combat. Deaths might amount to no more half a dozen . . . If both sides were evenly matched, a strategic withdrawal was made at the end of the day; but, if the men of one side were stronger, they chased their opponents from the arena, pursued them back to the nearest hamlets, and destroyed gardens and houses.

But the relation between warfare and politics has been clouded by the tendency to insist, by definition, that the units of social structure identified on the ground or in genealogies are the warring units, that they are permanent, and that their operations follow segmentary lineage principles. Berndt (1964) defines warfare as action occurring between named units of social structure: 'For the present purpose, warfare is defined as planned violence carried out by members of a political unit, in the name of that unit, against another'. He suggests that because of this, polities are thrown into sharper relief than in many other non-literate societies, mainly because of the prevalent warfare. But he concludes:

there was a conflict of loyalties, but not of an equally balanced kind: one centered on the group, the other on the person. Individual consideration of kin and trading partners, if these were distinguished, meant that in almost all fighting between two groups . . . there were some persons who would hold their hand in regard to some other persons. This in itself had a moderating effect on warfare. Warfare was never 'total'. Even apart from the issue of neutrality, participation of adult males was rarely complete. Non-participation was in some cases a conventional matter, as among Mbowamb. . . . In others . . . in any given encounter it was left very largely to individual choice. The apparent disregard for human rights in warfare outside a certain social range was, in fact, combined with a certain respect for such rights, and that respect was manifested in the provision for personal relationships even in the heat and excitement of actual combat. Flexibility, allowance for personal initiative within loosely defined limits, was apparent in this sphere of Highlands living no less than in others.

Now clearly, in a situation where individuals are allowed to act or not act independently of their group membership, where non-participation is a conventional matter, where there is a choice of loyalties, and where there are infinite numbers of temporary alliances possible, it is misleading to describe warfare as an affair between permanent corporate units of social structure in which members are jurally equal and the group or groups act with a common interest and a common purpose. Although this individual emphasis and flexibility has been repeatedly described in Papua New Guinea societies, those investigators who recognize it still ignore it when describing the social and political organization; they insist that the societies are just like units of social structure elsewhere. Reay (1967) writes that the Kuma

> have a segmentary lineage system of classical type, although to call their groups 'lineages' would give a misleading impression of their interest in genealogical reckoning, which they play down for reasons of expediency while emphasizing unequivocally the principles of unilineal descent.

Again, according to Salisbury (1956):

> To cite all the ways in which these descent groups conform with the characteristics of unilineal descent groups, as outlined by Fortes, would be a mere repetition of points brought out in the classic African studies. Suffice it to say that they are groups in which membership is by virtue of descent, and all members stand in real or fictitious kin relationships with all other members. They are corporate groups, as has been shown already in their corporate obligations in the blood feud. They are groups which, as far as an outsider is concerned, are internally undifferentiated.

This unilineal bias, as Leach (1961) calls it, has prevented workers in Papua New Guinea from coming to grips with the distinctive features of social and political organization, and makes the comparative study of politics in the area a difficult task.

If any understanding of Papua New Guinea political organization is to be achieved, particularly as it relates to warfare, it is crucial to cease considering warfare as a unitary phenomenon; and if this is true for the Highlands it is also true for the coastal regions. Even a cursory glance at the literature will show that in the Highlands there are at least two types of warfare. Both are mentioned by Ryan (1958–9): 'Apart from formal open battles, which were probably not very frequent, there was a constant series of sporadic guerila raids'. The differences between these two forms have been constantly ignored or treated as unimportant, and the emphasis has always been placed on the former. The best example can be seen in the following extract from Salisbury (1958):

Pitched battles consist of opposing clans lining the opposite ends of prepared battle grounds, firing occasional arrows, and shouting defiance, while champions joust with ten-foot spears of palm wood. Days may pass with no fatalities, and with hostilities ceasing at nightfall or in rain and beginning again around 9 a.m. the next day. In many ways such fighting seems to be regarded almost as a 'sporting event'. The fighting involving deaths and individual bravery occurs in ambushes or small raids. The height of bravado is to approach an enemy men's house at night, and to kill by firing arrows through the tiny doorway.

No further mention is made by this author of 'the fighting involving deaths and individual bravery', and he goes on to suggest that 'Football is a substitution of one sport for another'. Probably the best description of the formal warfare is found in Matthiessen's semi-popular account of the Baliem Valley peoples and in Gardner and Heider's *Gardens of War*.

But if it is clear that there were two types of warfare in the Highlands, we have no information on their distribution and importance. Although formal warfare could be contrasted with informal, a better choice of terms is probably 'restricted' and 'unrestricted'. By restricted warfare is meant that which (1) occurs only for a specific reason; (2) occurs only at certain seasons or times such as the headhunting period, initiation period, etc.; (3) is restricted in the sense of having defined goals such as one life for one life, to gain reputation, to obtain wives, etc.; or (4) a combination of these. Restricted warfare, as is implied here, takes place within a public in which there are known rules accepted by all participants. It is this type of warfare that is most usually described in terms of some sociological-equilibrium model. Unrestricted warfare occurs for a great variety of reasons, is not limited to any special season or motive, and does not take place within a system of rules. If the notion of totally unrestricted warfare is difficult to grasp for the European observer familiar with the rules of the Geneva Convention, the following quotations from Read (1954–5), Landtmann and Langness (1964) respectively, illustrate the situation with no exaggeration:

In warfare the aim is the complete destruction of an enemy and his means of livelihood, and each single tribe is opposed to other tribes which are regarded as traditional enemies and, consequently, as being permanently 'at war' with one another.

The purpose of the real wars, on the other hand, is to kill as many of the enemy as possible, destroy their property, and capture the heads of the slain.

In Bena Bena the stated aims of warfare were the complete and total destruction of the enemy, if possible. This included every man, woman, and child, whether old, infirm, or pregnant. Although it is true that most raids resulted in only one, or few deaths, cases are known in which entire groups were destroyed.

Ryan (1958–9) points out that although both types occur among the Mendi, unrestricted warfare seems to be the more important. It may be that restricted warfare is more typical of the Western than the Eastern Highlands, a fact that might in turn account for the different emphasis placed upon lineage and clan principles in the two areas, as noted by Langness (1964). Even if the two types occur in both areas the predominance of one would have the same effect.

The difference between the two types of warfare, and the necessity for examining the motives for war, are more apparent when the people of the lowlands are considered. Probably the best example of restricted warfare is that of the Arapesh and their neighbours, described by Fortune (1939):

[In] Arapesh warfare . . . the men of different localities were frequently on an explicit offensive and defensive in regard to their exclusive rights in women. . . . Land was little disputed, but, instead, more readily transferable goods. This broad characteristic of Arapesh warfare is not uncommon in the area. Neighbouring tribes of headhunters do not directly dispute the exclusive exploitation rights to land which they maintain. Their offensive takes heads, which are also more readily transferable than land. They remain content with their accessions of enemy heads, and, for lack of an expansionist land policy, even become disgruntled if neighbouring areas become depopulated of heads. . . . Without hypothesis, it is clear that Arapesh culture did not promote warfare to any vicious extreme. Warfare was made dependent upon women's sexual consent in extramarital liaisons outside locality borders, and it was regarded with considerable distaste. The chances for domestic peace, and for consequent peace abroad, were very high, and compare more than favourably with the chances for peace in other societies.

A similar kind of restricted warfare is reported by van der Kroef for the Marind Anim of the south-east of Irian Jaya (West Irian), but the information is not as complete:

The basic cause of head-hunting is the need for names [reputation] in a community, something that holds true uniformly for many of the New Guinea tribes that engage in it. . . . The dry monsoon is generally regarded as the most suitable time, but the hunt must not take place before the gardens have been properly cared for. . . . Traditionally the hunt culminates in an elaborate feast, celebrating the capture of the heads, which among the majority of the head-hunting communities of Southern New Guinea is also a focal point of religious observance and mythological commemoration. It is during this feast that rituals and traditions acquire meaning, and the social motives underlying the head-hunt are fitted into an overall pattern of approved behaviour. Preparations for the feast are elaborate, and may sometimes take as much as a year.

Although it is often difficult to judge accurately from the literature, the Kwoma (Whiting), Abelam (Kaberry 1940–1, 1941–2), perhaps the Kutubu (Williams 1940–1), the Kapauku (Pospisil), Sibil Valley people (Brongersma and Venema), Baliem Valley people (Matthiessen; Gardner and Heider) and Kuman (Nilles) are examples of societies with restricted warfare. The Kiwai (Landtmann), Gahuku-Gama (Read 1952–3), Bena Bena (Langness 1964), Huli (Glasse), Kamano (Berndt 1954–5, 1962), Mendi (Ryan 1958–9), Orokaiva (Williams 1930), Massim (Young) and the Mafulu (Williamson), all appear to be examples of societies in which unrestricted warfare was practised.

A thorough analysis of warfare and politics in any of these areas would have to take into account the nature of the publics, the motives for war, the prevailing or preponderant type of warfare, the specific rules or lack of rules, the limits of individual choice, as well as the nature of the polities. The public of which the Arapesh are a part (Fortune 1939) is clearly dissimilar to that in which the Gahuku-Gama (Read 1952–3) participate. One of the primary motives for war in the Western Highlands and Chimbu was the necessity or desire for land, a motive foreign to the Eastern Highlands and the Arapesh, where the reasons were more typically retaliation for sorcery, adultery or theft. The prevailing type of warfare for the Arapesh is restricted, whereas Bena Bena warfare is unrestricted. This implies for the Arapesh a set of rules about warfare. The limits of individual choice in the Highlands would seem to be far greater than for the Arapesh. This must, in turn, have profound implications for the nature of the respective polities.

The picture of warfare also highlights the importance of examining the relation of political action to non-political institutions such as economics. Warfare in the Western Highlands and Chimbu, in effect a struggle for land (Meggitt 1965; Brookfield and Brown), is clearly motivated by economic considerations. But few, if any, economic motives have been suggested for warfare in the Eastern

Highlands. Indeed, the image most often portrayed of Eastern Highlands peoples is that of people fighting and killing just for excitement. According to Berndt (1962) 'Fighting was, and remains, the "breath of life" to these people, one of their main preoccupations.' And 'fighting, revenge and counter-revenge are so commonplace that people become accustomed to this state of affairs and are often careless about their own safety.' This picture, consistent with the sociological game approach to warfare, ignores the possibility of economic motivation.

Consider, for example, this comment by Salisbury (1958):

> Only if one can give away 'valuables' can one gain prestige, and even then only if there is an 'audience' prepared to grant the recognition which is the counterpart of prestige. Thus for a clan to be 'one up' presupposes that the clan be surrounded by other clans on a quasi-equal footing to which 'valuables' can be given, and from which can come recognition; the only way to satisfy a desire to be 'top of one's league' is to keep the league in existence and composed of groups of about the same strength.

Such a statement overlooks an obvious alternative—that it is possible to obtain valuables by taking them away from a defeated group. Considering that the Highlanders valued shells, pigs and bird-of-paradise plumes, among other things, and that these were in short supply, it would not seem far-fetched to suppose that the people acquired them through warfare and that such acquisition was one of the motives for warring. Such a conclusion does not fit well with the equilibrium model. But considering that villages were burned and people killed or routed, it is legitimate to wonder what happened to their possessions. Indeed, among the Massim (Young) it appears that cannibalism was, at least at times, an economic factor of some significance. In any case, the failure to consider adequately the economics of warfare has influenced and perhaps prevented proper understanding of political organization.

A similar problem arises with regard to the relation between marriage, affinity, warfare and politics. Several writers have commented on this relationship. Elkin remarked that 'A sign that two groups intermarry is that they fight.' Salisbury (1962) said of the Siane 'They are our affinal relatives; with them we fight.' In this latter case it appears that clan groups can marry with all other clans except those of their own phratry; but the bonds of affinity so established do not prevent them from later fighting. At any point in time a clan is allied with a number of others for the purpose of exchanging women, but the alliances formed for this purpose are temporary and rapidly shifting. Thus a Siane clan not only potentially marries with all others but also fights with all others. This situation is similar in the Bena Bena, as noted by Langness (1964), except that there is no exogamous unit such as the phratry above the level of clans, and any clan may marry into any other provided a blood tie cannot be established between the two principals. The Bena Bena do not report any connection between those they marry and those they fight, and say that they fought everyone except the clans of their own tribe.

This does not appear to be true in all areas of the Highlands or in all other areas of Melanesia. In Mount Hagen, clans tend to avoid marrying traditional enemies to prevent their women from bearing them children. But according to A. and M. Strathern small clans deliberately marry out to keep up extra-tribal alliances. Likewise, among the northern Abelam where villages are the major political units, village solidarity is supported by a preference for marrying in, although some wives are taken from other villages. Such women usually come from places with which there are permanent alliances, even though the Abelam do not recognize the political motive for such marriages (Kaberry 1963–6). Among the Garia, also, relations with affines seem to be more important than among some Highlanders. Marriage contributes members to the security circle and establishes obligations that ensure collective action by one security circle against another, according to Lawrence (1963–6). That this was not always so in the Highlands can be seen in the following quotation from Fortune (1947):

> A man was certainly expected to serve his village in action against his sister's husband or against his wife's brother. I observed one case of a newly wed lad of our acquaintance taking the field against his bride's folk a few days after his wedding. I also overheard two or three instances of men shouting that they had just made their sisters war-widows, or their wives brotherless.

> Marriage among the Daribi, however, functions to bind two clans together into what Wagner (1969) calls a super-clan and is an important facet of political organization subject to conscious manipulation.

In the case of the Siane and Bena Bena it would seem that marriage has little in the way of political functions, at least long term ones. Marriage was no bar to fighting between clans, and each clan fought every other clan regardless of marital ties. Marriage can be seen as having political functions in that it is part of the machinery for establishing temporary alliances between groups. But even granted such a function, it is doubtful if the motive for marriage is to establish such alliances. Clearly no permanent alliance is established, and it is more likely that marriages took place as a result of alliances rather than the reverse.

In the case of the northern Abelam a situation obtains in which the function of marriage appears to be associated with permanent ties between groups, although Kaberry (1963–6) explicitly denies that the Abelam perceive this as the motive. But among the Daribi political functions are served by marriage, and the motive for marriage would seem to be the conscious intent to establish political relations between groups.

But here again the African model and the sociological tradition have brought about difficulties. Even Barnes, who has done most to call attention to the confusion resulting from the application of the model to Papua New Guinea, not only attributes political functions to all marriages but, by implication, assumes that the motive for marriage is to bring about political alliances (Langness 1964). A thorough analysis would have to examine both motive and function. We would then have a greater insight into the nature of Melanesian political systems as well as the institution of marriage.

Although our knowledge of the political systems is inadequate, partly for lack of intensive and systematic research and partly for the reasons mentioned above, certain features seem to be generally characteristic. Prior to European contact, the societies were, from the point of view of any one of them, units in an exceedingly small public with little knowledge of the world beyond a radius of a few kilometres. The units comprising the publics, both total communities and their component smaller polities, were relatively small, with probably two or three thousand individuals at most. The management of public affairs was carried out in some cases by what can be conceived of as relatively enduring corporate units, whether they be described as clans, villages or otherwise. But, as a result of the emphasis placed on individualism, choice, and the ethic of self-help, it appears that some public affairs were managed through a flexible system of security circles and temporary alliances, bringing together short-lived action groups. The corporateness of such groups is open to question. Although there was a formal machinery for settling disputes and for establishing and breaking alliances, this did not always result in joining corporate groups as such; it allowed the formation of groups specific to purpose. Leadership in matters of public concern was relatively informal and leaders emerged according to the circumstances, though qualities such as prowess in warfare could be generalized to other activities. Leaders, as big-men, almost always achieved their positions, but lesser authority was allocated on the basis of seniority. Leaders had no power of command, except by force of personality or by physical coercion, and they had no power to make binding decisions. Decisions were reached by consensus, with leaders and elders exerting more influence than others. Power and authority were diffuse and non-centralized, allocated on the basis of raw physical power as well as seniority, at least in some areas. They were not elaborated into political offices or other specifically governmental institutions.

These societies cannot be analysed in terms of existing theories of political organization. Such theories do not allow for a degree of flexibility unprecedented in the ethnographic literature. But it is true that some lend themselves to existing theories more readily than do others.

Bibliography

Balandier, G. 1970. *Political Anthropology*. New York.

Barnes, J. A. 1962. 'African models in the New Guinea Highlands', *Man*, vol. 62. Reprinted in H. I. Hogbin and L. R. Hiatt (eds), *Readings in Australian and Pacific Anthropology*, Melbourne, 1966.

Berndt, R. M. 1954-5. 'Kamano, Jate, Usurufa and Fore kinship of the Eastern Highlands of New Guinea', *Oceania*, vol. 25.

―――― 1962. *Excess and Restraint*. Chicago.

―――― 1964. 'Warfare in the New Guinea Highlands', *American Anthropologist*, vol. 66, special publication.

Berndt, R. M. and Lawrence, P. (eds) 1971. *Politics in New Guinea*. Perth.

Brongersma, L. D. and Venema, G. F. 1963. *To the Mountains of the Stars*. New York.

Brookfield, H. C. and Brown, P. 1963. *Struggle for Land*. Melbourne.

Brown, P. 1960. 'Chimbu tribes', *Southwestern Journal of Anthropology*, vol. 16.

―――― 1962. 'Non-agnates among the patrilineal Chimbu', *Journal of the Polynesian Society*, vol. 71.

―――― 1963. 'From anarchy to satrapy', *American Anthropologist*, vol. 65.

―――― 1967. 'The Chimbu political system', *Anthropological Forum*, vol. 2.

———— 1972. *The Chimbu: a study of change in the New Guinea Highlands*. Cambridge, Mass.

Brown, P. and Brookfield, H. C. 1959-60. 'Chimbu land and society', *Oceania*, vol. 30.

Bulmer, R. N. H. 1960-1. 'Political aspects of the moka ceremonial exchange system among the Kyaka people of the Western Highlands of New Guinea', *Oceania*, vol. 31.

———— 1965. 'The Kyaka of the Western Highlands', in P. Lawrence and M. J. Meggitt (eds), *Gods, Ghosts and Men in Melanesia*, Melbourne.

Burridge, K. O. L. 1963-6. 'Tangu political relations', *Anthropological Forum*, vol. 1.

Chowning, A. and Goodenough, W. H. 1963-6. 'Lakalai political organization', *Anthropological Forum*, vol. 1. Reprinted in Berndt and Lawrence (eds), *Politics in New Guinea*.

Cohen, R. 1970. 'The political system', in R. Naroll and R. Cohen (eds), *A Handbook of Method in Cultural Anthropology*, New York.

Easton, D. 1965. *A Framework for Political Analysis*. Englewood Cliffs.

Elkin, A. P. 1952-3. 'Delayed exchange in Wabag Sub-district, Central Highlands of New Guinea', *Oceania*, vol. 23.

Fortes, M. 1953. 'The structure of unilineal descent groups', *American Anthropologist*, vol. 55.

Fortes, M. and Evans-Pritchard, E. E. (eds) 1940. *African Political Systems*. London.

Fortune, R. F. 1939. 'Arapesh warfare', *American Anthropologist*, vol. 41.

———— 1947. 'The rules of relationship behaviour in one variety of primitive warfare', *Man*, vol. 47.

Gardner, R. and Heider, K. 1968. *Gardens of War*. New York.

Glasse, R. M. 1954-62. 'Revenge and redress among the Huli', *Mankind*, vol. 5.

Glasse, R. M. and Lindenbaum, S. 1971. 'South Fore politics', in Berndt and Lawrence (eds), *Politics in New Guinea*.

Gluckman, M. 1956. *Custom and Conflict in Africa*. Oxford.

———— 1965. *Politics, Law and Ritual in Tribal Society*. Oxford.

Harding, T. G. 1967. *Voyagers of the Vitiaz Strait*. Seattle.

Hau'ofa, E. 1971. 'Mekeo chieftainship', *Journal of the Polynesian Society*, vol. 80.

Hogbin, H. I. 1938. 'Social reaction to crime', *Journal of the Royal Anthropological Institute*, vol. 68.

———— 1951. *Transformation Scene*. London.

——— 1969-70. 'Food festivals and politics in Wogeo', *Oceania*, vol. 40.

Hogbin, H. I. and Wedgwood, C. 1952-4. 'Local grouping in Melanesia', *Oceania*, vols 23-4.

Kaberry, P. M. 1940-1. 'The Abelam tribe, Sepik District, New Guinea', *Oceania*, vol. 11.

——— 1941-2. 'Law and political organization in the Abelam tribe, New Guinea', *Oceania*, vol. 12.

——— 1963-6. 'Political organization among the northern Abelam', *Anthropological Forum*, vol. 1. Reprinted in Berndt and Lawrence (eds), *Politics in New Guinea*.

Landtmann, G. 1927. *The Kiwai Papuans of British New Guinea*. London.

Langness, L. L. 1964. 'Some problems in the conceptualization of Highlands social structures', *American Anthropologist*, vol. 66, special publication. Reprinted in H. I. Hogbin and L. R. Hiatt (eds), *Readings in Australian and Pacific Anthropology*, Melbourne, 1966.

——— 1969. 'Courtship, marriage and divorce: Bena Bena', in R. M. Glasse and M. J. Meggitt (eds), *Pigs, Pearlshells, and Women: marriage in the New Guinea Highlands*, Englewood Cliffs.

——— 1971. 'Bena Bena political organization', in Berndt and Lawrence (eds), *Politics in New Guinea*.

——— 1972. 'Violence in the New Guinea Highlands', in J. F. Short jr. and M. E. Wolfgang (eds), *Collective Violence*, New York.

Lawrence, P. 1965. 'The Ngaing of the Rai coast', in P. Lawrence and M. J. Meggitt (eds), *Gods, Ghosts and Men in Melanesia*, Melbourne.

——— 1963-6. 'The Garia of the Madang District', *Anthropological Forum*, vol. 1.

Leach, E. R. 1954. *Political Systems of Highland Burma*. London.

——— 1961. *Rethinking Anthropology*. London.

Lowman-Vayda, .C. 1967-70. 'Maring big men', *Anthropological Forum*, vol 2. Reprinted in Berndt and Lawrence (eds), *Politics in New Guinea*.

McArthur, M. 1966-7. 'Analysis of the genealogy of a Mae-Enga clan', *Oceania*, vol. 37.

Macridis, R. C. 1955. *The Study of Comparative Government*. New York.

Maher, R. F. 1961. *New Men of Papua*. Madison.

Maine, H. S. 1861. *Ancient Law*. London.

Mair, L. 1962. *Primitive Government*. Harmondsworth.

Matthiessen, P. 1962. *Under the Mountain Wall*. New York.

Mead, M. 1947. *The Mountain Arapesh III: socio-economic life*. Anthropological Papers of the American Museum of Natural History, vol. 40.

Meggitt, M. J. 1962. 'Growth and decline of agnatic descent groups among the Mae-Enga of the New Guinea Highlands', *Ethnology*, vol. 1.

—— 1965. *The Lineage System of the Mae-Enga of New Guinea*. Edinburgh.

Middleton, J. and Tait, D. (eds) 1958. *Tribes Without Rulers*. London.

Morgan, L. H. 1877. *Ancient Society*. New York.

Newman, P. L. 1965. *Knowing the Gururumba*. New York.

Nilles, J. 1943-4. 'Natives of the Bismarck Mountains New Guinea', *Oceania*, vol. 14.

—— 1950-1. 'The Kuman of the Chimbu region, Central Highlands, New Guinea', *Oceania*, vol. 21.

Ploeg, A. 1969. 'Government in Wanggulam', *Verhandelingen van het Koninklijk Instituut voor Taal-, Land-, en Volkenkunde*, vol. 57.

Pospisil, L. 1958. 'Kapauku Papuan political structure', in V. F. Ray (ed.), *Systems of Political Control and Bureaucracy in Human Societies*, Seattle.

—— 1963. *Kapauku Papuan Economy*. New Haven.

Radcliffe-Brown, A. R. 1940. Introduction to Fortes and Evans-Pritchard (eds), *African Political Systems*.

Rappaport, R. A. 1967a. 'Ritual regulation of environmental relations among a New Guinea people', *Ethnology*, vol. 6.

—— 1967b. *Pigs for the Ancestors*. New Haven.

Read, K. E. 1946-7. 'Social organization in the Markham Valley', *Oceania*, vol. 17.

—— 1949-50. 'The political system of the Ngarawapum', *Oceania*, vol. 20.

—— 1952-3. 'Nama cult of the Central Highlands, New Guinea', *Oceania*, vol. 23.

—— 1954. 'Cultures of the Central Highlands, New Guinea', *Southwestern Journal of Anthropology*, vol. 10.

—— 1954-5. 'Morality and the concept of the person among the Gahuku-Gama', *Oceania*, vol. 25.

—— 1959. 'Leadership and consensus in a New Guinea society', *American Anthropologist*, vol. 61.

Reay, M. 1959. *The Kuma*. Melbourne.

—— 1967. 'Present-day politics in the New Guinea Highlands', in R. Cohen and J. Middleton, *Comparative Political Systems*, New York.

Ryan, D. J. 1958-9. 'Clan formation in the Mendi Valley', *Oceania*, vol. 29.

—— 1961. Gift Exchange in the Mendi Valley. Ph.D. thesis, University of Sydney.

Sack, P. G. 1971-2. 'Kamara: self-help, group solidarity, and law enforcement', *Oceania*, vol. 42.

Sahlins, M. D. 1961. 'The segmentary lineage: an organization of predatory expansion', *American Anthropologist*, vol. 63.

Salisbury, R. F. 1956. 'Unilineal descent groups in the New Guinea Highlands', *Man*. vol. 56.

—— 1958. Political Organization in Siane Society. Ph.D. thesis, Australian National University.

—— 1962. *From Stone to Steel*. Melbourne.

—— 1964. 'Despotism and Australian administration in the New Guinea Highlands', *American Anthropologist*, vol. 66, special publication.

Schapera, I. 1956. *Government and Politics in Tribal Societies*. London.

Smith, M. G. 1956. 'On segmentary lineage systems', *Journal of the Royal Anthropological Institute*, vol. 86.

Strathern, A. J. 1968. 'Descent and alliance in the New Guinea Highlands: some problems of comparison', *Proceedings of the Royal Anthropological Institute*.

—— 1971. *The Rope of Moka: big men and social change in Mount Hagen*. Cambridge.

—— 1972. *One Father, One Blood*. Canberra.

Strathern, A. J. and Strathern, M. 1969. 'Marriage and marriage patterns in Mount Hagen, Western Highlands District, Australian New Guinea', in R. M. Glasse and M. J. Meggitt (eds), *Pigs, Pearlshells, and Women: marriage in the New Guinea Highlands*, Englewood Cliffs.

Strathern, M. 1972. *Women In Between*. London.

Swartz, M. J., Turner, V. W. and Tuden, A. (eds) 1966. *Political Anthropology*. Chicago.

Uberoi, J. P. Singh 1962. *Politics in the Kula Ring*. Manchester.

van der Kroef, J. M. 1952. 'Some head-hunting traditions of southern New Guinea', *American Anthropologist*, vol. 54.

Vayda, A. P. 1971-2. 'Phases of the process of war and peace among the Marings of New Guinea', *Oceania*, vol. 42.

Vicedom, G. F. and Tischner, H. 1943-8. *Die Mbowamb.* 3 vols. Hamburg.

Wagner, R. 1967. *The Curse of Souw.* Chicago.

—— 1969. 'Marriage among the Daribi', in R. M. Glasse and M. J. Meggitt (eds), *Pigs, Pearlshells, and Women: marriage in the New Guinea Highlands,* Englewood Cliffs.

Watson, J. B. 1970. 'Society as organized flow: the Tairora case', *Southwestern Journal of Anthropology,* vol. 26.

—— 1971. 'Tairora: the politics of despotism in a small society', in Berndt and Lawrence (eds), *Politics in New Guinea.*

Wedgwood, C. H. 1958-9. 'Manam Kinship', *Oceania,* vol. 29.

Whiting, J. W. M. 1941. *Becoming a Kwoma.* New Haven.

Williams, F. E. 1930. *Orokaiva Society.* London.

—— 1940-1. 'Natives of Lake Kutubu, Papua', *Oceania,* vol. 11.

—— 1941. 'Group sentiment and primitive justice', *American Anthropologist,* vol. 43.

Williamson, R. W. 1912. *The Mafulu.* London.

Young, M. W. 1971. *Fighting with Food: leadership, values and social control in a Massim society.* Cambridge.

Law*

A. L. Epstein

In many former colonial territories the official recognition and status accorded to 'native law and custom', and provision for the administration of justice through formally constituted 'native courts', gave direct encouragement to the study of indigenous legal institutions. In Papua New Guinea administrative policy has always favoured a more 'direct' form of rule. It is true, of course, that for many years a number of Territory of New Guinea ordinances and regulations, affecting principally the conduct of subordinate courts concerned with the affairs of the indigenous communities, directed these courts to apply native custom save where it was repugnant to the local laws. But until the Native Customs (Recognition) Ordinance came into force in 1963 such directions had been in very general terms: they did not specify what customs were intended nor how they were to be ascertained. More strikingly, there has been no formal provision of any kind for the setting up of native tribunals, composed of indigenes and administering customary law. In these circumstances it is not surprising that, from the point of view of systematic research, law has been one of the most neglected aspects of indigenous Papua New Guinea culture.

Yet this lack of interest in customary law, as revealed in the paucity of literature on it, is not to be explained simply in terms of administrative policy. Account has also been taken of the social structure of indigenous communities and the way in which this has encouraged anthropologists to approach the subject of law. Traditional society is fragmented and essentially parochial; there is nothing corresponding to the institution of kingship or chieftainship, widespread, for example, throughout Africa. There is a concomitant lack of judicial law-enforcement mechanisms comparable with our own or those of many parts of Africa. It was this which led Malinowski, working in the Trobriand Islands, to ask how, in the

* Entitled *Law, Indigenous* in the *Encyclopaedia*.

174

absence of those specialized institutions which we tend to regard as basic to a legal system, social cohesion is maintained. *Crime and Custom in Savage Society*, the small book in which Malinowski first attempted to tackle this problem, was an important and influential work. However, with its emphasis on the principle of reciprocity, its lasting significance is now generally seen to lie in its contribution to general sociological theory rather than in its furtherance of our understanding of primitive law as such. For Malinowski tended to equate the problem of law with that of social control and thus obscured many of the issues of more immediate jurisprudential interest. But his mode of formulating the problem is only one of a number available to us. For example, if we regard courts of law as specialized institutions which decide disputes by reference to rules recognized as valid within the society, and in a given society find that there are no such bodies, we can proceed to enquire as to what disputes arise within it and what measures are taken for their settlement.

Focusing attention on disputes and their resolution at once opens up a number of possibilities. For instance, in his detailed study, *Kapauku Papuans and their Law*, Pospisil has presented the first major account of the *corpus juris* of a Papua New Guinea people by examining the rules stated for him by his informants in the context of disputes. More important, perhaps, is that since there is likely to be less variation in the modes of settlement than in the details of custom, concentrating on the dispute process enables us more readily to pinpoint the characteristic features which Papua New Guinea legal systems, despite their diversity in other respects, appear to share. It is clear from Pospisil's account, and also from the earlier work of Thurnwald, that the traditional societies recognize a body of rules of binding obligation governing family relations, the use and disposition of land or personal property, inheritance and succession, and so on. Where notions diverge most sharply from those usually accepted as necessary to the workings of a modern legal system is in regard to jural classification. For what is crucial in New Guinean thought is that the nature of an offence is defined not so much by the act itself as by the social context within which it occurs. Hence, for example, acts of adultery with different persons, which we would regard as instances of the same kind of offence, are (except perhaps by the offended spouse) not necessarily so regarded. What determines the mode of settlement in any given situation, therefore, is only partly a function of the character of the offending act; equally, if not more, important are the status and social relations of the people involved in the dispute. Much of what is most characteristic of Papua New Guinea legal systems may be derived from this proposition.

Broadly speaking, three main situations may be distinguished: offences concerning parishes that are at a distance from one another; offences concerning different parishes within the same general locality; and cases arising within the small local community. A more definitive analysis would probably also have to take account of disputes between kin, including affines, as yet a further category. Traditionally, parishes were independent autonomous units whose relations were marked by suspicion and the constant threat of open hostility. Accordingly, the killing of a man from another area, the theft of his property or interference with his womenfolk, were always likely to incite the aggrieved party to an act of vengeance, and fighting might break out. Yet warfare was not always the inevitable outcome of such hostile acts, even in those areas of the Highlands where physical violence and aggression were cardinal values. It is difficult to avoid the analogy with contemporary international relations. For the rivalry and mutual antipathy that appear as the primary mark of relations between parishes represent only one side of the coin; as with modern nations, the hostility between parishes is tempered by the complexity of their social interests as reflected in the cross-cutting and constantly changing patterns of alliance between groups. Papua New Guinea big-men, no less than the leaders of modern nation-states, have to be able to recognize that there are times when their aims will not be served by fighting, and call for amicable settlement and payment of compensation. The dispute process is nearly always deeply tinged by political considerations.

An act that might lead to serious fighting between the residents of different areas will usually be regarded in a different light when it occurs within one area. On Wogeo, for example, adultery with a woman from a village several kilometres away would usually have led in the past to fighting with spears; within the locality it might be settled in the course of a ceremonial fight of the kind staged before an initiation rite or on some other festive occasion. Yet here too it is noticeable that the sanction did not follow in any automatic fashion. The villages of this general area are linked by close social ties; co-operation is emphasized, and the pressures towards a peaceful settlement are correspondingly greater. Here, as on Wogeo, the matter is likely to be publicly discussed within the village of the offender, and agreement may be reached for payment of compensation. But much will depend on the culprit's record and position within the group; if he is unable to win the support of his local

leaders he may well be left to face severe punishment in a ceremonial fight.

It is within the parish or local community that the most complex
disputes are likely to arise, and it is here too that the essentially
political character of many disputes can be seen most plainly.
Describing modes of redress for wrongs in south-west New Britain,
Todd has observed how discussion and argument arise over land
ownership problems and economic transactions, and recriminations
are made and countered without end. This complexity has its roots
in the conditions of village life. The members of a local community
are linked and divided by a multiplicity of ties. Tensions develop
within such a closely knit group, and grievances, often of an
apparently trivial kind, erupt into violent quarrels. These are all the
more difficult to resolve because the grievances of the parties are
compounded of so many ingredients, and because what is really at
issue between the disputants is not declared openly for fear of giving
too great offence.

An excellent illustration of this is found in Hogbin's account of
a dispute over heirship at Wogeo. The matter first came to his
notice when the eldest son of the village headman discovered the
loss of a small sum of money he had deposited for safe-keeping in
his father's house. The incident triggered a long and bitter wrangle
within the village, in the course of which it soon became clear that
the angry protests of the son on the discovery of the theft were
linked with a quarrel he was embroiled in with his father over the
choice of a spouse for a younger sister. Since in Papua New Guinea
societies marriage provides a major means of fostering political
alliances, it seems here that the dispute was a reflection of the
cleavage of political interests of father and son. But this was still
only the surface expression of a deeper source of tension in their
relationship and, since the matter was never discussed explicitly, it
was not until some time had elapsed that the ethnographer came to
realize that the heart of the matter lay in the question of succession
to the village headmanship. The situation that had developed
between father and son had its roots in the rules of succession
themselves which did not specify a particular heir but allowed a
choice between a number of possible candidates. In this case the
eldest son felt that he was entitled to succeed whereas the father
appeared to favour a younger son. Such lack of specificity in the
rules of succession to office is common in pre-literate societies, and
it has a number of important implications. In the first place, it
introduces a measure of flexibility into the social system. Secondly,
the fact that the rules allow for alternative candidates, each of

whom can usually marshal valid arguments in support of his case, frequently provides the major focus of the political process within the village.

It is interesting to note that throughout the report of this long dispute there is no indication that the issues were ever debated before some kind of public forum. And perhaps this is not surprising, for the issues were not of a kind readily amenable to settlement by juridicial means; essentially a political dispute, the matter would have to be settled by political means in the end.

It would be wrong to conclude from the Wogeo example that the settlement of disputes in Melanesian communities always takes so inchoate a form. Local leaders or big-men frequently enjoy considerable power and authority within their own communities. Disputes within the group will be brought before the big-man for formal adjudication, and he will normally have a variety of sanctions at his command by which to enforce his judgement. However, the point worth stressing is that even where a public forum for the hearing of cases exists, situations similar to that described are always likely to arise.

For example, among the Tolai of the Gazelle Peninsula it has been the long-established practice, possibly going back to pre-contact times, for disputes to be brought for hearing before the village assembly or moot. Today the proceedings are presided over by the village councillor assisted by a 'committee' of elders. Their role has certain affinities with that of a bench of judges. They maintain decorum and the conditions for orderly debate. They also take the leading part in questioning the litigants on their statements, and intervene to bring them back to the point when they appear to be straying too far afield. Yet it is also clear that to describe them as judges would be misleading. In many cases it seems that their task is merely to hold the ring, so to speak, allowing the disputants to place their arguments freely before the assembled village. Then, by discreet intervention at appropriate moments, as they gauge the feeling of the moot, they try to persuade one or other of the parties to yield gracefully. In these cases the whole emphasis of the procedure lies in working towards a decision by consensus. To the trained lawyer it might seem that decisions reached in this way are likely to result in variation in or departure from the established or recognized rules. In fact, where a decision is reached it is almost invariably because one of the parties has been persuaded to accept the strength of the case against him. More illuminating for an understanding of the nature and function of the moot are the many instances where agreement cannot be reached and the hearing has to be abandoned without any 'judgement' being entered. Many of the cases of this kind are concerned with litigation over land, and their analysis suggests that the failure to reach a decision can be only partly explained by the present lack of legal authority vesting in the moot. A more important consideration is that often the parties are able to invoke rules of customary law which are equally valid and fundamental to the social system, and between which there is no means of deciding on priorities. In these circumstances the apparent failure of the 'judges' to reach a decision only serves to emphasize the point that such disputes cannot be regarded simply as cases between individual litigants seeking to establish their proper legal entitlements. The moot here functions not so much as a court of law but as an arena for a trial of strength between opponents who are seeking to advance or defend their political interests. A further point is that few cases can be regarded as bounded or isolated events; rather they have to be understood in the context of a developing social process.

It is clear then that the modes of settlement of disputes in a Papua New Guinea community differ in important respects from those typically prevailing in Western society. What may be less easy to appreciate is that Western judicial methods may not always be the most appropriate to Papua New Guinea conditions. It may be useful to emphasize this point a little. Fundamental to Western legal procedure is the preliminary narrowing down of the legal issues between the parties so that the court has before it a clear-cut statement of claim and counter-claim on which it can proceed to hear argument on either side. It is on this basis that the court is able to adjudicate between the litigants, apportion liability, and enter a finding for one party or the other. This form of procedure requires in turn a rigid concept of relevance, so that what does not appear to have direct bearing on the issues before the court can be excluded. The conditions under which disputes arise in a Papua New Guinea community demand a different approach. In the first place, as we have seen, the aetiology of disputes is often extremely intricate and complex. Rather like family quarrels among ourselves, they are compounded of many ingredients difficult to disentangle; the overt issues may have little direct bearing on the underlying tensions between the parties. In seeking to get to the heart of the matter an indigenous moot has to take cognizance of many matters an Australian court would be required to ignore or exclude. Secondly, a serious dispute within a village is likely to disturb the whole social life. In so far as people have to live together in spite of the quarrels that divide them, the aim of the moot is the reconciliation of the parties and the restoration of amity in social relationships. As we have seen, this is not always easy to achieve, particularly where the disputants are political rivals. It is even less likely to be achieved when Western techniques of settlement are administered: a finding that one party is right and the other wrong, without the latter's acquiescence in his guilt, is only likely to exacerbate tensions within the village. It is, of course, true that since first coming under European influence great social and political changes have overtaken indigenous Papua New Guinea society.

As the country approaches independence the need for the development of more appropriate legal institutions becomes urgent. Those concerned with matters of policy are undoubtedly correct in stressing the importance of creating a modern legal system uniform for the whole country. Yet these wholly valid aims may well be thwarted if no adequate provision is made for the administration of justice at the local level in a form the villager can understand and appreciate. To paraphrase the comment a Solomon Islander once made to an anthropologist, it is important that there should be no wall built between the law of yesterday and the law of today.

Bibliography

Berndt, R. M. 1962. *Excess and Restraint*. Chicago.

Derham, D. P. 1963. 'Law and custom in the Australian Territory of Papua and New Guinea', *University of Chicago Law Review*, vol. 30.

Epstein, A. L. 1970-1. 'Dispute settlement among the Tolai', *Oceania*, vol. 41.

Hogbin, H. I. 1938. 'Social reaction to crime', *Journal of the Royal Anthropological Institute*, vol. 68.

—— 1940-1. 'The father chooses his heir', *Oceania*, vol. 11.

—— 1943-4. 'Native councils and native courts in the Solomon Islands', *Oceania*, vol. 14.

Kaberry, P. M. 1941-2. 'Law and political organization in the Abelam tribe, New Guinea', *Oceania*, vol. 12.

Malinowski, B. 1926. *Crime and Custom in Savage Society*. London.

Pospisil, L. 1958. *Kapauku Papuans and their Law*. Yale University Publications in Anthropology no. 54. New Haven.

—— 1965. 'A formal analysis of substantive law', *American Anthropologist*, vol. 67.

Sack, P. G. 1971-2. 'Kamara: self-help, group solidarity, and law enforcement', *Oceania*, vol. 42.

Thurnwald, R. C. (ed.) 1929-30. 'Papuanisches und melanesisches Gebiet südlich des Äquators einschliesslich Neuguinea', in E. Schultz-Ewerth and L. Adam (eds), *Das Eingeborenenrecht* (2 vols), vol. 2, Stuttgart.

Todd, J. A. 1935-6. 'Redress of wrongs in south-west New Britain', *Oceania*, vol. 6.

Sorcery and Witchcraft

Leonard B. Glick

Sorcery and witchcraft have to do with malevolent use of super-human powers. Although the two are closely linked and in many cultures inseparable, anthropologists sometimes distinguish between sorcery as the use of powerful rites or poisonous objects and witchcraft as the projection of harmful personal power. A sorcerer's capacity to harm, in other words, depends on his ability to control extrinsic powers; whereas a witch, who can inflict sickness or death on others simply by staring at them or willing evil on them, possesses powers—inherited or acquired—as an intrinsic part of his or her person. Beliefs in witchcraft are not uncommon in Melanesian cultures, but among most peoples of Papua New Guinea sorcery beliefs are decidedly predominant; moreover, where witchcraft is encountered it is likely to appear as part of a complex of ideas centring on sorcery. But more important than these academic distinctions are those features characteristic of both sorcery and witchcraft. Both have to do with malevolent power; both lead to accusations by one person or group against another; and both arise in situations marked by tension, conflict and varying degrees of social instability.

Sorcery and witchcraft are popular topics nowadays in college and university circles, and some readers may reject interpretations that deny the actual existence of such practices. Be that as it may, it must be emphasized that most anthropologists and other students of the subject do not believe that a few anti-social individuals possess special knowledge and powers or are especially predisposed to attack others; rather, they begin with the premise that sorcery and witchcraft refer to ideas held by everyone in a society about the potential ability of other people to inflict harm and misfortune on their enemies. To interpret sorcery and witchcraft accusations it is not enough, therefore, to analyse the personalities or psychological peculiarities of the accused or their accusers, although these may

182

be of interest and may help to explain particular incidents. But total recourse to psychologically-slanted explanations centring on the mental status of particular individuals may obscure more fundamental insights, namely, those to be derived from approaching accusations as social events. For such accusations do not occur in a vacuum: they emerge in the context of a particular community's culture, economic conditions, and social history, and they are the means by which people may express, dramatically and memorably, their most fundamental conflicts and anxieties. As such, they call for enquiry reaching well beyond single episodes or the peculiarities of single individuals.

The first questions that are likely to arise have to do with what people believe, or say they believe. What forms of mystical evil power are potentially available in the community? Are certain people, or certain kinds of people, said to be sorcerers or witches? Whom do they harm? What provokes them to act? How can they be controlled or resisted?

In Papua New Guinea, answers to such questions usually focus on sorcerers and the ways in which they poison their enemies. In many communities, however, one encounters a distinction between two forms of sorcery, both feared but for different reasons. The more usual form, which I call 'projective sorcery', has three distinct features. First, the sorcerer is almost always a single individual: he may act either on his own initiative or on behalf of another person or group, but he works alone. Second, the sorcerer and his victim do not come into direct physical contact; instead, he attacks by some form of remotely-directed or projective action such as propelling disease objects into his victim, cooking bits of bodily refuse or food scraps with poisons, and so on. Finally, illnesses attributed to projective sorcery are usually marked by gradual onset, a prolonged course, and a measure of optimism: the victim knows that he is ill, seeks help, and hopes to recover. Likewise, whoever assumes responsibility for curing him presumably does so with some confidence in his own ability to oppose the will of the sorcerer.

In the second form of sorcery, sometimes known by the Pidgin term *sangguma*, and which I call assault sorcery, we find almost the precise reverse. First, assault sorcery is said often, though not necessarily, to require several assailants, whose foremost purpose may be aggression or revenge on behalf of their own descent group against that of their victim. Second, the attack is personal, immediate and uncompromisingly vicious. The assailants spring on their victim from ambush, brutally overpower him, jab poisons directly into his body, sometimes twist or rip out organs, and perpetuate similar crimes against his person. They are not satisfied until he is thoroughly befuddled, unable to remember who or what has afflicted him. A characteristically sadistic touch is to ask simple questions or set simple tasks to test the victim's mental state—'Who are we?' 'Where are you now?' 'Point to where the sun rises'—and resume the attack if he responds sensibly. Thus assault sorcery includes an element of irony: the victim is permitted to stagger home but only as a shell, a mocking sign to kinsmen and neighbours that in this man's person they have all in a sense been assaulted and are now helpless to resist. Finally, a foreseeable corollary: it is immediately evident to everyone except the victim that the illness is hopeless. Curers may attempt to reverse its course, but only half-heartedly it would appear, for the patient's physical and mental integrity are damaged beyond the range of their powers.

To understand these beliefs in depth one must enquire into their role and significance in social life. For although sorcery and witch-craft may not exist as objective realities, sorcery and witchcraft accusations are not irrational. They arise in situations characterized by stress and insecurity, and they often turn out to be a vivid reflection of real tensions and emergent cleavages in social systems: potential realignments, incipient role redefinition, and similar social phenomena especially characteristic of periods of rapid or intensive change. Moreover, as Forge reminds us in his recent study of Abelam sorcery, to be a big-man is tantamount in many Papua New Guinea societies to having some form of control over sorcery, for mystical power is the reverse side of a medal whose obverse is political power. Hence, accusations may highlight struggles in the central political arena, and what may at first appear to be an individual's personal misfortune may in time be related to the political fortunes or misfortunes of an entire community. It is obvious, then, that such accusations should not only be taken seriously but also be studied for the insights they may afford into the social fabric as it responds to the shifting stresses of present-day life.

If sorcery and witchcraft were nothing more than naive forms of expression—primitive exotica—they might be expected to disappear as people became more modern in outlook; and it might be thought that they would decline in Papua New Guinea as more and more communities enter the market and wage-earning economy, develop better communications with one another and the rest of the world, and move generally in the direction of Westernization. But there is good reason for saying that often precisely the opposite will be the case. For, as Marwick points out in a provocative article on the declining productivity of anthropologists in this field, the unavoidable conflicts that arise in societies undergoing change— conflicts arising from altered roles, newly-defined relationships, ambivalence toward neighbours and kin as potential competitors, and so on—are not unlike those that have always underlain sorcery and witchcraft accusations, even though the sources of tension may be less apparent in times of relative stability. And it is not improbable that traditional modes of dramatizing such conflicts may survive for a long time.

To illustrate this point with just one example, we may consider briefly the community of Hanuabada, near Port Moresby, studied some twenty years ago by Belshaw and probably representative of the kind of community that will emerge increasingly as the country achieves independence and enters the modern world. Hanuabada was even then a rapidly changing community. Many of its inhabitants were wage-earners in Port Moresby, and Belshaw characterized it as truly urban. Yet sorcery beliefs were as prevalent as ever. Sorcerers were said to have a kind of power, or 'heat', similar to that of a frenzied dancer or a charismatic orator. Such power might be projected from a distance; or the sorcerer might sneak up to a house at night and induce sickness through spells, or charm a sleeping victim into wandering later to a place where an accident would befall him. The villagers maintained that sorcery knowledge originated in neighbouring rural communities, but this did not preclude their accusing one another of being sorcerers. Belshaw seems to have been impressed by the persistence of such beliefs. He viewed them as a reflection of social tensions and an expression of chronic distress associated with poverty and disease, implying that they would probably disappear when social conditions improved.

If Hanuabada is indeed suggestive of what we may expect to encounter in a changing Papua New Guinea, it is possible that more, rather than less, sorcery and witchcraft accusations will be part of the social scene. What are the implications for social planners and other persons concerned with the on-going life of communities?

Here we enter a less well-defined area, one in which responsible people may reasonably disagree. My own position, and that of the great majority of anthropologists today, derives from what has already been said, namely, that energies should not be wasted on efforts to eliminate sorcery and witchcraft accusations through education or fiat. Rather, every effort should be made to understand such events, in their own social contexts, as manifestations of genuine, perhaps necessary and functional, conflicts rooted in the social history of a community. Sorcery and witchcraft accusations, in this view, may turn out to be responses to deprivation, absolute or relative, for which remedies may then be sought. They may reflect newly-emerging conflicts of interest, or needs—perhaps only dimly perceived and otherwise poorly articulated—for redefinition of roles and relationships. They may be the idiom in which struggles for new forms of political and economic power are expressed. They may, in short, be keys to the most fundamental problems confronting a people. I would argue, therefore, that whatever one's personal feelings about such ideas and practices, it is appropriate, indeed essential, that they be examined in their own social and cultural contexts rather than in the light of Western values and premises. To do less is to deny people their essential right to cultural and personal equality.

Bibliography

Belshaw, C. S. 1957. *The Great Village*. London.

Forge, A. 1970. 'Prestige, influence, and sorcery: a New Guinea example', in M. Douglas (ed.), *Witchcraft Confessions and Accusations*, London.

Lawrence, P. and Meggitt, M. J. (eds) 1965. *Gods, Ghosts and Men in Melanesia*. Melbourne.

Marwick, M. G. 1964. 'Witchcraft as a social strain-gauge', *Australian Journal of Science*, vol. 26.

——— 1972. 'Anthropologists' declining productivity in the sociology of witchcraft', *American Anthropologist*, vol. 74.

Ethics

L. L. Langness

The term as here used means the system of morals of a particular group, including not only the current ideals of what is right but also the sanctions that secure conformity with those ideals.

In the first half of the nineteenth century, prior to the emergence of anthropology as a special study, the peoples to whom the word primitive is now sometimes applied were regarded simply as immoral or uncivilized. Later, under the influence of the theory of evolution, there was an attempt to show that they were, rather, pre-moral, amoral, or 'slaves of custom'. This attitude resulted in the neglect of ethics or morality as a field of enquiry. The reaction against evolutionism, the so-called functional movement of the 1920s, which Spiro also referred to as the 'Copernican Revolution' of anthropology, although demonstrating convincingly that primitive peoples were not in fact slaves of custom and that their lives were less simple than had been supposed, did little to stimulate work on ethics *per se*. The tendency was to regard morality as part of religion, and where moral rules lacked backing by supernatural sanctions of some sort, as is sometimes the case in primitive societies, they were omitted from study. If on the other hand there were such sanctions, morality was discussed under the general heading of religion instead of being treated as an independent subject.

A revival of interest in ethics and values occurred in the late 1930s, particularly in the United States, and since that time extensive studies of particular moral systems have been undertaken. Although these have restored consideration of ethics to a legitimate place in anthropology and stimulated much interest, there has been as yet no intensive investigation of the subject in Papua New Guinea. Such information as is available is usually embedded in some more general ethnographic text or is marginally covered in a treatment of social control, law or politics. As Hogbin's *Island of*

187

Menstruating Men (1970) is the first full-length treatment of a Papua New Guinea religious system since Fortune's *Manus Religion* published in 1935, there has been little help from students of comparative religion. Nevertheless, certain facts are known, and it is now possible to perceive important variations in the moral systems of the country as well as certain features that appear to be universal.

SUPERNATURAL SANCTIONS

One aspect of variation concerns the presence or absence of such sanctions for breaches of the moral code. Among the Huli, according to Glasse (1965), there is a specific supernatural being, Datagaliwabe, whose particular function is the supervision of ethical conduct:

> Datagaliwabe is no ordinary deity and indeed the Huli never call him a *dama* [a class of invisible deities possessing supra-physical powers to control the weather, cause sickness and infertility, etc.] but refer to him only by name. His special province is punishing breaches of kinship and for this purpose he continually observes social behaviour. One man described him as a giant who, with legs astride, looks down upon all and punishes lying, stealing, adultery, murder, incest, breaches of exogamy and of taboos relating to ritual. He also penalizes those who fail to avenge the deaths of kin slain in war. He has no concern, however, with the behaviour of unrelated persons.

But in general the belief in supernatural beings who validate morality is relatively uncommon. Sanctions of a supernatural type, where they exist, are more commonly associated with ghosts. Perhaps the best example is to be found among the Manus of the Admiralty Islands, recorded by Mead (1937):

> Each Manus household is governed by a ghost of a recently dead male relative. In conception this ghost is a father, but a son may actually be raised to this position after death. The skull of the ghost is kept in the house and presides over the moral and economic life of the household. He punishes sex offences, scandalmongering, obscenity, failure to pay debts, failure to help relatives, and failure to keep one's house in repair. For derelictions in these duties, he sends illness and misfortune.

Still another form of supernatural sanction, noted by Berndt (1965), perhaps a more indirect and less efficacious one, is related to mythology. Here mythological nonhumans of various kinds, as

well as humans in some cases, are held up as examples of how
human beings should behave:

> Each [myth] ends with a moral injunction, to the effect that 'we,
> story characters, have done this; you, men, should not.' In many
> cases men behave as the story characters do, and not as the
> moral dictates. But generally speaking this type of myth deals
> (negatively) with what people should not do, rather than (posi-
> tively) with what they should.

Wagner comments similarly on the Daribi near Mount Karimui:

> Models of correct courteous actions are given by a pair of stock
> characters in Daribi legends, generally portrayed as two cross-
> cousins . . . the *bidi mu,* or 'true man,' and *peraberabidi,* or 'man
> who breaks things'.

The above comments by no means account for the complexity of
belief and action regarding supernatural sanctions. Nor are the
types ever found in pure form. Among the Huli, for example, it is
not only Datagaliwabe who is concerned with the moral affairs of
the living but also, albeit to a lesser degree, the *dama,* as well as
the ghosts of both recent and distant ancestors. Among the Fore,
Kamano and others is found, along with the mythology, a belief in
ghosts, although how functional these are in the moral sphere is not
entirely clear. In looking at the country as a whole, one finds a
remarkable complexity of belief regarding supernatural beings:
gods, ghosts, spirit-beings, sky-dwelling creatures, demons and
others. And in each case the limits of action for any specific supernatural being, as well as the limits for all supernatural beings, can
vary. Sometimes the ghosts are concerned only with the morality of
their surviving kinsmen and not that of others; sometimes a god is
concerned only with violations of incest rules but not with stealing;
sometimes the supernatural beings intervene only upon the failure
to perform certain rituals, and so on. The distribution of various
types of supernatural beings and the specifics of their influence
upon the moral behaviour of the living are not well known.

In contrast with the above there are many societies in which
there is no relationship between moral rules and supernatural
sanctions or, indeed, between religion and morality. Even where a
belief in ghosts exists, for example, such things are not necessarily
believed to affect the moral affairs of the living. The Gururumba
are a good case in point. According to Newman:

In other words, ghosts are not moral agents punishing the living for acts of wrongdoing. Neither are they thought of as vengeful. Wrong between living individuals is not made right by ghostly attack when the wronged individual dies and becomes a ghost. In general terms, ghosts act because of affronts to their physical person, as in the case of wanting their bones cleaned; to their esteem, as in the case of not wanting to be forgotten; or to express some strong personal desire, as in the case of not wanting to have one's name spoken.

Meggitt (1965) notes that the Enga also, with a similar belief in ghosts, do not associate them with morality. Enga dogmas about other types of supernatural beings likewise do not associate them with morality. The sky beings, conceived of as the 'causal and originating people', responsible for good and bad luck, are not concerned with the ethical conduct of their putative descendants:

> Although some people assert that a dishonest man is more likely to experience bad luck than is an honest man, they do not believe that the sky beings are concerned consistently to punish the evil and reward the good. The popular tendency is to define right and wrong behaviour in terms of what currently serves the particular interests of corporate groups in the lineage hierarchy.

The Wogeo (Hogbin 1938, 1970) and the Orokaiva (Reay) appear to be even clearer examples of societies in which there is no connection between morality and religion. This situation, and many more examples could be cited, has given rise to obvious questions, the most fundamental being what sanctions do exist to maintain the moral order. A number of explanations have been offered. For convenience these can be classified as follows: retaliation, group identification, self-regulation and quasi-legal sanctions. As will become obvious these are not precise categories. Each can be sub-divided, and one category tends to merge into the next.

RETALIATION

A widespread sanction, it expresses itself in at least two ways. In its simplest form, retaliation takes the character of direct physical violence (Langness 1972). Among most groups, for example, a woman found guilty of adultery would simply be beaten by her husband. He might beat the guilty man also or, as among the Bena Bena, shoot him in the thigh with a special arrow kept for this purpose. Likewise, to avenge a death, either by sorcery or through some physical act, the relatives of the deceased must kill someone in the group presumed responsible. The knowledge that reprisals can be expected encourages observance of the moral prescriptions.

As Reay has shown for the Orokaiva, retaliation can also take the form of withdrawal, as in the case of a woman who leaves her adulterous husband to fend for himself. There is also the with-holding of goods and services as, for example, when an uncle refuses to contribute to a youth's bride price.

A more indirect form of retaliation involves sorcery, the threat of which can act as a sanction for proper conduct. This was apparently of some significance among the Busama at one time, as recorded by Hogbin (1963):

> In earlier days sorcery was another factor to be reckoned with. The fear of black magic spurred people to overcome temptation and meet the legitimate claims of their kin; and, in addition, it served as an innocuous outlet for feelings of irritation. By this means the man harbouring a grievance obtained satisfaction without jeopardizing his position, hurting his enemy, or upsetting the life of the village.

Although sorcery beliefs exist almost universally throughout Melanesia, sorcery is not always employed as a sanction, nor is it always associated with morality. The Bena Bena, with strong beliefs about sorcery, view it as emanating only from enemies, and as such it is an activity having nothing to do with their own moral conduct, either right or wrong. According to Read, the same is true for the Gahuku-Gama. Nor does there appear to be any clear-cut relation-ship between the presence of beliefs about sorcery and the presence or absence of religious sanctions for moral behaviour (Lawrence and Meggitt).

GROUP IDENTIFICATION

In this category must first be placed what Williams defines as group sentiment. This phenomenon, he believed, accounts for much of the conformity found in primitive societies, including conformity to moral rules. In brief, Williams argues, there is a basic 'sentiment of fellowship', which is strong in men and particularly strong among 'primitives', who characteristically live in relatively small groups. This is not something of which people are aware, and it is related to what Williams regards as an 'unconscious imitativeness'. But it is much more than merely imitativeness, it is also 'an often-expressed desire, even duty, to do things in the approved manner, in the "way of our fathers".' Although Williams was aware that there was

a limited range of choice for primitives, and that there were
practical reasons as well for conformity, he did not believe these
were sufficient to explain the degree of conformity he observed:

> It may be claimed that there are ample reasons of a more
> practical kind why a man should behave with special considera-
> tion towards his own group-members—e.g. the prospect of
> mutual assistance, the necessity for co-operation and mutual
> restraint, etc., which the individual is supposed to keep in mind.
> But to lay all the stress on this aspect seems to the present writer
> to embody the intellectualistic error. It is not to be supposed that
> the native is so calculating in his conduct, so keen a student of
> self-interest. Without unduly discounting this factor in his
> motives, the writer is disposed to believe that the native acts, or
> refrains from acting, with less intellectual finesse than it implies.
> At any rate it can hardly be denied that the group sentiment
> which we have called that of fellowship exists; and if it exists, it
> does not exist for nothing. It must influence conduct, and we
> need not entirely disbelieve such oft-repeated statements as 'I
> would not do so and so an injury because he is my brother, my
> kinsman, my neighbour, etc.'

Although group sentiment is a difficult concept to define and
work with, and although Williams himself only asserts its existence,
the basic position is part of a wider tradition that still exists in
sociology and anthropology. Many scholars (Redfield; Foster)
would argue that among primitives there is a kind of mystique or
sense of solidarity not present in more complex societies, but there
are now beginning to be dissenting opinions (Edgerton).

In the same category, group identification, can be justifiably
placed attempts to explain moral behaviour in terms of shame.
Shame is an apparently universal concept among the peoples of
Papua New Guinea. It should be made clear, however, that this is
not shame in precisely the sense that Westerners are accustomed to
think of it. The feeling as an emotional experience is perhaps more
akin to what Westerners would call intense guilt. It is unlike guilt,
perhaps, in that it is related to the fear of being found out rather
than to purely private pangs of conscience over having sinned or
committed an unpardonable offence. There is no doubt that it has
an effect on the personalities of those who experience it, driving
them to extremes of behaviour and even to suicide.

In the most intensive account of shame to date, Hogbin (1946–7)
has shown both its overwhelmingly social character and its relationship to morality. The Busama, with whom he deals, clearly regulate
much of their conduct in terms of the avoidance of shame. This

regulation extends from the most fundamental of daily interpersonal relations to sexual behaviour, magic, and even legal and political behaviour. In this particular case, paradoxically, shame also operates at times to inhibit the punishment of those who do wrong. Hogbin cites the case of a man, obviously unsuitable for office, being appointed because the people were ashamed to say anything against him once his name had been submitted.

Hogbin maintains that the content of shame is similar everywhere but that the actions that arouse it vary with the moral code. While this may be true it is of less importance as a sanction in some areas than in others. Burridge, for example, reports that shame, although present, is relatively unimportant among the Tangu.

SELF-REGULATION

This also can be considered from more than one point of view. First, it is implicit in the notion that primitive folk act only in terms of custom. Indeed it is implicit in the concepts of society and of culture themselves, for no matter how these are defined the definitions always imply some regularity of behaviour. But beyond this are usually enumerated characteristics of small-scale societies that automatically constrain action within narrow limits. There is the relative absence of choice so often noted; the need to help others if a person is to expect help in his turn; the fact that co-operation is a necessity for survival in an inhospitable environment with only a crude technology; and the psychological and social limits imposed by kinship as the primary principle of organization. But to see self-regulation in this way it is necessary to make one of two extreme assumptions about human behaviour. Either, as Williams noted, people must be seen as acting always in terms of conscious self-interest—I will help him only because I expect something in return —or else they are seen as acting with virtually no conscious awareness at all—this is the way people have always acted so I will act in this way—neither a very satisfactory view of human nature.

Nadel has offered a more penetrating explanation of the process of self-regulation by adding the concepts of value and maximization as necessary conditions for even customary behaviour to occur:

Rather, traditional or customary behaviour operates reliably only when two other conditions apply and derives its force and apparent self-propulsion from them. Either acting in accordance with tradition (i.e. in accordance with old inherited models) is as such considered desirable and good; or, this way of acting happens also to be safe, known routine. In the first case the traditional action is also value-oriented, being indeed short-lived without this support, as is instanced by changing fashions and fads. In the second case the custom remains such because its routinized procedure affords maximum success with least risk. It is, I suggest, in these two conditions that we find the true elements of self-regulation.

He then goes on to show that any activity that is socially important is, simply by virtue of its importance, automatically protected from violation. This is so, he argues, from two different points of view. From the point of view of the participant in the action, an important activity is one that is valued and, as people do not readily give up their values and convictions, that which is important is by that measure protected. More important, Nadel argues, is that from the point of view of the observer the social importance of an activity is determined by its focal position among all other social activities. This is because an action can, of course, serve many ends or interests other than those for which it is primarily intended. If it is truly focal the failure to perform it will result in more undesirable consequences and greater dislocation of the system than if it is not a focal activity. This works as follows:

> Consider for example, a society, patrilineally organized, where marriage is prohibited between agnatic kin, is contracted by the payment of bride price, and entails specific duties towards the offspring on the part of both father's and mother's kin. If any man married in disregard of the first rule, the others would fail to work also. The bride price would have to be paid within the same descent group, while in the people's conception it is a payment suitable only between such groups, being meant (among other things) to indemnify the bride's group for the loss of her prospective progeny. The offspring of such an irregular union would forfeit the double assistance from two kin groups since the father's and mother's kin now coincide, and would be less advantageously placed than the offspring of customary marriages. And there would be various other, minor but no less confusing, complications; for example, rules of avoidance (obligatory towards in-laws) and intimacy (towards blood relations) would now apply to the same people. In short, one breach of routine disrupts routine all round, and the individual is faced with a wide loss of social bearings.

That this is self-regulation can be seen in that the punishment for the violation of the marriage rule is intrinsic in the situation rather than extrinsic. That is, no formal or legal sanction is necessarily involved: the man does not face a gaol sentence or execution, he simply does not get satisfaction from the social system.

The process here cannot be separated from the values of the society, for the self-regulation implied in the notion of multiple consequences is part of a system that continuously feeds back upon itself. That is, any conduct that conforms to the norm stimulates further positive actions which keep the system going, becomes a model exhibiting its efficacy, and thereby gets its positive value reinforced. For a further discussion of this type of process see Bateson's *Steps to an Ecology of Mind*.

Nadel believed that self-regulation was characteristic of small primitive societies:

> In more general terms, the regulative effects must vary inversely with the separation of social roles, with the specialization of offices and tasks, and, implicitly, with the size of groups (since only small groups can function adequately without considerable internal differentiation). It is precisely the small scale and lack of internal differentiation which characterize the societies we commonly call primitive and hence enable them to lean more heavily on such machinery of self-regulation.

Thus, following Nadel, it would be unusual to find highly developed legal institutions or procedures of law enforcement in the traditional societies of Papua New Guinea. This is precisely the case; and hence the last category, quasi-legal sanctions.

QUASI-LEGAL SANCTIONS

Here are found various forms of institutionalized behaviour, other than simple retaliation, that can be used against those who violate the moral rules. Often these come into play only when the principle of retaliation threatens to become overly disruptive. Hogbin (1963) reports that among the Busama, for example, it is up to the individual to secure redress by personal retaliation. However, if serious argument ensues and it appears that someone may be hurt, formal machinery is brought into play. This consists of a headman, preferably not a relative of either party to the dispute, and a council of elders who are empowered to suggest punishments in the form of fines. They seem to have had no power to impose punishments if the weight of public opinion behind them was not sufficiently strong and if one or both of the disputants did not defer to their judgement. This situation appears to have been fairly uniform over the country. Leadership was characteristically based more upon strength of personality, success and knowledge than upon inheritance or election; and although leaders could influence and suggest, they could not command. They had little or no authority over individuals who did not wish to obey. Thus, although leadership and authority are present, as they must be in all societies, intervention in the moral or legal sphere occurs only under certain conditions. It is, as Nadel suggests, only when self-regulation fails to operate that quasi-legal or legal sanctions appear.

There are other mechanisms for dealing with violations of moral rules. These are sometimes built into the economic life of the community. Kaberry records that among the Abelam, for example, a man who suspects his wife of adultery can challenge the accused man to an exchange of yams:

> The husband, with the object of shaming the other man, sends yams and pigs to him, with the challenge that he make an equivalent return. The implication is that the adulterer is more interested in sexual intercourse than in growing yams, and that he will not be able to meet the challenge. An avoidance is established between them, and they no longer sit and talk together. They are *wauna-ndu*, men who mock and abuse one another on public occasions. Such quarrels have wide repercussions, for unless a man can exonerate himself he is placed in the position where his relations become strained with a number of individuals in the village, and he has also to make additional efforts as a gardener if he is to meet his adversary's challenge and produce yams to vindicate his reputation. Thus the yam cult, with its taboos on sexual intercourse during part of the year, ambition and a jealous regard for prestige act as sanctions to preserve marital fidelity.

Here, then, is an institutionalized way of punishing a breach of morality without unnecessarily disrupting the foundation of social life through physical assault or murder. This method of maintaining the moral system through exchange and equivalence is fundamental to many societies. It is so basic to the Tangu, for example, that Burridge reports there would be no amity without it:

> The critical axiom which governs all Tangu relationships through a variety of contents, bases and motives is amity. No vague and emotional goodwill, amity depends on and is expressed by equivalence, a principle of moral equality which must be continually reaffirmed and reiterated lest someone become dominant. Without equivalence there can be no amity in Tangu. The focal assertion of equivalence is at food exchanges at every level whether the exchange is completed in a day, weeks or months.

The principle here, which Burridge refers to as a 'principle of moral equality', operates not only at the level of individual behaviour but is also invoked at a level of action more properly termed political (see, for example, Berndt 1962; Glasse 1954-62; Read 1959). This merely emphasizes the difficulty of distinguishing between such concepts as morality, law and politics in societies of this type, a distinction always more analytical than real.

Some moral prescriptions are probably universal: those dealing with stealing, adultery, murder, incest, rape, bad behaviour towards kinsmen and friends, etc. But there is variation, of course, and what is considered ethical conduct by one group is not necessarily so considered by another. Among the Bena Bena, for example, consuming the dead bodies of certain kinsmen was considered right and proper, whereas among the peoples further to the west such conduct was thought to be horrifying. Pre-marital intercourse is relatively common among the Bena Bena (Langness 1969) whereas among the Enga (Meggitt) it is improper. Violence towards a grey-haired man is unthinkable to the Kapauku people (Pospisil) whereas senicide occurred in other groups. The extent of this variation has not been systematically determined.

Beyond the specific universal content of the codes, whatever that may prove to be, there are certain universal features of the moral systems *qua* systems. Shame, as noted, is probably universally present. In that sense they might be categorized as 'shame cultures' as opposed to 'guilt cultures' (Piers and Singer) assuming that is a valid distinction. Another universal feature is that the moral code, along with whatever sanctions support it, is always group specific. That is, the moral rules do not apply beyond some known and finite boundary—the clan, the parish, an alliance of parishes, or perhaps at most a language group. Read (1954–5) has made by far the most cogent and penetrating analysis of this aspect of tribal morality. Although he is speaking only of the Gahuku-Gama his remarks would apply to all known peoples in Papua New Guinea prior to European contact:

> We may note, however, that people do not assert that 'it is wrong to kill', or that 'it is right to love everyone', while of the other universal commands of Christianity a large number are conspicuously absent. The Gahuku-Gama, for example, do not say that one should practise forbearance in all circumstances; indeed, their injunctions against adultery, against lying, thieving and slander should not be accepted as applying to all the situations

in which the individual may find himself. There is nothing unusual in this. It is simply another way of saying that we are dealing with a tribal morality as distinct from the universal morality of Christian teaching. In other words, Gahuku-Gama assertions of what is right or wrong, good or bad, are not intended to apply to all men; they are stated from the position of a particular collectivity outside of which the moral norm ceases to have any meaning.

Still another universal feature is that moral rules are not abstracted from their social context or their locus in the system. The people themselves do not think of a category 'morality' as opposed to other aspects of behaviour. They have thus no theology and no ethics, if we restrict this latter term to its strictly philosophical meaning. The moral rules are simply part of social life itself as are the accompanying sanctions.

Retaliation, group identification, self-regulation and quasi-legal sanctions are, of course, merely convenient categories for outlining different mechanisms working to ensure conformity with moral, and other, rules. No society exhibits only one of these and, indeed, it is likely that their presence and mixture in all societies of Papua New Guinea is a further universal feature of their moral systems.

Perhaps the most curious and important ethical feature of many Papua New Guinea societies is the capacity for allowing a maximum amount of individual freedom, even in spite of significant threats to group survival. Thus it is possible for individuals to refuse to fight against groups in which they have kinsmen while simultaneously remaining members in good standing of their own groups. Likewise there is a minimum of interference with the lives of others in general. There would appear to be useful lessons for the rest of the world here, and a genuine need for extensive comparative studies.

Bibliography

Bateson, G. 1972. *Steps to an Ecology of Mind*. San Francisco.

Berndt, R. M. 1962. *Excess and Restraint*. Chicago.

—— 1965. 'The Kamano, Usurufa, Jate and Fore of the Eastern Highlands', in Lawrence and Meggitt (eds), *Gods, Ghosts and Men in Melanesia*.

Burridge, K. O. L. 1965. 'Tangu, northern Madang District', in Lawrence and Meggitt (eds), *Gods, Ghosts and Men in Melanesia*.

Edgerton, R. E. 1973. *Social Deviance*. Reading, Mass.

Fortune, R. 1935. *Manus Religion: an ethnological study of the Manus natives of the Admiralty Islands*. Philadelphia.

Foster, G. M. 1953. 'What is folk culture?', *American Anthropologist*, vol. 55.

Glasse, R. M. 1954-62. 'Revenge and redress among the Huli', *Mankind*, vol. 5.

———— 1965. 'The Huli of the Southern Highlands', in Lawrence and Meggitt (eds), *Gods, Ghosts and Men in Melanesia*.

Hogbin, H. I. 1938. 'Social reaction to crime', *Journal of the Royal Anthropological Institute*, vol. 68.

———— 1946-7. 'Shame: a study of social conformity in a New Guinea village', *Oceania*, vol. 17.

———— 1963. *Kinship and Marriage in a New Guinea Village*. London.

———— 1970. *The Island of Menstruating Men: religion in Wogeo*. Scranton.

Kaberry, P. M. 1941-2. 'Law and political organization in the Abelam tribe, New Guinea', *Oceania*, vol. 12.

Langness, L. L. 1966-7. 'Sexual antagonism in the New Guinea Highlands', *Oceania*, vol. 37.

———— 1969. 'Marriage in Bena Bena', in R. M. Glasse and M. J. Meggitt (eds), *Pigs, Pearlshells, and Women: marriage in the New Guinea Highlands*, Englewood Cliffs.

———— 1972. 'Violence in the New Guinea Highlands', in J. F. Short jr. and M. E. Wolfgang (eds), *Collective Violence*, New York.

Lawrence, P. and Meggitt, M. J. 1965. Introduction to *Gods, Ghosts and Men in Melanesia*. Melbourne.

Mead, M. 1930. *Growing Up in New Guinea*. New York.

———— 1937. 'The Manus of the Admiralty Islands', in M. Mead (ed.), *Cooperation and Competition among Primitive Peoples*, New York.

Meggitt, M. J. 1964. 'Male-female relationships in the Highlands of Australian New Guinea', *American Anthropologist*, vol. 66, special publication.

———— 1965. 'The Mae Enga of the Western Highlands', in Lawrence and Meggitt (eds), *Gods, Ghosts and Men in Melanesia*.

Nadel, S. F. 1952-3. 'Social control and self-regulation', *Social Forces*, vol. 31.

Newman, P. L. 1965. *Knowing the Gururumba*. New York.

Piers, G. and Singer, M. B. 1953. *Shame and Guilt: a psychoanalytic and a cultural study*. Springfield.

Pospisil, L. 1958. *Kapauku Papuans and their Law*. Yale University Publications in Anthropology no. 54. New Haven.

Read, K. E. 1954-5. 'Morality and the concept of the person among the Gahuku-Gama', *Oceania*, vol. 25.

―――― 1959. 'Leadership and consensus in a New Guinea society', *American Anthropologist*, vol. 61.

Reay, M. 1953-4. 'Social control amongst the Orokaiva', *Oceania*, vol. 24.

Redfield, R. 1953. *The Primitive World and its Transformations*. Ithaca.

Spiro, M. 1972. 'An overview and suggested reorientation', in F. L. K. Hsu, *Psychological Anthropology*, Cambridge, Mass.

Wagner, R. 1967. *The Curse of Souw*. Chicago.

Williams, F. E. 1941. 'Group sentiment and primitive justice', *American Anthropologist*, vol. 43.

Religion and Magic

Peter Lawrence

Religion is important in all Papua New Guinea societies. Allowing for regional variations, virtually all serious events are seen as in some way connected with it. Nevertheless it is difficult to define. The people themselves have no general term for it, and it cannot be regarded, as it is in the Western world, as a separate culture entity, something pertaining to a special supernatural or transcendental realm within the cosmos. Its explanatory mythology or scripture is not different or set apart from other forms of knowledge, nor is its ritual reserved for and performed on specified individual occasions. It is not something removed from the ordinary world of secular human affairs: it is best examined as one aspect of the total cosmic order that the people believe to exist.

This order has two parts: the empirical and the non-empirical. The empirical part consists of the natural environment, its economic resources (including animals), and its human inhabitants. The non-empirical part includes spirit-beings, impersonal occult forces, and sometimes totems. The total cosmic order can be examined from three analytically separate yet functionally interdependent points of view: men in relation to the environment and its resources, or the economic system; men in relation to other men, or the socio-political system; and men in relation to spirit-beings, occult forces and totems, or religion. Thus religion is men's putative relationships with beings and forces in the non-empirical part of the cosmos. We can look at it initially in two ways: first, as a set of human beliefs about the nature of spirit-beings, occult forces and—where they are acknowledged—totems, all generally contained in explanatory myths and legends which are regarded as the repositories of un-questionable truth; second, as a system of ritual techniques which men use in the attempt to communicate with these beings and forces to their own advantage.

It should be stressed at once that this definition incorporates magic within the general framework of religion and does not try to separate them. None of the three classic distinctions between the two—propounded by Tylor, Frazer, Malinowski and Durkheim—can be consistently substantiated by the evidence available.

For Tylor and Frazer, religion was essentially man's belief in spirit-beings who were superior to himself, whom he endeavoured to appease by means of ritual, and to whom he thereby accorded freedom of action. Spirit-beings could help or harm mankind as they saw fit. Pure magic was man's belief that he himself, without the aid of spirit-beings, could control impersonal occult forces by using specialized ritual techniques. This distinction is untenable for two reasons. In the first place, many people, such as the Dobu Islanders and the inhabitants of the southern Madang District, perform ritual with the clear intention not of appeasing spirit-beings but of ensuring that these will automatically do as man desires. In the second place, ritual techniques which, according to Tylor's and Frazer's definitions appear to be pure magic, are often, in fact, believed to have been given to mankind by spirit-beings. Any classification that adhered scrupulously to these definitions would be thrown into disorder by the continual appearance of aberrant hybrid forms.

For Malinowski, who based his approach on his field work in the Trobriand Islands, the distinction was to be found in the goals sought by those engaged in any ritual activity. Thus a religious rite was an end in itself and had no other immediately obvious objective. The aim of magic, however, was 'always clear, straightforward, and definite'. Magic was pragmatically oriented: it was directed towards such things as the production of crops, raising pigs, hunting, fishing, trading and warfare. This view would make it virtually impossible to define any aspect of Papua New Guinea life as religious, for nearly every myth and ritual act has some specific practical purpose in view.

Durkheim tried to distinguish between religion and magic on the basis of the people holding particular beliefs and performing particular rites. For him, religion was social and collective: its beliefs symbolized and its rituals reinforced the social order. Magic was individual and isolative: it was based on a purely personal relationship between the practitioner and his followers and, unlike religion, had no congregation or 'church'. This position also is untenable in Papua New Guinea. It would be difficult to distinguish between the two categories on the basis of the number of people associated with any belief or ritual. First, allowing for some degree of group and individual monopoly of myth and ritual, virtually all members of a society subscribe to all its beliefs. Second, all these beliefs tend to rely on a common set of intellectual assumptions. Third, the number of persons engaged in any ritual activity is determined by how many are necessary to carry it out efficiently. This varies with the situation. A large garden demands a large team of experts for planting ritual. For a small garden, one expert is enough.

A more flexible approach is that of Goode who sees religion and magic as the two ideal poles of a continuum, to either of which actual beliefs and practices only approximate. Yet even this has doubtful heuristic value because it is still based on categories which bear little resemblance to reality and are not recognized by the New Guineans themselves. Religion and magic, as cultural isolates, are Western concepts and must not be regarded as universal. New Guineans have special words for such things as myths, totems, deities or culture heroes, the dead, various forms of ritual, and sorcery. Yet, as has been remarked, they have no collective terms for religion; nor do they have terms separating religion from magic.

The definition of religion offered at the outset is an attempt to avoid using preconceived ideas from an alien culture and to examine the facts through the eyes of the people themselves, taking into account only their own experiences and the forces that have shaped their socio-cultural order. Nevertheless it incorporates and endorses many important views of the scholars mentioned. Like Goode's approach it is sufficiently flexible to allow for a variety of forms. From Tylor and Frazer it adopts a cognitive or intellectualist approach and sees religion as part of a people's mental life, emphasizing their understanding of the world around them. With Malinowski it stresses the role of religion in the economic system. From Durkheim it takes a social approach, seeing religion as part of the social process or stressing its relation to the social order. Again, with Malinowski and Durkheim it sees religion also as an index of people's anxiety about different aspects of their total environment —geographic, economic and socio-political. Where an activity or institution is strongly validated by myth and buttressed by ritual, it is obviously of great general concern. Where no myth or ritual is associated with it, the people ignore it or take it for granted.

For a clearer understanding of this integrated approach it is essential to describe at once the main characteristics of some of the terms already used: spirit-being, totem, ritual, occult forces, magic, sorcery and ritual experts.

Spirit-beings fall into three categories. First, there are autonomous spirit-beings such as culture heroes, gods and goddesses who, in most cases, are believed to have existed virtually from the time of the creation or from an early period and to be the primary operative forces in the cosmos. Associated with gods and goddesses, and included in the broad class of deities, are demigods. Culture heroes are only creative. They are said to have established the cosmic order—or significant parts of it—but thereafter to have lost interest and to have disappeared to a land across the sea or a sky world. They are enshrined in myth but have no importance in ritual. Some gods and goddesses are both creative and regulative. They are thought to be responsible for the creation of the whole or vital parts of the cosmic order, still to be in close contact with human society, and still to influence its concerns. Other gods and goddesses are purely regulative. They are given no creative role but are important in the direction of human affairs. Demigods were originally ordinary human beings to whom gods, goddesses, or even culture heroes delegated limited creative and regulative powers—as in the creation of crops and artefacts. Like gods and goddesses they are important in the ritual associated with the items of culture they are thought to have invented. Second, in some societies there are autonomous spirit-beings who have no creative or regulative functions: tricksters, demons, pucks and quasi-human imps, all of whom may steal human children or cause annoyance, harm or even death. Third, there are the dead, who can be subdivided into the recent dead— ghosts or spirits of the dead; and the remote dead—ancestors, ancestral spirits or ancestral ghosts. Both classes of the dead are regarded as distinct from the two categories of autonomous spirit-beings described. Even demigods do not become spirits of the dead before turning into deities.

Totems cannot be categorized as spirit-beings in that they have an actual as against a putative existence. They are usually animals, birds, plants, objects, or natural phenomena with special qualities and special relationships to human beings. This may be expressed in either of two ways. Totems may be putative ancestors or ancestresses of patrilineal or matrilineal descent groups: clans, phratries or moieties. On the other hand, they may be merely heraldic badges or emblems which these descent groups adopt because of an assumed association, but with which they do not claim any genealogical connection.

Ritual, as noted, is any means taken to communicate with or manipulate spirit-beings and occult forces. Often it must be supported by the observance of taboos on sexual intercourse, eating, drinking and washing on the part of those performing it. Without these taboos, ritual may be deemed useless. No ritual as such is performed for totems, but they are protected by strong taboos:

their putative descendants or followers must not harm, destroy, kill or eat them.

The most important types of ritual are those connected with spirit-beings and occult forces. In the case of most spirit-beings (gods, goddesses, demigods and the dead, although not, of course, culture heroes) ritual is regarded as a substitute for the face-to-face dealings that characterize all associations between human beings. It may emphasize or combine any of three approaches: propitiation by means of prayers and sacrifices (offerings of cooked food, areca nut, tobacco and even pigs); bargaining with offerings; or to creation by invocation, spell and offerings of reciprocal relationships modelled on those in human society, in which spirit-beings should automatically confer material benefits on men. The last has often been called the attempt to coerce.

Occult forces are impersonal and, initially at least, fall within the province of sympathetic magic. This takes the two classic forms described by Frazer: homoeopathic (imitative) magic and contagious magic. Homoeopathic magic assumes that like creates like: that where two objects are superficially similar, any action taken on one of them will affect the other in the same way. Contagious magic assumes that the part always remains in sympathetic contact with the whole, or that where two objects have been in close contact they will remain in sympathetic contact even when separated. Hence, any action taken on either the part or one of the two separated objects will have identical effects on the whole or the other object. Both forms of sympathetic magic may be thought to derive their power purely from the ritual itself or, as is probably more common, from the deities or culture heroes who invented the techniques and gave them to mankind. In the latter case, they are no longer pure sympathetic magic.

Many forms of sorcery have been recorded. Except for one type, which relies largely on physical techniques, the general aim is to perform ritual to harm or kill human beings. The most common form, known as *poisin* in Pidgin English, is an example of contagious magic. The sorcerer steals from his victim a cigarette butt, a piece of clothing, some excreta, a lock of hair, or nail parings— anything that has been in close contact with or is part of him, and is thought to be impregnated with his soul-stuff. The sorcerer then places the stolen object in a bamboo container. Breathing spells, he burns it or heats it over a fire, depending on whether he intends to cause death or illness—that is, to destroy or merely injure his victim's life force. The spells may be simple expressions of wish-fulfilment ('I destroy the soul of . . .') or invocations to the deity thought to have invented this type of sorcery. Other forms of sorcery are called *sangguma* in Pidgin English. A widespread technique is for the practitioner to turn invisible or take animal form, invoke the name of the creator deity, and then project missiles —arrowheads, stones, or bundles of bones and sticks—into his victim's body. Yet another technique is for the sorcerer to confront and bemuse his victim, then 'remove' his head or entrails, which he replaces with vegetable material, and finally send him home to die. There is, in addition, the form of *sangguma* which is essentially physical murder, although elements of ritual may be associated with it. The sorcerer renders his victim insensible and then inserts into strategic parts of his body—under the tongue and between important joints—slivers of bamboo (or nowadays pieces of wire), thereby causing dumbness and paralysis. The victim staggers home to die. Cures for *poisin* and *sangguma* are thought to be achieved by various types of counter-sorcery, such as removal of missiles from the body.

There are also types of sorcery for the theft of property. A man who can turn invisible or take animal form can steal as well as kill. There is also a kind of sorcery, as on Dobu Island and in the Bagasin area, whereby deities presiding over staple crops such as yam or taro can be induced to make them travel from one garden to another. The Garia of the Bagasin area perform ritual at the end of the agricultural year to bind gardens and prevent this sort of eventuality.

Beliefs in witchcraft are not widespread and are found mainly in parts of the central Highlands and the Massim area. These are not as elaborate as in other parts of the world, such as Africa. Among the Huli in the Southern Highlands, female witches are said to cause death. Among the Siane in the Eastern Highlands, males are said to practise witchcraft by inhaling and exhaling tobacco smoke and simultaneously pronouncing formulae which cause witchcraft-substance to attack other people's souls. The Kyaka of the Western Highlands have a mild form of witchcraft, and the practice is known also among the neighbouring Kuma.

Love philtres, which are closely associated with sorcery and witchcraft, have many forms. The most common is for a man to roll a cigarette, mixing one of his own pubic hairs with the tobacco. He gives it to the woman he intends to seduce. It is believed that after she has smoked it she will dream that she has slept with him —an event that should soon occur in reality. In some cases the cigarette may be thought to be effective on its own; in others it is impregnated with sympathetic spells; and in others a creator deity is invoked.

In the practice of ritual, adult males play the predominant role. They either have a complete monopoly, performing ritual themselves to the absolute exclusion of women, or take the lead and relegate women to a secondary position. This varies throughout the country. In one case, however, women are said to have a monopoly to the complete exclusion of men—in abortion techniques which, although they appear to have a pragmatic base, are regarded as a form of ritual. They are women's most closely guarded secret and are said to be revealed to a girl at marriage. Men know little about them.

Among males, ritual is generally in the hands of experts or specialists, although in the majority of societies this does not denote the existence of definite offices such as priesthoods. In some cases, as on Wogeo Island and among the Trobriand Islanders, ritual is regarded as an essential if not exclusive possession of hereditary headmen or chiefs. Yet in most indigenous societies, strongly egalitarian as they are, leadership is democratic. Aspiring men force their way competitively to the surface of affairs. Their roles tend to be generalized: they should be expert in many fields—war, agriculture, hunting, dancing, oratory, and organizing feast exchanges or trading expeditions—rather than just one. Yet it is not enough to master only the secular aspects of these activities. Leaders must also know and use the ritual secrets that guarantee success.

Religion as an operative system

Religion in Papua New Guinea is best seen as a dynamic or functioning process as is illustrated by a number of examples chosen from all over the country, especially from the two major geographical areas: the central Highlands of the mainland, and the seaboard—the mainland coast and the islands to the east. To understand how religion operates within the cosmic order, it must be examined from two points of view. First, it can explain and validate the origin and existence of the cosmic order, the physical environment, the economic system, and the socio-political system, by recounting in a series of myths the creative activities of a number of spirit-beings and totems. Thus, completely fictitious and historically worthless though they may be, myths in Papua New Guinea have the same intellectual importance as the Scriptures had in mediaeval Europe. They differ from legends, which combine imagination with a certain amount of fact and are, thus, partly historical accounts. Second, religion gives man the assurance that he can control, regulate or manipulate the cosmic order by means of ritual. He is master of his own destiny. Like myths in the intellectual field, ritual is regarded, in the field of action, as an expression of absolute unquestioned power and truth. It is the guarantee of success in all important economic, social and political undertakings. Hence, the extent to which religion is used in either of these two ways—as a form of explanation and as a form of control —indicates those aspects of the cosmic order about which a people feels the greatest anxiety. These general principles are now examined in the light of ethnographic examples from the central Highlands and the seaboard in the following contexts: the realm of spirit-beings and occult forces; religion and the physical environment; religion, economics and society; religion, social values and knowledge.

THE REALM OF SPIRIT-BEINGS AND OCCULT FORCES

Papua New Guinea religions have two areas of broad similarity. The first, which is correlated with the view already expressed that religion must be examined as one aspect of the total conceived cosmic order, is that the realm of the non-empirical is always closely associated with, in many cases part of, the ordinary physical world. It is supernatural in only the most limited sense, if at all, and transcendental in no sense whatever. The various classes of spirit-beings described, which are its most important representatives, are said almost invariably to reside on the earth, generally in their own sanctuaries near human settlements. They are superhuman in that they can do things beyond ordinary human capabilities, such as travelling huge distances in a moment and, in the case of deities, performing creative miracles. Yet, emotionally and often physically they have the same nature as ordinary men. Although they can appear as a variety of animals, birds and insects, they normally assume human corporeal form. Even when they are thought to live away from the earth, as in the case of Mae Enga sky people, or to have no fixed abode, as in the case of the Ngaing creator god Parambik, they are hardly supernatural or transcendental. Either their world is a physical replica of the earth or they are assumed to dwell somewhere on the earth. Moreover, both types of totem, and the impersonal non-spiritual occult forces harnessed by sympathetic magic, are conceived as terrestrial: they belong to the natural environment and no other realm.

The second common feature is that, allowing for exceptions noted below, there is a wide similarity of belief in spirit-beings. Gods, goddesses, demigods and culture heroes are generally envisaged as the same kinds of beings wherever they are recognized. The same applies to demons, pucks, tricksters, totems and the dead. Again, virtually all groups in the country acknowledge the power of sorcery and of love philtres, and have some forms of sympathetic magic either as an independent part of their ritual or as a part of the ritual given them by their deities or culture heroes. When they are away from home, people have little difficulty in recognizing the broad nature of spirit-beings and occult forces described by members of other societies.

Nevertheless, there is considerable geographically random variation in the degree to which the various types of spirit-beings described are stressed as important, in certain ideas about the nature of the dead, and in the recognition of totemism. Although future research may force us to revise our position, at present the rough distinction between the central Highlands and the seaboard will be useful.

In the Highlands, beliefs in autonomous creative and regulative spirit-beings are unevenly emphasized. To the south and west, the Huli and Kuma attach considerable importance to their deities, whereas the Melpa and various Enga groups, while acknowledging such beings, do not. Again, the Mae Enga and Kyaka, who are close neighbours and speak related dialects of Enga, both recognize numerous sky people. Yet the Mae attribute to them a distinct creative role while the Kyaka are little interested in them. Indeed, the Kyaka have only one important deity, a goddess whom they imported from the Melpa and to whom they attribute only regulative functions. In the Eastern Highlands, the Kainantu peoples, Fore, Usurufa, Jate and Kamano, have two dominant creative deities, Morofonu and Jugumishanta. The Siane recognize only one, whose primary duty is guardianship of the dead; and the Chimbu and Gahuku-Gama, who are close neighbours of the Kainantu peoples and the Siane, acknowledge only vaguely or expressly deny the existence of autonomous creative and regulative spirit-beings.

In the lowlands, however, what may be called the theistic principle is widely established. There are, indeed, a few peoples who appear to acknowledge no major autonomous creative or regulative spirit-beings, for whom the principal spirit-beings recognized are the dead, and whose geographical distribution is again inexplicably random: the Orokaiva of the Northern District; the Ngarawapum inland from Lae; the Manus of the Admiralty

Islands; and the people of Lesu in northern New Ireland. Otherwise, most seaboard societies, including the immediate neighbours of the groups just mentioned, have creative deities or culture heroes of some kind. The main differences are in the number of such beings recognized. The Ngaing and Garia have pantheons with many deities. Yet their relatively close neighbours, the coastal peoples of Madang and Astrolabe Bay, acknowledge only two great creative spirit-beings, Kilibob and Manup, who delegated power over various artefacts and foodstuffs to minor gods and demigods, and who also gave sympathetic magic to the people. Further south from Madang, the Sengam and Som, who acknowledge Kilibob and Manup, have also many gods of their own of equal status as well as several demigods. Other coastal peoples are content with few deities or culture heroes. Thus the Nakanai recognize about three, of whom only one is in any way significant.

Beliefs about the dead are relatively consistent throughout the country, although it is possible to draw one basic distinction between Highlands and seaboard peoples. Most Highlanders appear to make a sharp division between the recent and remote dead, attributing different importance and attitudes to each. Seaboard peoples, however, normally ignore remote ancestral spirits and concentrate on those of the recent dead. The Garia, for instance, believe that ghosts become flying foxes, which may be killed and eaten with impunity, after about three generations. Yet the neatness of this cultural division between seaboard and Highlands is partially obscured in another respect. Beliefs which could be interpreted as a form of reincarnation are reported irregularly from both the Highlands and the seaboard, among such widely scattered groups as the Siane, Kyaka, Iatmül, and Trobriand Islanders. Among the Siane the spirit of a living person, the *oinya,* becomes his *korova* after death. Later, the individual *korova* becomes part of an undifferentiated pool of ancestral spirits, elements of which can ultimately enter another human body and become its *oinya.* In other societies the belief is unknown. Most important, the concept of reincarnation might be regarded as a means of transmitting status and distinctions of rank from one generation to the next. Reincarnation and rank are found together in the Trobriand Islands, but the other societies mentioned have no marked systems of social stratification. Moreover, stratified societies such as the Manam and Wogeo have no beliefs in reincarnation.

Totemism is not reported from the central Highlands, and its distribution on the seaboard is irregular. Many groups in the latter area have no totemic beliefs, and there are marked differences between those that do. In the Bismarck Archipelago, for example, the Nakanai and the Lesu both have matrilineal totemic emblems. But the Nakanai associate them with matri-clans, and the Lesu with matri-moieties. Again, the Ngaing, a people with a form of double unilineal descent, acknowledge totemic ancestresses for their matri-clans but no totems of any kind for their patri-clans. Their immediate neighbours, the Sengam and Som, as well as the peoples of Astrolabe Bay such as the Yam (whose social structure is similar to that of the Ngaing although it emphasizes only patrilineal descent) have patri-clan totemic emblems but not ancestors. The Orokaiva have patri-clan totemic emblems, while their island neighbours of Milne Bay have matrilineal totemic ancestresses. In the Sepik Districts, the Arapesh have totemic emblems for their patri-moieties but not their patri-clans. Of their neighbours, the Abelam have patri-clan totemic emblems, and the Iatmül patri-clan totemic ancestors.

RELIGION AND THE PHYSICAL ENVIRONMENT

No Papua New Guinea society pays great attention in religion to the physical environment. Most treat it as something that can be taken for granted. It is no cause for anxiety except on the relatively rare occasions when it is threatened by disasters such as volcanic eruptions. Hence there are no elaborate myths to explain its origin or, except at times of crisis, rituals to ensure its continuance. Those peoples who have no interest or beliefs in creative spirit-beings—the Kyaka, Chimbu, Gahuku-Gama, Orokaiva, Manus and Lesu—assume, of course, that the earth always existed. But this is true also of other groups which acknowledge creative spirit-beings: the Huli, Mae Enga and Siane in the Highlands, and the Busama, Arapesh and Trobriand Islanders on the seaboard. The Wogeo say that their island always existed but that their culture heroes created all other places in Papua New Guinea. Other groups, such as the Ngaing and Garia, attribute the origin of the earth to creator gods but dismiss the matter in one or two sentences. In yet other cases—for example, the Kainantu and Astrolabe Bay peoples—contradictory beliefs may be held by members of the same society, some asserting that the earth always existed and others that gods or culture heroes brought it into being. Around Astrolabe Bay some people believe that the earth was from the beginning, although the great creative spirit-beings Anut (Dodo), Kilibob and Manup subsequently added certain natural phenomena. Others insist that these spirit-beings brought the whole earth into existence. Apart from occasional myths for the sun, moon, and a few of the major constellations (such as the Pleiades) in some societies, there is even less interest in the heavenly bodies. The major exceptions in this context are seafaring peoples such as the Trobriand Islanders.

RELIGION, ECONOMICS AND SOCIETY

Religion is especially important in the realm of economic and certain socio-political activities. The whole economic system and some socio-political relationships are always sources of anxiety and cannot be taken for granted. They can easily become unstable or collapse, and hence they must be validated by mythology and reinforced by ritual.

In the field of mythological explanation, the country's religions fall into three categories: those that attribute the origin of the economic and socio-political systems to only one or two creator deities or culture heroes; those that attribute them to a large number; and those that entirely or almost entirely disregard the problem. The Kainantu, Nakanai, Trans-Fly, Trobriand Island and Astrolabe Bay peoples belong to the first category. These groups have, generally speaking, mythologies which explain their economic and socio-political structures as total systems. Thus the inhabitants of Astrolabe Bay have the famous Kilibob-Manup myth cycle which describes how the two brothers were born on Karkar Island (or, in some versions, near Madang), quarrelled, and had to leave. Before they departed, they invented men, canoes, woodcarving, food plants, bows and arrows, adzes, rain and important dances. They invented ritual for each of these cultural items and also sorcery. They then sailed away, one to the north and the other to the south, to Madang and the Rai Coast to its east. The brother who journeyed south put in at each of the many village sites, leaving behind men to whom he gave the power of speech, food plants, artefacts and ritual. Thereby he was responsible for the different socio-cultural systems in the area, for these men became the ancestors of the various linguistic, political and descent groups. Apart from establishing subsistence agriculture, he set up one of the major economic institutions in the region: he taught the inhabitants of Yabob and Bilbil Islands to become master potters, and so brought into being the trade in clay pots and wooden bowls between Madang and the Rai Coast. To the second category belong the following peoples: the Huli, Mae Enga, Ngaing and Bagasin-area peoples, and the Arapesh and Wogeo Islanders. In contrast to the peoples in the first category, these groups, with the exception of the Mae Enga, do not attempt to explain their economic and socio-political systems *in toto*. They are content to emphasize in their mythology only single aspects that they regard as vitally important: food plants and artefacts that are a source of worry; and key points in the social structure where conflict and instability can arise, such as land tenure, feast exchanges, and initiation. Each of these institutions may be validated in a separate myth about a separate creator deity. The Siane, Chimbu, Gahuku-Gama, Kyaka, Orokaiva, Tangu, Lesu and Manus belong to the third category. It is important to note that the possession of an elaborate mythology does not mean that a society must acknowledge many deities or culture heroes. It is true that some groups with many deities or culture heroes have many myths. Yet other societies, such as the Kainantu and Astrolabe Bay peoples, who each recognize only two or three real creative spirit-beings, have—as in the Kilibob-Manup cycle—most complex mythologies.

In the sphere of ritual, the general economic and socio-political needs that religion must satisfy are the fertility of crops and animals, success in the manufacture and use of artefacts, and the well-being of society. The ritual for economic undertakings is probably more elaborate than that for socio-political purposes, for risk and failure in this field cause the greater worry. There are three main types of ritual: ritual performed for creative or regulative spirit-beings, which may involve placation, bargaining, or what we have called coercion; sympathetic magic; and ritual in honour of the dead.

Techniques in the first two categories are not uniform throughout the country and are often combined. Thus, in the Highlands, the Huli and Kuma use ritual with the intention partly of placating and partly of bargaining with their deities. The Huli also employ sympathetic magic. The Kainantu peoples invoke the two great deities, Jugumishanta and Morofonu. On the seaboard, the Nakanai try to placate their major god but also use much sympathetic magic, while the peoples of the Rai Coast, Astrolabe Bay, and the Bagasin area invoke their deities in the expectation of an automatic and immediate response. Their ritual formulae are based on the secret names of gods and goddesses, but also incorporate some sympathetic magic which in most cases they assert was taught them by their deities. The Arapesh, however, use only sympathetic magic, which they believe to be powerful in its own right. Those groups that do not acknowledge deities rely on sympathetic magic. These types of ritual are used variously for promoting the growth of crops, fecundity of pigs, success in the manufacture of slit-gongs and other major artefacts, lethal qualities in bows and arrows, good weather at sea for fishing and trading voyages, and the satisfactory completion of trade deals. In trading, it is important to ensure that partners act honourably and have the requisite goods in ample supply. One example of such ritual is that used in Ngaing agriculture. The ritual expert makes a shrine of stones in the garden and performs, first, a purely magical act, rubbing a *Canarium* almond on the shrine and digging sticks so that its flavour will permeate the crops. He then plants shoots of the crops, which the agricultural goddess is said to have given mankind, in and around the shrine. Simultaneously he silently breathes a spell based on the secret name of the goddess, and then audibly invokes the spirits of his forbears who used to work on the land and are its true guardians. Occasionally food offerings are left for the goddess and the dead.

The third type of ritual, in honour of the dead, is performed by all peoples, although technical details differ throughout the country. Broadly speaking, it consists of mourning at funerals, the offering of food, areca nut and tobacco, and the performance of the ceremonies of the male cult—dances and exchanges of pigs, vegetables and valuables—the secrets of which are reserved for initiated men. The aims of the rituals are to ensure that the dead will protect crops from wild pig and landslides, ensure the fertility of domesticated animals, provide hunters with plenty of game, bring their descendants gifts and messages about the future, and ward off enemy missiles in time of war. Most important are the ceremonies of the male cult, in which the spirits are invited to return to the villages. These are described in greater detail below. This category of ritual is especially important in those societies which do not acknowledge deities as the originators and guarantors of their economic systems.

There are two major differences between Highlands and seaboard attitudes to and ritual for the dead. First, as has been mentioned, both groups of peoples regard the remote and recent dead as having different degrees of importance for the living. Highlanders tend to expect economic benefits from the spirits of the remote rather than the recent dead. They regard spirits of the recent dead as malevolent and primarily interested in punishing the transgressions of their descendants. Seaboard peoples—with some exceptions, such as the Nakanai who are never quite certain in the matter—generally take a reverse view. They tend to regard the spirits of the recent dead as potentially well-disposed towards their living descendants, although not descendants of their former enemies, provided that the requisite honour is accorded them. They tend to dismiss the remote dead as unimportant or, as in the case of the Garia, non-existent. Second, there are differences in the character of ritual for the dead. These appear to correspond with differences in human social relationships in the two areas, for the dead are seen as an extension of human social structure. In the Highlands, ritual emphasizes bargaining and bribery—the social techniques for manipulating aggressive egalitarian rivals. On the seaboard, the prevailing view is that, just as the rule of reciprocity should operate in dealings between human beings and between human beings and deities, so the fulfilment of ritual obligations to the dead should meet with an immediate and automatic response. Highlands ritual assumes that the dead have freedom of choice in helping mankind, whereas seaboard ritual tends to leave them no option but to do so.

Religion can ensure the welfare of society in two ways. First, ritual in the field of action, like myth in the field of validation, buttresses key groups and social relationships likely to become unstable, and is intended to promote the fertility of human beings. Second, in some societies—although by no means all—religion may be regarded as the source of social morality. In addition, the place of sorcery in the social order must be taken into consideration.

From the point of view of reinforcing social groups and relationships and promoting human fertility, deities are relatively unimportant. Among some peoples, culture heroes and deities and their associated ritual symbolize and are believed to maintain specific socio-political groups, as in the case of ritual designed to ensure that war gods bring their followers success in battle. Occasionally, ritual may be performed to an important god when an epidemic strikes. Generally speaking, however, it is ceremonies honouring the dead—especially those of the male cult which solemnize birth, initiation, marriage and death—that are principally concerned with the well-being of society. Apart from the economic benefits mentioned, the aim of the ceremonies is that the dead should give strength to the novices experiencing them for the first time, and guarantee the health of children and the fecundity of women. Their latent function is probably more important. They operate in the same way as trade ritual, which consolidates trading groups and personal ties between individual trade partners. That is, they reinforce clans or equivalent groups by mobilizing them to produce the wealth to be handed over in the feast exchanges that are an intrinsic part of the ceremonies. They also strengthen the affinal and kinship bonds that are the axes of the exchanges. They reflect the different social roles that men and women are expected to play.

The Ngaing will serve as an example. Male cult ceremonies and feast exchanges are held on the occasions of birth, initiation, marriage and death. They begin when each of the participating patri-clans has assembled the pigs, food and valuables it intends to give away in the exchange. Men of each patri-clan go to their sacred pools where they wash and decorate their gourd trumpets which are used in the ensuing musical festival. They invoke the gods presiding over the ceremony and the sacred pools to send the spirits of the dead back with them to the village. As soon as it is dark and they cannot be seen by the women and children, they return home, leading the spirits by playing patri-clan melodies on their trumpets. When the party reaches the village, both men and women welcome the spirits with a dance which lasts until dawn. Thereafter the men kill the pigs, and both men and women cook them with the other food. When the exchange has taken place and everyone has eaten, the men honour the dead by playing music on the trumpets and the slit-gongs in the cult house. They continue with this every night from dusk till dawn for about three months. Finally, they escort the spirits out of the cult house, in which they are believed to have resided during this time, back to their sanctuaries.

As indicated, women are debarred from the inner secrets of these ceremonies, especially the ritual washing of the trumpets and the festivities in the cult house. Yet they are never wholly excluded: there is social difference yet interdependence between the sexes, for women must take part in the dance to welcome the spirits and in the work of the feast exchange. Other societies have special rites which point to the indispensable role that women play in society. Nevertheless, throughout the country all ceremonies honouring the dead stress male dominance, although, as always, there is variation. In the Eastern Highlands, male-female antagonism is extreme and is reflected by severe initiatory ordeals for men which underline the values of male superiority—penis-bleeding, nose-bleeding and cane-swallowing. Nubile women have to undergo similar ordeals. In the Western Highlands, sex antagonism is not so intense and women have a more secure social position. The techniques of initiation and education are less traumatic and repressive. Harsh and obligatory rites give way to voluntary associations, such as a bachelors' cult which imposes less severe taboos and practices on its members. On the seaboard, attitudes towards sex range from extreme puritanism to extreme laxity, with corresponding differences in the relationships between men and women. In some areas, such as the Madang hinterland and parts of the Sepik area, women are regarded as vastly inferior to men and as physically and ritually dangerous. In other areas, such as the Rai Coast and the Trobriand Islands, women enjoy some degree of equality with men and have a definite, if less prominent, role in ritual life.

Initiatory ceremonies on the seaboard are sometimes harsh but are never as violent as those of the Eastern Highlands. They involve segregation from women, taboos on food and water, and in many places some form of blood-letting, such as scarification of the body which is practised in the Sepik area, and penis-bleeding which is common around the mainland coast. A special feature of initiation in the Sepik area is that the novices are 'swallowed' and 'regurgitated' by a deity who presides over the ceremonies. As in the Eastern Highlands, in some places girls have to undergo comparable rites at puberty. The Ngaing may be quoted once more as an example of initiatory procedures. First, the novices' fathers and mothers' brothers—who act as the chief initiators—bring up their respective patri-clan spirits to the cult house in the way already described. Second, the boys—who now have to observe taboos on eating meat, drinking water and washing—are shown the sacred instruments, such as the gourd trumpets, and given a basic introduction to mythology and ritual secrets. Third, they are segregated for about a month and are taught to play the sacred instruments and given a symbolic beating by their mothers' brothers. In one Ngaing village only, as among the neighbouring Sengam, Som and Gira whose initiatory rites are similar, the mothers' brothers perform the operation of penile supra-incision on the novices. At last, dressed in fine ornaments, the boys are brought home and presented to the women. As they have been under the special protection of the dead during the ceremony, they should thereafter grow up healthy and attract wives.

In the context of morality, religion helps to stabilize some, although by no means all, societies by specifying and upholding the codes of behaviour on which they depend. The pattern is clearest in the central Highlands, where some groups, such as the Kainantu peoples, have a special mythology for inculcating such norms. Other groups, such as the Huli, have a deity who is the guardian of ethics. The pattern is implied also by the predominant attitude that deities should be propitiated and that the dead will respond to ritual only if the laws of clanship and kinship are scrupulously observed. On the seaboard, the issue is less obvious. Some peoples, such as the Manus and the Nakanai, believe that their spirit-beings have the greatest concern for human morality. Thus the Manus believe that each family has a tutelary ghost (Sir Ghost), who is symbolized by the skull of a recently deceased forbear kept in the rafters of the house. The ghost is said to protect the family's interests, especially in the all-important activity of trade, but only if its members observe a most stringent moral code. If they break the rules the ghost withdraws his support at once. In other societies, ghosts are said to punish a variety of offences: trespass, adultery, murder, and marriage between close kin. Among many peoples, however, there is no recognized connection between religion and morality: good conduct is regarded as being virtually human in origin and is enforced by secular sanctions alone.

The final way in which religion is linked with the social order is through sorcery, in the fields of both explanation and action. Sorcery explains the occurrence of deaths that would be otherwise incomprehensible—those of young people which are not obviously attributable to natural causes—and so assures man that for bad as well as good he is in command of every aspect of his life. It helps to consolidate socio-political groups and friendly relationships between individuals, and to delineate and maintain traditional cleavages, which are also part of the socio-political system. Virtually all the societies acknowledge the power of sorcery, but the importance attached to it varies throughout the country. Some have marked sorcery complexes, while others are not particularly interested. Even close neighbours speaking related dialects, such as the several Enga groups, are divided in this way. Again, the incidence of sorcery is not in inverse proportion to the degree to which religion seems to uphold the moral code, nor can it be attributed to lack of coherence and explanation in religious doctrine. Sorcery is often found among peoples who have elaborate religious beliefs with detailed ethical content. As was noted at the outset, it has many forms, both intricate and straightforward. Provided there is a felt need, it can be incorporated in any religious system and tailored to suit its intellectual expression. We must look for its source, therefore, in the socio-political context.

Sorcery functions in the socio-political system as a strain-gauge and safety valve. It expresses and helps to relieve tensions in intergroup and interpersonal relationships. Its operation can be demonstrated in two general types of society: those with fluid, and those with stable, local organizations. In the first type—peoples such as the Dobu Islanders and the Garia—sorcery accusations are a convenient means of easing strained relations between individuals who lack the security of membership in solidary groups and are not bound to each other by personal ties. On Dobu Island, for example, every settlement contains a number of mutually unrelated persons as the result of a bilocal residential pattern. This engenders suspicion and hostility which must find an outlet. Hence, accusations of sorcery are common. In the second type of society, local organization is based, generally speaking, on permanently settled descent groups or congeries of descent groups which, in the absence of wars for territorial or other forms of economic aggrandizement, must preserve their unity and identity by means of rivalry. This rivalry is expressed partly through feast exchanges but also, very largely, through sorcery accusations, which act both as an important medium for expressing enmity and as an excuse for initiating warfare. The latter is, of course, ultimately the most effective means of relieving feelings of aggression. Sorcery is often seen—as is football in the modern situation—as a substitute for warfare, and there is evidence from two places at least (the Bagasin area and Kainantu, which represent the first and second types of society respectively) that the rate of sorcery accusation has risen since the Australian Administration banned blood feud and warfare. It is the only effective avenue left to the people for relieving tension. Yet this argument does not explain every situation. There are some societies, such as the Mae Enga and Ngaing, which were most warlike in the past yet never had great interest in sorcery and, what is most significant, have not so far developed such an interest as a result of pacification. At the moment, there is no satisfactory explanation of these cases.

RELIGION, SOCIAL VALUES AND KNOWLEDGE

The relationship between religion and social values has been stated implicitly throughout and needs only a brief reiteration here in the contexts of the natural environment, the economic system, and the socio-political structure. That between religion and knowledge needs greater analysis.

An examination of social values is tantamount to an examination of the degree of anxiety which a people feels about certain aspects of the cosmic order, and which it expresses through mythological and ritual elaboration. As was seen, the emphasis throughout the country is uneven. Most peoples appear to pay minimal attention to the natural environment, and even to the economic and socio-political structures as total systems. Even those groups that attribute the origin of the whole cosmic order to the actions of only one or two deities or culture heroes do not stress them in myth and ritual as complete entities. They accept them as they are and, as they do not know of any world order other than their own, regard them as immutable and stable. Generally speaking, it is only when people recognize parts of the cosmic order as vital for the continuance of life and likely to go wrong, thereby weakening the total system, that they become concerned. These things are then emphasized in myth and ritual: star constellations by seafarers; individual geographical features such as mountains and rivers that are given special meanings; agriculture, manufacture of artefacts; pig-raising; hunting, fishing; trading expeditions; the rules of land tenure; descent and local groups, affinal and kinship ties, and partnerships essential for the provision and distribution of wealth in feast exchanges and trade and for cementing relationships within the society and with other societies; and, finally, aggression, sorcery, warfare and death. Of all these probably the most stressed are economic factors, but the emphasis that each receives, even in a single society, varies according to the needs of individual situations and is rarely, if ever, constant.

To understand the relationship between religion and knowledge it is necessary to distinguish, within the people's total cognitive framework, between two categories: technical or empirical knowledge on the one hand, and sacred or revealed knowledge on the other. The first is knowledge that the people actually possess. The second is knowledge that they believe was revealed to their forbears by deities or culture heroes during the period of creation. Yet this is a distinction based essentially on Western epistemological categories. New Guineans appear to conceive the sources of their knowledge in a radically different way. Seaboard peoples certainly tend to regard both these types of knowledge as a single complex within which, far from being relegated to the background, sacred knowledge assumes a role of overwhelming importance not only as an intellectual possession but also as education for boys and a qualification for leadership. In the central Highlands, especially to the west, these attitudes, although present, appear to be less extreme; empirical knowledge receives greater emphasis.

Seaboard peoples have in fact accumulated, in relation to their environment and the resources at their disposal, a modest but sound body of technical or empirical knowledge which they use with considerable efficiency. The sea-going canoes of coastal and island peoples, the slit-gongs used by such peoples as the Ngaing to send elaborate messages over long distances, and widespread practical expertise in agriculture, hunting and fishing are ample evidence.

Europeans regard this sort of knowledge as the result of secular human endeavour. The seaboard peoples, however, tend to believe that empirical knowledge exists because it was revealed to men by deities and culture heroes. At the time of the creation, deities and culture heroes actually lived with men or appeared to them in dreams, visions or other extraordinary experiences. They showed men the items of culture they had invented and the practical skills necessary for their production or performance: how to plant crops; raise pigs; make canoes, slit-gongs, bullroarers and bows and arrows; and perform dances. Yet they also gave men something of far greater importance: the esoteric knowledge, mythology and ritual formulae essential for success in secular undertakings, the element without which these would fail.

Indeed, not only is the whole corpus of knowledge believed to be derived from deities or culture heroes but sacred knowledge is stressed as paramount. Secular techniques are described as 'knowing', but only at an elementary level—as something that anybody can assimilate through mundane experience. The hard core of knowledge is regarded as the mastery of myths and especially of ritual, such as the repetition of complex spells based on the secret names of deities or sympathetic magical formulae. This, as suggested, is the dominant theme in education and leadership.

The upbringing of male children is largely free of the formal education found in Western society. As soon as he can walk, a boy is given toilet training and instruction in basic kinship usage, property rights, and respect for the religious code. But he is given no specific teaching in economic and technical skills. He is expected to grow into this part of his culture by a process of imitation. Thus, between the ages of six and ten, boys are rarely forced to work. They are frequently indulged and rarely disciplined. Yet, perhaps out of boredom, they accompany their parents to work in the gardens or elsewhere. Here they are still left to their own devices, but it is not uncommon for them to pick up axes and bush knives and copy the work their elders are doing. They are never discouraged and often complimented. Hence, as they grow older they gradually become adept in the use of tools and basic technical skills. When they are adolescents, they have, without formal education of any kind, mastered all the essential technical knowledge in their society. Unlike their counterparts in the West, who often regard education as a waste of time because it is generally in advance of the stage of social maturity they have reached, these lads can always see the direct significance of what they are doing. Their activities are clearly related to survival.

The technical achievements of boys at this period are not regarded as important. They are not rated as 'true knowledge'. Boys acquire 'true knowledge' only during and after adolescence, when they are initiated. One of the aims of initiation is to give them special instruction. Yet virtually none of this instruction has to do with purely secular skills, most of which they have mastered already. What is emphasized is sacred or religious knowledge. The boys are introduced to the important myths of origin of the material and social culture. They learn sacred songs and, if they are old enough, the spells that harness the power of the deities. If they are too young, they are told that the spells exist and that they may learn them later on. In those societies in which it is important, they are given instruction in sorcery. The stress on religion in education is apparent also in the importance attached to the imposition of taboos. These are believed to ensure the retention and successful use of sacred knowledge far more effectively than mere human intellectual capacity. It is believed that the deities decreed that young men learning myths and ritual should observe these taboos, by refraining from contact with women of child-bearing age, from drinking water and from washing, from eating most kinds of meat and vegetables cooked in water, and by eating only sugar-cane and roasted vegetables. Should the taboos be ignored, the boys' training will be useless. They will never learn the spells or use them properly.

Again, as was stressed earlier, it is mastery of sacred rather than secular skills that is essential for leadership. The big-men of sea-board societies are essentially the men who 'know', who can direct the activities of others—those who do not 'know'—to the best possible advantage by the competent performance of ritual. Physical weakness or temporary poverty is not necessarily a handicap provided that a man has the patience to learn and the courage to accept responsibility. The greatest obstacle is failure in an under-taking because of unforeseen hazards. Thus, in any set of novices, factors of personality and chance tend to eliminate all but the stead-fast and lucky. In each generation, such men are relatively few, so that in any local group—village, village section or localized clan—there are normally no more than two or three leaders. The power of each may be limited by competition. A really energetic man whose consistent success has demonstrated his skill may lure followers away from his rivals within his own community and even in other communities.

Seaboard peoples' predilection for sacred knowledge might suggest a high degree of mysticism in their thinking. Yet this would be an interpretation purely in Western terms. The thinking of these peoples, however dominated by religion, is pragmatic. This is best understood by considering the spatial and temporal dimensions of the cosmos as the people conceive them. In spatial terms, as has already been emphasized, there is no distinction between the realms of the natural and supernatural. Gods and spirits of the dead are human in character, often corporeal in form, and reside in the ordinary physical world. Man sees himself as the focal point of two systems of relationships set out in the initial definition: between himself and other human beings, or the socio-political system; and between himself and gods and spirits, or religion.

The pragmatic content of both systems of relationships tends to be understood and expressed in roughly the same terms. A man fulfils his social obligations so as to make other persons with whom he has human relationships 'think on' him and fulfil their obligations to him. Similarly, the aim of ritual is to make deities and the dead 'think on' human beings and confer material benefits on them. But the activities of gods and spirits in helping mankind have no mystical quality. They are believed to take place on the same plane of existence and to have the same validity as those of human beings working at any joint task. Work is regarded as a compound of secular and ritual techniques, both having the same empirical reality: both derive from a common source—deities or culture heroes—and both require co-operation between inhabitants, humans and spirit-beings, of the same geographical environment.

In its temporal dimensions the cosmic order is conceived as essentially fixed and static. There is no continuing historical tradition, with a system of recording dates, in the Western sense. Time can be measured in two ways: as ecological time or cosmic time. Ecological time is the annual succession of the seasons and is reckoned by means of rough calendars used for fixing the time when feasts and ceremonies are to be held. Cosmic time represents the recognized age of the cosmos, consisting of known genealogical time plus the period of antiquity: the time of the emergence of the natural environment, human beings, and their economy, culture and society.

Yet even cosmic time has limited chronological utility. The depth of empirically recordable genealogies—the period of remembered events—in most societies is not only shallow but also kept more or less constant. With each new generation, distant forbears are forgotten. Time depth, therefore, does not increase. Moreover, the period of antiquity is, in a sense, timeless. There is no clear concept of a fixed order of creation; after the initial establishment of the natural environment (if this is mentioned in the mythology), food plants, artefacts, domesticated animals, ceremonies and even human beings, emerge at random.

Even individual myths as well as the general mythology reflect the absence of the concept of time depth. There is no tradition of a gradual advance from a rudimentary to a more elaborate way of life. Each part of the culture is generally described at the time of its invention in exactly the same form as at present. There is no idea of improvement by experimentation. Also, each myth depicts the people's culture during the period of antiquity as quite recognizably up to date and complete except for that part which the relevant god, goddess or culture hero has to introduce and explain. Thus events of antiquity are the events of today and will be the events of tomorrow as well. The relationships between men, gods and the dead within the cosmos are finally established, for all have their unalterable roles to play towards each other. The religion is utopian or chiliast in the Panglossian rather than the Marxist sense: it has achieved the best of all possible worlds and does not express the hope of achieving such a world in the future in exchange for an inferior present.

By the same token, the body of knowledge, as the people see it, is as static and finite as the cosmic order within which it is contained. It was brought into the world ready-made and ready to use. It can be augmented only by further acts of invention and revelation by old or new creative spirit-beings who inhabit the natural environment. Hence, it is hardly surprising that the epistemological system has taken this form. The religion is intellectually satisfying, for it operates within a framework that guarantees its validity. Because of the monotonous repetition of economic and social life, there is hardly any event which cannot be explained by or attributed to it. The whole visible world—the annually ripening crops, the fertility of pigs and human beings, and even death as the apparent result of sorcery—far from allowing it an aura of mysticism, proclaims that it is solidly based on empirical and verifiable fact. There is no need, in fact no room, for an independent secular human intellect.

As suggested earlier, the peoples of the central Highlands share the foregoing principles of religion with the inhabitants of the seaboard but appear to give them less emphasis. They rely on religion, of course, for the same kinds of economic and socio-political welfare, but in many important tasks they appear to regard purely secular techniques as the only valid avenue to success. This is particularly true of peoples of the Western Highlands, such as the Mae Enga. On the whole, Highlanders stress hard physical work, astuteness in conducting exchange and trade deals as well as the ability to provide ample supplies of valuables for these occasions, flamboyant oratory and keenness in litigation, and power deriving from personal and military strength, as qualities which a leader must possess in as great a measure as ritual knowledge.

The reasons for this difference of emphasis are as yet not fully understood. One factor that should not be ignored is contact with the West. The impact of the Australian Administration and especially of European missions has been less severe on the peoples of this area than on those of the seaboard, so that they have not become as self-conscious about their religion. But the difference is probably rooted in the people's culture. Highlanders may be comparatively recent immigrants who have had to fight their way into the country. This would impose the necessity of making ad hoc decisions in a continually changing situation, prevent the epistemological system from being fossilized in religion, and contribute to the general secularization of life. It may be reflected in the general Highlands attitude towards ritual in contrast to that of the seaboard. Highlands secularism seems to correlate with the widespread close association between religion and morality, and the assumption that success in ritual is not automatic and immediate but depends on securing the goodwill of spirit-beings, who are accorded freedom of choice and action in dealing with mankind. Deities, where they are important, and ghosts and ancestors have to be propitiated or manipulated by bargaining. Man cannot invariably rely on their support and is, therefore, often thrown back on his own purely secular intellectual resources. He is forced to think for himself. The greater prominence of religion in the epistemological systems of the seaboard could perhaps be correlated with the less general association between religion and morality, and with the more pronounced view that spirit-beings must react immediately to ritual correctly performed. In this area, spirit-beings are accorded less freedom of choice and action in their dealings with mankind; and man, satisfied that they are largely under his direction, regards ritual techniques, as against his own intellectual endeavour, as the most valuable knowledge in his possession.

Bibliography

Allen, M. R. 1967. *Male Cults and Secret Initiations in Melanesia.* Melbourne.

Bodrogi, T. 1953. 'Some notes on the ethnography of New Guinea', *Acta Ethnographica,* vol. 3.

Burridge, K. O. L. 1960. *Mambu: a Melanesian Millenium.* London.

Durkheim, E. 1947. *The Elementary Forms of the Religious Life.* Glencoe, Ill.

Fortune, R. F. 1932. *Sorcerers of Dobu: social anthropology of the Dobu Islanders.* London.

—— 1935. *Manus Religion: an ethnological study of the Manus natives of the Admiralty Islands.* Philadelphia.

Frazer, J. G. 1913. *The Golden Bough,* vol. 1. London.

Goode, W. J. 1951. *Religion among the Primitives.* Glencoe, Ill.

Guiart, J. 1962. *Les Réligions de l'Océanie.* Paris.

Hogbin, H. I. 1951. *Transformation Scene.* London.

—— 1970. *The Island of Menstruating Men: religion in Wogeo.* Scranton.

Lawrence, P. 1952. 'Sorcery among the Garia', *South Pacific,* vol. 6.

—— 1965. *Road Belong Cargo.* Melbourne.

—— 1971. 'Statements about religion: the problem of reliability', in L. R. Hiatt and C. Jayawardena (eds), *Anthropology in Oceania,* Sydney.

Lawrence, P. and Meggitt, M. J. (eds), *Gods, Ghosts and Men in Melanesia.* Melbourne.

McArthur, M. A. 1971. 'Men and spirits in the Kunimaipa Valley', in L. R. Hiatt and C. Jayawardena (eds), *Anthropology in Oceania,* Sydney.

Malinowski, B. 1948. *Magic, Science and Religion.* Glencoe, Ill.

Meggitt, M. J. 1962. 'Dream interpretation among the Mae Enga of New Guinea', *Southwestern Journal of Anthropology,* vol. 18.

Newman, P. L. 1964. 'Religious belief and ritual in a New Guinea society', *American Anthropologist,* vol. 66, special publication.

Oliver, D. L. 1955. *A Solomon Island Society.* Cambridge, Mass.

Powdermaker, H. 1933. *Life in Lesu.* London.

Read, K. E. 1952-3. 'Nama cult of the Central Highlands, New Guinea', *Oceania,* vol. 23.

—— 1954-5. 'Morality and the concept of the person among the Gahuku-Gama', *Oceania,* vol. 25.

Reay, M. 1959. *The Kuma.* Melbourne.

Schmitz, C. A. 1960. *Historische Probleme in Nordost-Neuguinea. Huon-Halbinsel* (with summary in English). Wiesbaden.

Tylor, E. B. 1903. *Primitive Culture.* 2 vols. 4th ed., London.

Valentine, C. A. 1961. *Masks and Men in Melanesian Society.* Lawrence, Kan.

Vicedom, G. F. and Tischner, H. 1943-8. *Die Mbowamb.* 3 vols. Hamburg.

Williams, F. E. 1924. 'The natives of the Purari Delta', *Territory of Papua, Anthropology Report* no. 5.

—— 1930. *Orokaiva Society.* London.

—— 1936. *Papuans of the Trans-Fly.* Oxford.

—— 1940. *Drama of Orokolo.* Oxford.

Changing Indigenous
Societies and Cultures*

Charles A. Valentine

Social and cultural change are twin aspects of the dynamics by which social and cultural systems maintain their existence and coherence. Alteration and persistence are equally natural and normal processes of cultures and societies in general. Change should not be understood as intrinsically separate from the regular workings of organized social existence in human groups.

In Papua New Guinea, nevertheless, Europeans have long sought an embodiment of the myth that an unchanging primitive man still exists. Actually few branches of humanity provide less factual support for this stereotype than the peoples of Melanesia, who include all indigenous New Guineans. The available evidence indicates that there was a lengthy evolution of local societies and cultures in the islands before Europeans discovered the region. This is the most plausible explanation for the diversity: variability of human populations, indigenous languages, and traditional cultures. All these must have grown out of adaptations to unstable varied habitats and many movements of diverse groups through the region.

Nor is this simply an ancient diversity preserved by isolation or conservatism. Among indigenous villagers there is a striking openness to change from sources outside their immediate system. Trade commodities, art motifs, linguistic forms, ritual patterns, mythological themes and social customs apparently all flowed from one group to another long before Westerners added another great source of change. There is much more here than mere imitation of old neighbours or new overlords. New Guineans have well developed indigenous mechanisms for forming cultural innovations and social inventions when there is a need for change. The cult process, for example, has provided continuity in adaptive responses to stressful conditions ranging from pre-European natural catastrophes to the crises flowing from Western impact (Valentine). The

* Entitled *Social and Cultural Change* in the *Encyclopaedia*.

227

cultural worlds of New Guineans, like those of other peoples, foster creativity as well as conservatism.

Today, the small-scale societies are being integrated into emerging global economic, social and political systems. Economic penetration profoundly alters the villagers' productive systems through new patterns of technology, exchange and labour. The islanders' material fate becomes tied to the structure of world financial and commercial interests. Political change is not confined to revolutionary alterations in local and territorial power systems; New Guineans are becoming participants in international politics. Incipient nationalism, nascent urbanization, emerging secular education, are all bringing them structurally and culturally into the modern world.

It is remarkable that the country's small societies and little traditions have not been overwhelmed by these great forces. To understand what has happened we must recognize that New Guineans traditionally have allowed many alternatives and choices in social relationships, modes of organization, and established solutions to human problems. Higher and lower status are generally not set by birth. Rules of conduct recognize numerous options. There is a pragmatic tendency to judge behaviour by results as well as by established legitimacy. Curiosity, and a disposition to revise belief systems or create new ones, help to make the unfamiliar intelligible and balance universal anxieties about the unknown.

Effective military or political resistance to European domination was never a long-term possibility. The technology of the New Guineans was simple, stratification minimal, political sovereignties narrow, and there were few full-time specialists in any sphere. Yet associated qualities have helped save them from the shattering fate of other non-Western peoples such as the Australian Aborigines (see, for example, the recent revealing work of Pierson) and the Polynesians whose traditional systems, each unique in many ways, were generally less flexible. Papua New Guinea cultural elasticity is also reflected in the range of approved personalities. These societies have traditionally fostered and rewarded a variety of talents and temperaments. They define and treat as big-men, individuals who have autonomous and flexible characters. These qualities have been highly adaptive under modern conditions requiring change. Big-men have often been leaders of innovative cults and modernizing development schemes, as well as movements of traditionalist resistance (Valentine 1960, 1963).

Initial indigenous reactions of fear and flight from Westerners have been as brief as early attempts to hold off the outsiders by force. Europeans in the islands had, by the nineteenth century, accepted Melanesians as more adaptable and exploitable as labourers than were Asians or Polynesians. Not only were islanders becoming adherents of Christianity; but already they were reinterpreting Western religious themes to fit into their own emerging cultural syntheses. With the last century not yet ended, movements which were wrongly called 'nativistic' cults were beginning to emerge all the way from Irian Jaya (West Irian)—the Mansren Movement—through and beyond Papua New Guinea itself to Fiji —the Tuka Religion. These political-religious initiatives for change combined social features and cultural content from alien and traditional sources with local innovations. These and similar movements have been misunderstood by many outsiders ever since. Nevertheless, by the 1920s Reed discerned a developing territory-wide way of life which he labelled 'Kanaka culture' (cf. 'contact culture' as later described by Mead and Schwartz). Island workers and native policemen from widely scattered districts demonstrated in 1929 their capacity to carry out a general strike at the important port of Rabaul.

During the time between the two world wars, dozens of political-religious change movements, many classifiable as cargo cults, came to the attention of the outside world. Being denied meaningful secular education, New Guineans thus created their own ideological versions of the local and wider modern world, its history and future. Blocked from an economic modernization that would serve their interests, they devised ceremonial and organizational approaches to attaining many material and political goals that were realistically beyond their grasp within the country's emerging plural society. With only partly relevant indigenous models and under authoritarian colonial regimes, New Guineans thus created new forms of wider political unity, as Worsley made clear. Their ambitious expectations received many expressions, from elaborate millenarian prophecies to what Stanner termed 'Symbolic Europeanism'. Many rebellions against the several colonial governments arose from these sources. There were observers such as Guiart who, seeing that these were movements both for internal change and for new wider intergroup relations, identified them as the forerunners of Melanesian nationalism. Through such means, many New Guineans had, by World War II, achieved their own complex collective emotional, intellectual and organizational responses to world realities comprehending Germany, Japan and the United States.

It is often noted that change in Papua New Guinea is uneven. Some indigenous groups are still going through the earliest stages of Western influence. Others are succeeding in expanding enterpreneurial or co-operative commercial efforts. Some of the evidence can be interpreted to mean that movements for change are becoming increasingly practical and programmatic by Western standards. Examples include the Paliau Movement as reported by Mead and Schwartz, and the Tommy Kabu Kompani as described by Maher. Yet even in groups whose first contact with Occidental strangers is well within living memory, leaders may take part in the territorial central government or meet with United Nations representatives. To understand this change it is essential to recognize that the society as a whole is a complex multi-racial system. Its prime structural feature is ethnic stratification, a socio-economic hierarchy of Europeans, Asians and Melanesians. It is within this structure that the last have had to cope with experiences historically new to them.

First among these is Western technology, which they have grasped enthusiastically. Indeed, demands for its fruits are often well in excess both of those that Europeans are willing, or able, to grant, and those that can be effectively supported by indigenous knowledge and organization. The second great area of new experience is long-term political conquest by aliens. This is un-precedented in terms of traditional intergroup processes and has therefore imposed difficult problems of adaptation. Third is the closely related imposition of ethnically defined classes cutting across the entire emerging complex society, again outside the framework of any historically relevant indigenous experience.

In general, European policies have followed the principle of dual development. According to this doctrine, 'natives' should play their part in the developing complex society as directed from above by the ethnically superior political masters. How the long-standing tendencies of this structure will ultimately be reconciled remains to be seen. It has been nearly a decade since the country had its first national election. The results and prospects of this and subsequent exercises in imposed parliamentarianism are naturally ambiguous. It has been suggested that 'In the context of modern colonialism, the Australian administration of New Guinea has been one of the most benign and progressive' (Schwartz 1968). Yet in the early 1970s the population remained a congeries of subject colonial peoples.

Meanwhile, the impressive achievement by New Guineans is that they have developed authentically independent responses to this array of new experience and unprecedented problems. It should be no surprise that United States politics of the 1960s evoked the seemingly exotic echo of a Johnson Cult in New Hanover (north-west of New Ireland), or that in 1972 a leader from the Sepik area, committed to the cargo ideology in nationalist form, should be elected to the official House of Assembly. These responses—and many others only lightly touched upon here—have been consistently misunderstood and underrated by outsiders, including many scholars and specialists on the region. These misinterpretations have prevailed partly because scholars have focused too narrowly on elements that seem bizarrely unrealistic from a Western viewpoint, as in the cargo ideology.

Another source of misunderstanding is that interpretations worked out for seemingly similar situations elsewhere do not apply here. Thus it is suggested, by Mair and others with African experience, that difficulties arise in changing small-scale societies because people with traditionally prescribed high status tend to be conservative. For indigenous New Guineans with so few ascribed status differences this analysis is essentially irrelevant. A closely related expert view is that traditional societies with positions of authority set by birth are generally being replaced, despite local resistance, by modern systems with wider opportunities through achieved positions. The broad historical shape of imposed change in Papua New Guinea has been just the opposite.

Preconceived judgements and hasty analyses of evidence from the country itself have not helped. Adaptive, innovative Papua New Guinea cultures have been dismissed as representing rudimentary levels of development with broad evolutionary shortcomings, leading to poor historical performance (Sahlins). Highly organized but flexible traditional social structures have been stigmatized as anarchy, while leaders of cargo movements and village councils alike have been labelled mere satraps (Brown). These and comparable misconceptions persist. Recently Schwartz (1968) has adopted the hypothesis, with explicit credit to the earlier work of Fortune, that Melanesian change movements involving cargo ideology are best understood as expressing a regressive paranoid ethos rooted in traditional cultures of the region. Cochrane perpetuates the established notion that cargo-oriented movements represent traditional values focused on indigenous status-giving goods as opposed to Western utilitarianism. Counts follows this analysis by positing a generalized opposition between cargo activities on the one hand and village councils or other modernization measures on the other (cf. Valentine 1960).

Such formulations are most difficult to square with the factual record summarized here so briefly. These and many other specialized constructions consistently tend to underestimate the changes already achieved by Melanesians in Papua New Guinea and their creative potential. This potential can be expected to surprise many external observers and to serve the indigenous peoples well in an uncertain future.

Bibliography

Barnes, J. A. 1960. 'Indigenous politics and colonial administration with special reference to Australia', *Comparative Studies in Society and History*, vol. 2.

Belshaw, C. S. 1957. *The Great Village*. London.

Brown, P. 1963. 'From anarchy to satrapy', *American Anthropologist*, vol. 65.

—— 1972. *The Chimbu: a study of change in the New Guinea Highlands*. Cambridge, Mass.

Burridge, K. O. L. 1960. *Mambu: a Melanesian millennium*. London.

Cochrane, G. 1970. *Big Men and Cargo Cults*. Oxford.

Counts, D. E. A. 1970. Cargo or Council: two approaches to development in northwest New Britain (mimeograph, American Anthropological Association).

Fortune, R. F. 1932. *Sorcerers of Dobu: social anthropology of the Dobu Islanders*. Revised ed., London, 1963.

—— 1935. *Manus Religion: an ethnological study of the Manus natives of the Admiralty Islands*. Philadelphia.

Guiart, J. 1951-2. 'Forerunners of Melanesian nationalism', *Oceania*, vol. 22.

Harding, T. G. and Wallace, B. J. (eds) 1970. *Cultures of the Pacific: selected readings*. New York.

Hogbin, H. I. 1951. *Transformation Scene*. London.

—— 1970. *Social Change*. Melbourne.

Keesing, F. M. 1945. *The South Seas in the Modern World*. New York.

—— 1953. *Culture Change*. Stanford.

Lawrence, P. 1965. *Road Belong Cargo*. Melbourne.

Lawrence, P. et al. 1964. 'New Guinea's first national election', *Journal of the Polynesian Society*, vol. 73.

Lawrence, P. and Meggitt, M. J. (eds) 1965. *Gods, Ghosts and Men in Melanesia*. Melbourne.

Leeson, I. 1952. *Bibliography of Cargo Cults and Other Nativistic Movements in the South Pacific*. South Pacific Commission Technical Paper no. 30.

Maher, R. F. 1961. *New Men of Papua*. Madison.

Mair, L. P. 1964-5. 'How small-scale societies change', *Advancement of Science*, vol. 21. Reprinted in L. P. Mair, *Anthropology and Social Change*, London, 1969.

—— 1970. *Australia in New Guinea*. Melbourne.

Mead, M. 1956. *New Lives for Old*. New York.

—— 1964. *Continuities in Cultural Evolution*. New Haven.

Meggitt, M. J. 1971. 'From tribesmen to peasants: the case of the Mae Enga', in L. R. Hiatt and C. Jayawardena (eds), *Anthropology in Oceania*, Sydney.

Oliver, D. L. 1962. *The Pacific Islands*. Revised ed., New York.

Pierson, J. C. 1969. The Australian Aborigine: an anthropological perspective. M.A. thesis, Sacramento State College.

—— 1972. Aborigines in Adelaide: a study of urban adaptations. Ph.D. thesis, Washington University.

Reed, S. W. 1943. *The Making of Modern New Guinea*. Philadelphia.

Rowley, C. D. 1958. *The Australians in German New Guinea 1914–1921*. Melbourne.

Sahlins, M. D. 1963. 'Poor man, rich man, big-man, chief', *Comparative Studies in Society and History*, vol. 5. Reprinted in H. I. Hogbin and L. R. Hiatt (eds), *Readings in Australian and Pacific Anthropology*, Melbourne, 1966.

Salisbury, R. F. 1962. *From Stone to Steel*. Melbourne.

—— 1970. *Vunamami: economic transformation in a traditional society*. Melbourne.

Schwartz, T. 1962. *The Paliau Movement in the Admiralty Islands, 1946–1954*. Anthropological Papers of the American Museum of Natural History, vol. 49.

—— 1968. Cargo Cult: a Melanesian type-response to culture contact (mimeographed paper, International Congress of Anthropological and Ethnological Sciences, Tokyo).

Stanner, W. E. H. 1953. *The South Seas in Transition*. Sydney.

Valentine, C. A. 1960. 'Uses of ethnohistory in an acculturation study', *Ethnohistory*, vol. 7. Reprinted in Bobbs-Merrill *Anthropology Series*, New York, 1965.

—— 1961. Review of Burridge, op. cit., *American Anthropologist*, vol. 63.

—— 1963. 'Men of anger and men of shame: Lakalai ethnopsychology and its implications for sociopsychological theory', *Ethnology*, vol. 2.

—— 1963-6. 'Social status, political power, and native responses to European influence in Oceania', *Anthropological Forum*, vol.

1. Reprinted in Harding and Wallace (eds), *Cultures of the Pacific.*

—— 1965. 'The Lakalai of New Britain', in Lawrence and Meggitt (eds), *Gods, Ghosts and Men in Melanesia.*

Wallace, A. F. C. 1956. 'Revitalization movements', *American Anthropologist*, vol. 58.

Watson, J. B. (ed.) 1964. 'New Guinea: the Central Highlands', *American Anthropologist*, vol. 66, special publication.

Worsley, P. M. 1968. *The Trumpet Shall Sound.* 2nd ed., New York.

Glossary of
Anthropological Terms

Affines: persons to whom an individual is related through marriage, i.e. the spouses of his cognates and the cognates of his spouse. The spouse's siblings' spouses, often important to him, are not affines; they are marriage connections.

Age group: in many societies persons of the same sex and of approximately the same age are formally grouped into distinctive sets, which are usually formed at successive intervals. The age set is an organized group of age-mates, youths or girls, men or women. An age set may pass through a series of stages each of which has a distinctive status and defined public duties to perform. Such stages are known as age grades.

Agnates: persons descended in the male line from a common ancestor. The same as patrilineal kin.

Bilateral: on both sides, that of the father and that of the mother.

Bride price: in traditional Papua New Guinea societies the wealth, foodstuffs, ornaments, valuables etc. collected from a bridegroom's relatives and distributed among his bride's relatives; often the latter offer a smaller gift in return. But once a money economy has been accepted the bride's parents tend to prefer cash to goods; moreover, they may demand increasing amounts and insist on spending it on themselves rather than giving shares to their kinsmen. Correspondingly the bridegroom's kinsmen may be unwilling to part with their cash on his behalf, and he is forced to provide most of it himself. No portion of the bride price, whether in a traditional or a Westernized marriage, goes to the couple as a contribution to the expenses of setting up the new household.

Recently some writers have substituted 'bridewealth' for the conventional Papua New Guinea 'bride price'. The term was invented by Evans-Pritchard when he was writing about the Nuer, a cattle-keeping people of the Sudan. The cattle payments at marriage have so many distinctive features unknown in Papua

New Guinea that 'bridewealth' is best left for accounts of the stock-raising peoples of Africa.

Clan: a term used with the utmost vagueness by English-speakers in Papua New Guinea, brown and white alike (cf. 'Tribe'). It may refer to an extended family, the descendants of a set of early settlers, an entire population sharing a language and culture, or something else.

Properly speaking the clan is a unilineal descent group, patrilineal or matrilineal, within which the specific genealogical connections with the founding ancestor, real or putative, are unknown; many of the members are therefore unable to say exactly how they are related to one another. Usually the clan has a name. The members may have a ritual relation with some natural species, e.g. a bird or a plant—their totem—and be subject to particular dietary taboos. A clan is said to be 'localized' when the adults of one sex, generally the men, live together as neighbours (the members of the opposite sex join their spouses at marriage and hence are scattered); it is said to be 'dispersed' when both sexes are scattered over a wide area. A clan may be divided into sub-clans, and often it is then dispersed and the sub-clans localized. The sub-clans may be divided in turn into lineages. Usually the clan is exogamous.

Cognates: persons descended from a common ancestor. The descent may be traced through males exclusively, through females exclusively, or through males in some generations and females in others.

Corporate group: a recognized body of persons who for some purpose or purposes act together as a single entity. They may hold land or other property jointly, they may be obliged to assemble from time to time to perform a ceremony, or their appointed leader may be the sole representative in dealings with outsiders. In certain parts of the world, though not in Papua New Guinea and probably nowhere in the Pacific, some groups, e.g. clans, are corporate in the sense that the members are jurally equal; hence they are answerable for each other's misdeeds and under the obligation to seek blood revenge should one of their number be slain. Usually in Papua New Guinea, perhaps always, the entire circle of the deceased's kin, as well as his affines, are responsible for exacting vengeance.

Cousins: children of siblings of the same sex are said to be 'parallel' cousins; children of siblings of opposite sex, 'cross' cousins.

Descent: a relationship mediated by a parent between a person and an ancestor, defined as a genealogical predecessor of the grandparental or an earlier generation. If descent is traced exclusively through one line it is said to be 'unilineal'—'patrilineal' when the line is of males, 'matrilineal' when of females. In some places descent is 'double unilineal', i.e. traced simultaneously through males for some purposes and through females for other purposes. When descent is traced through males and females indifferently, it is said to be 'non-unilineal' or 'cognatic'.

Descent group: a kin unit in which descent, unilineal or non-unilineal, is the necessary criterion for recruitment. Unilineal descent groups are often exogamous. Where a society is organized on a basis of non-unilineal or cognatic groups each person is potentially a member of more than one and can make a choice, limited though that choice may be. He may be able to choose his father's group or his mother's or perhaps that of any of his grandparents. In the course of his life he may change his membership two or three times.

Dowry: wealth that the father presents to his daughter on her marriage. Usually she then has no further claim on his estate. When dowry consists of land, in Papua New Guinea generally in the care of the men, its management may be entrusted to the husband; but if divorce occurs the woman retains the property as her own. It is inherited by her children. Dowry is not the reverse of bride price, nor is it a form of 'husband price'. It is also not to be confused with 'trousseau', the household goods and utensils, as a rule gifts from the bride's kin, that she brings to her new home.

Dual organization: division of a society into halves, to one of which each person belongs. Recruitment may be on the basis of descent (*see* Moiety organization), residence, allocation by an authority, or choice.

Exogamy: the rule of marrying out: the insistence that everyone must seek his or her spouse outside a particular group of which he or she is a member. Often the moiety, the clan and the lineage are exogamous. It is wrong—and misleading—to speak of marriages as exogamous if by chance husband and wife belong to different groups. The opposite of exogamy is 'endogamy', the rule of marrying in. Again, it is both wrong and misleading to speak of marriage as endogamous if by chance husband and wife belong to the same group. In a given society one set of groups may be exogamous and simultaneously another set endogamous, as for instance where exogamous clans are coupled with endogamous castes.

Family: the need to define the varieties of family becomes evident when the use of the word in English is analysed. In common parlance 'family' may mean a group composed of a married couple and their children, a group of relatives with the same surname, a person's kinsmen, a person's ancestors, or a group of relatives living as one household.

In anthropological literature the term 'simple', 'elementary' or 'nuclear' family refers to a group consisting of a father, a mother and their children, whether or not they are all living together. 'Polygynous family' refers to a group consisting of a man, his wives, and their children. 'Extended family' refers to the group formed when two or more lineally related kinsfolk of the same sex, their spouses, and their children occupy a single dwelling or set of neighbouring dwellings and act together as a single social unit: for example, a man and his wife, their married sons, and the sons' wives and children; or a woman and her husband, their married daughters, and the daughters' husbands and children.

Filiation: the fact of being the child of a specified parent and hence deriving rights, privileges or responsibilities from him or her. It is 'patrifiliation' if the parent concerned is the father, 'matrifiliation' if the mother.

Incest: sexual intercourse between persons related in specified prohibited degrees of kinship. The prohibited degrees differ widely from society to society; for instance, sexual intercourse between uncle and niece is incestuous in Scotland but not in England. Within the one society incest and marriage prohibitions do not necessarily coincide, and often sexual relations are tolerated between persons who are forbidden to marry.

Inheritance: the transmission, according to recognized principles, of the property of a person, usually deceased, to an heir or heirs. It is 'patrilineal inheritance' when the property has to go to the son or sons, 'matrilineal inheritance' when to a sister's son or the sisters' sons.

Kindred: a set of a person's cognates recognized for social purposes A kindred is always centred on a single individual and is reckoned through male and female links. The members of a person's kindred need not be, and often many of them in fact are not, related to one another. In a small community the kindreds of different persons, unless they are full siblings, necessarily overlap.

Kinship: genealogical relationship, real or putative, recognized and made the basis of the regulation of social relations between individuals. Except for illegitimate persons unacknowledged by the father, kinship ties are always bilateral.

Lineage: a descent group in which the members can give the specific genealogical connections with the founding ancestor; ideally each person is therefore able to say how exactly he is related to the rest. A lineage may be divided into segments each founded by an ancestor of a less remote generation. These units are referred to as lineages themselves or as lineage segments. A large lineage segment may also be divided into small lineage segments each founded by an ancestor of a recent generation. Usually the lineage is exogamous.

Matrilateral: on the mother's side. 'Matrilateral kin' are the cognates on the mother's side.

Matrilineal: in the female line. 'Matrilineal kin' are the person's cognates who trace their descent through females exclusively from the same ancestress as himself.

Moiety organization: the division of a society into halves on the basis of descent. Every person must belong to one moiety, and usually the two groups are exogamous, i.e. a member of one moiety is obliged to marry a member of the other. The division may be associated with reciprocal economic or ceremonial duties.

Parish: the largest local group forming a political unit, i.e. the largest unit within which regular institutions exist for the maintenance of law and order; usually also the smallest war-making unit. As a rule the members regularly combine for certain economic tasks, for feast giving, and for the more important religious ceremonies. Statistics are lacking, but probably the average parish in the Papua New Guinea lowlands numbers 200 to 300 persons, though some are smaller and a few have over 1000. The Highland figures are higher, with perhaps 300 to 500 as the average.

Parish settlement: the collection of dwellings occupied by the members of a parish. The houses may form a compact village, or they may be scattered over a defined area in a series of small homesteads or hamlets.

Patrilateral: on the father's side. 'Patrilateral kin' are the cognates on the father's side.

Patrilineal: in the male line. 'Patrilineal kin' are the person's cognates who trace their descent through males exclusively from the same ancestor as himself.

Phratry organization: the division of a society into three or more large groups each usually composed of several clans. The divisions may or may not be descent groups, and they may or may not be exogamous.

Phyle: a large body of people speaking the same language and practising the same customs but lacking political cohesion. The linguistic groups of Papua New Guinea are best referred to as phylae. The names by which they are known today are usually of recent origin.

Polygamy: the marriage of one person to more than one spouse. If a man has more than one wife his marriage is 'polygynous', if a woman has more than one husband her marriage is 'polyandrous'.

Prestation: gift giving that entails the establishment or maintenance of social relations.

Residence after marriage: when a man and a woman marry she may leave her kin and join the husband and his kin ('virilocal residence'), or he may leave his kin and join the wife and her kin ('uxorilocal residence'). These terms have replaced those formerly current, respectively 'patrilocal' and 'matrilocal', now mainly used in compounds. 'Patri-virilocal residence' refers to couples living among the husband's patrilineal kin; 'avunculo-virilocal residence' to couples living among his matrilineal kin; 'matri-uxorilocal residence' to couples living among the wife's matri-lineal kin. If the married pair alternate between the husband's kin and those of the wife, regularly spending long periods with each, residence is said to be 'bilocal'; if they move away from both sets of kin and set up a home in a new place it is said to be 'neolocal'; and if they refrain from setting up a common house-hold and continue to live in their respective natal homes it is 'duolocal'.

Sibling: persons of either sex who have the same parents are said to be full siblings; if one parent only is shared they are half siblings; and if a man with a family marries a widow or divorcee with a family, the two sets of children are step siblings.

Succession: the transmission, according to recognized principles, of the office, status, rights and privileges of a person, usually deceased, to an heir. It is 'patrilineal succession' when the office or the like has to go to a son, 'matrilineal succession' when to a sister's son, 'adelphic succession' when to a brother.

Totem: the natural species, natural phenomenon, or object with which the members of a group, e.g. a clan, have a ritual relation. If the totem is edible, often the group members are not allowed to eat it. Sometimes a group is named after its totem.

Tribe: a term used with utmost vagueness by English-speakers in Papua New Guinea, brown and white alike (cf. Clan). It may refer to the descendants of a set of early settlers, a political unit, an entire population sharing a language and culture, or something else.

Properly speaking the tribe is a politically or socially coherent and autonomous group occupying or claiming a particular territory. The members have a strong feeling of unity.

Uterine kin: persons descended in the female line from a common ancestress. The same as matrilineal kin.

List of Peoples
and Where They Live

Abelam	Inland, East Sepik District
Arapesh	Inland and coast, East Sepik District
Aroma	Coast, Central District
Baktamin	Fly River headwaters near junction of boundaries of Papua, New Guinea and Irian Jaya
Baliem Valley	*See* Dani
Bena Bena	Eastern Highlands District
Busama	West coast, Huon Gulf (near Lae), Morobe District
Chimbu	Chimbu District
Dani	Baliem River Valley, central Irian Jaya
Daribi	Chimbu District
Dobu Islanders	Milne Bay District
Doura	Inland, Gulf District
Elema	Orokolo Bay (west of Kerema), Gulf District
Eltimbo	Division of the Melpa *q.v.*
Enga	Western Highlands District
Faiwolmin	Inland, West Sepik District, near junction of boundaries of Papua, New Guinea and Irian Jaya
Fore	Eastern Highlands District
Gabadi	Inland, Gulf District
Gahuku-Gama	Eastern Highlands District
Garia	Inland, Madang District
Gira	East coast, Madang District
Goodenough Islanders	Milne Bay District
Gururumba	Eastern Highlands District
Hanuabada	Port Moresby, Central District

Hula	Coast, Central District
Huli	Southern Highlands District
Iatmül	Sepik River, East Sepik District
Ipili	Western Highlands District
Jate	Eastern Highlands District
Kainantu	Eastern Highlands District
Kamano	Eastern Highlands District
Kapauku	Central western Irian Jaya, east of Geelvink Bay
Kawelka	Division of the Melpa *q.v.*
Keraki	Western District
Keveri	Central District
Kimam	Frederik Hendrik Island, south-eastern Irian Jaya
Kitepi	Division of the Melpa *q.v.*
Kiwai	Coast, Western District
Koita	Coast, Central District
Korofeigu	Eastern Highlands District
Kove	North coast, West New Britain District
Kuma	Western Highlands District
Kuman	Chimbu District
Kunimaipa	Inland, Central and Morobe Districts
Kurtatchi	Buka Passage, Bougainville District
Kutubu	Southern Highlands District
Kwoma	Sepik River, East Sepik District
Kyaka Enga	Division of the Enga *q.v.*
Labu	Near Lae, Morobe District
Lakalai	North coast, West New Britain District
Lesu	East coast, New Ireland District
Lutu	Near Lae, Morobe District
Mae Enga	Division of the Enga *q.v.*
Mafulu	Inland, Central District
Mailu	Island, eastern Central District
Manam Islanders	Madang District
Manus	Coast, Manus District
Marind Anim	Coast, south-eastern Irian Jaya
Maring	Inland, Madang District
Massim	Northern islands of Milne Bay District
Mbowamb	Near Mount Hagen, Western Highlands District
Melpa	Near Mount Hagen, Western Highlands District
Mendi	Southern Highlands District

Motu	Coast, Central District
Möwehafen	South coast, West New Britain District
Mundugumor	Yuat River, East Sepik District
Nakanai	*See* Lakalai
Ngaing	Madang District
Ngarawapum	Central Markham Valley, Morobe District
Oklembo	Division of the Melpa *q.v.*
Orokaiva	Inland, Northern District
Purari	Coast, Gulf District
Rossel Islanders	Louisiade Archipelago, Milne Bay District
Sengam	Coast, east of Madang, Madang District
Sengseng	South coast, West New Britain District
Siane	Eastern Highlands District
Sibil Valley	Star Mountain, central eastern Irian Jaya
Sio	North coast, Huon Peninsula (near Lae), Morobe District
Siuai (Siwai)	Southern Bougainville District
Som	Coast, east Madang District
Suau Islanders	Near Samarai, Milne Bay District
Tabalu	Division of the Trobriand Islanders *q.v.*
Tangu	Inland, Madang District
Tchambuli (Tshambuli, Chambri)	Sepik River, East Sepik District
Telefolmin (Telefomin)	Inland, West Sepik District, near junction of boundaries of Papua, New Guinea and Irian Jaya
Tolai	Rabaul area, East New Britain District
Trans-Fly	Western District
Trobriand Islanders	Milne Bay District
Tsembaga	*See* Maring
Usiai	Inland, Manus District
Usurufa	Eastern Highlands District
Wain	Mountains north of Lae, Morobe District
Ware	Milne Bay District
Waropen	Geelvink Bay, Irian Jaya
Wogeo	Schouten Islands (north-east of Wewak), East Sepik District
Yagaria	Eastern Highlands District
Yam	Astrolabe Bay, Madang District